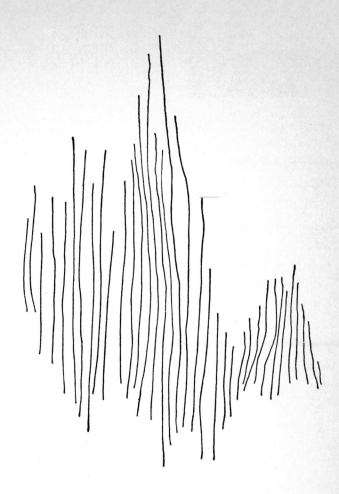

Harry Roskolenko

Prentice-Hall, Inc., Englewood Cliffs, N. J.

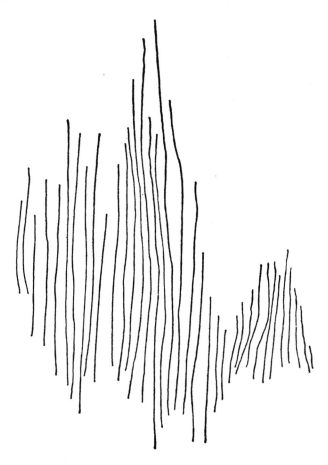

THE TERRORIZED

COLLEGE OF THE SEQUOIAS
LIBRARY

The Terrorized, by Harry Roskolenko © 1967 by Harry Roskolenko Copyright under International and Pan American Copyright Conventions All rights reserved. No part of this book may be reproduced in any form or by any means, except for the inclusion of brief quotations in a review, without permission in writing from the publisher. Library of Congress Catalog Card Number:67–23506 Printed in the United States of America T 90350 Prentice-Hall International, Inc., *London* Prentice-Hall of Australia, Pty. Ltd., *Sydney* Prentice-Hall of Canada, Ltd., *Toronto* Prentice-Hall of India Private Ltd., *New Delhi* Prentice-Hall of Japan, Inc., *Tokyo*

Henry Treece

TO

The Poet reveals . . .

The Doctor heals . . .

Dr. Arthur Schifrin

Other Books by Harry Roskolenko • WHEN I WAS LAST ON CHERRY STREET • POET ON A SCOOTER • WHITE MAN GO! • LAN-LAN • BLACK IS A MAN • PARIS POEMS, *Illustrated by Zao Wou-ki* • SEQUENCE ON VIOLENCE • I WENT INTO THE COUNTRY • A SECOND SUMMARY, *Illustrated by Sidney Nolan* • NOTES FROM A JOURNEY, *Illustrated by Sidney Nolan*

Acknowledgment is hereby made for brief quotations of material from: *Perspective,* Winter 1949. "The Terrorized" by Harry Roskolenko. *The New Leader,* April 5, 1947. "Report From Japan" by Harry Roskolenko. *The Voice of America,* 1949. Chang Family Script No. 15, by Harry Roskolenko and Diana Chang. *Congress Bi-Weekly,* "A Literary Anti-Semite," Jan. 30, 1950; "The Celine Mish-Mash," Mar. 30, 1950. "Germany Today," Oct. 9, 1950. "Jewish Writers In Paris," Jan. 2, 1950, by Harry Roskolenko. *Readers and Writers in Japan* by Harry Roskolenko. 7/13/47 Book Review, © 1947 by *The New York Times Company.* Reprinted by permission. *Frankfurter Hefte,* 5.Jahrgang Heft 11 November 1950. "In der braunen Hitze Indochinas" by Harry Roskolenko. *The Sewanee Review,* Autumn 1947. "Letter From Japan" by Harry Roskolenko. *Canadian Forum,* "Literature and Art in Japan," September 1947. "From Kure to Hiroshima," July 1947, by Harry Roskolenko. *Poetry,* August 1950. "From The 14th Arrondissement," by Harry Roskolenko. *The Diaries of Theodore Herzl,* edited by Marvin Lowenthal. Reprinted from *The Diaries of Theodore Herzl* edited by Marvin Lowenthal. Copyright © 1956 by The Dial Press, Inc. and used by permission of the publisher. *Nietzsche, Philosopher, Psychologist, Antichrist* by Walter A. Kaufmann, 1950. From "The Madman." Princeton University Press, Princeton, New Jersey. *The Proustian Vision.* "The Crippled Giant" by Milton Hindus. "My World Is Pyramid" from *The Collected Poems of Dylan Thomas.* © 1953 Dylan Thomas. Reprinted by permission of New Directions Publishing Corporation.

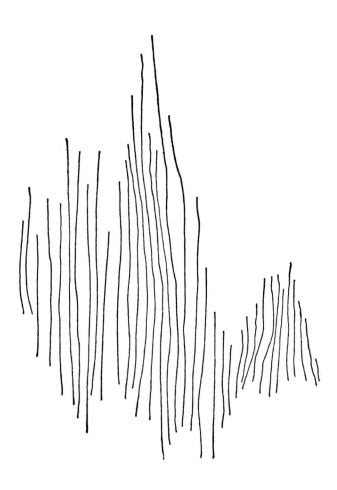

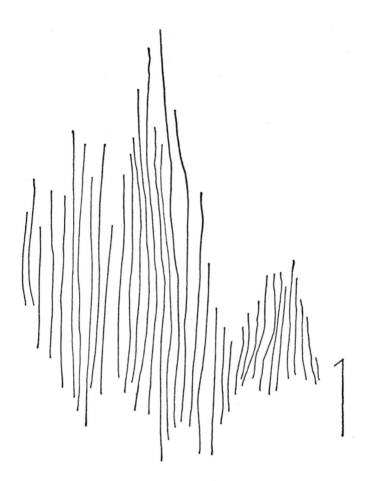

WE WHO CAME BACK

IT WAS POSTWAR—1946. The dead were gone; and I, like so many
returning Americans, had come back from that war. Some of us
were still whole people—self-contained, proud of our little military wounds, our single battles, our uniforms with a bullet hole,
and our estimable thoughts regarding the final outcome. It took
only three years from you—and if you were not really hurt, you
were only a postwar something else on the streets of our great
country.

I defined myself as a private Jewish statistic, nevertheless. I
had whole eyes, a whole head, and a much leaner body. In
Europe, there had been gas chambers for the children of Abra-

3

ham. Physically, the war had done little to me; and, like others, I had danced with the girls, here and abroad, during the war. It was natural enough, despite the casualties, everybody said. You soldiered and you played. It was part of you when you got down to yourself; the boy, the man, the uniform—and the American, above all.

I was the man, however, who had come back to the American cities. I was older and I had picked up some slightly bizarre ways. But though I was whole and intact, I was, at age 38, too old to romanticize our postwar national magnificence. For the country was not a woman. The country was a continent wide; but it was, too soon after all the killing, pregnant with the universalisms of the bastards. We had not reached Abraham's bosom in 1946.

We were, now, venerating too little in the *heart*—and we could no longer use such an ignoble word. You were shallow or naïve if you talked about any kind of honesty. It was not in our new language; but I had learned another one during the Thirties. Now we had telescoped words and meanings for our most active, immediate superficiality, in our tightening cities.

We had always acted as if we were just growing up. And, once again, we were becoming majestic, like our suddenly shot-up straight buildings; and once, too, our church spires had been the tallest buildings in America. Now, with all our immediacy, we were dedicating everything to man, to build the newest illusion to greatness—postwar.

I knew, or so I thought, the nature of our passionate politics and the greatness of our universally admired industries. We had the marketplace for everything. Above all, we were becoming socially concerned with everything human. We had our bastards but we also had our non-bastards—to talk about our bastard ways; and it was, too, so very American. With the dissenters came the non-dissenters. With the people who had made the money came the poor people. It was the way money divided in the American way . . . and the flags waved every day over our magnificent, burgeoning, rebuilding, prospering, occasionally individualistic, yet united and venerable 48 states of America. It was a strange, big land, we said.

I knew the land. I had ridden and walked over its once-dirt roads, its plains, and through its younger cities. I'd had my wandering years as a boy before the Depression, before another war—and before the American earth was bastardized en route to greatness. And now, once again, we were emerging as a greater nation.

The postwar, however, was in the streets with other illusions; it was in the newspapers of New York, with other savageries— and in Washington there were stranger scandals. One went after the other, in compact war words. Mathematically, the people of the scandals were called five-percenters, but most of us called them patriots. There were ten-percenters and we called them *bigger* patriots. We could see the national humor in this: some of us were killed, and others, between five-percenting and cost plus, had made a killing. And so we knew about money, we said . . . and the scandals were as Yankee as they were Southern and as Middle Western as they were Far Western. We were a continent wide—and money was a bitch not confined to a whorehouse.

We heard other words to qualify the whoring heart; and many gray men, the preachers in dark pulpits, were saying terrible things. Whores, pimps, madams—they were all Americans. It was the way of money and the way a country grew into more than a whore, eventually. Some preachers, who had antique thoughts, said that America was overgrown. It was Mongoloid —due to its exaggerated spaces, its overwhelming richness, its varieties of people; and other gray men, who thought spiritual things, said that we were essentially undernourished, though the stomach was our religion. Our morals, too, had filled up the un-collected garbage cans . . . and an agricultural scientist, eager to salvage part of our magnificent garbage, suggested that we would, by 1970, need to reuse our refuse for the next stage of our national development as a people of plenty.

Of course, apologetically, everything in America had happened too soon for all of us in our cities, and just as we were improving on our native science for progress. Naturally, too, since we'd all had hard-working fathers and latter-day frontier mothers, we could not, in 1946, call ourselves, spiritually or statistically, a crude bunch of American bastards. Yet it fitted us so well in the interim, before we matured into perfected, cultural, capable American heroes. We were therefore just en-route bastards. You heard that word in anger among men, women and children. It was a hate-love word at its highest and lowest conceit. When it was Jew bastard, it was hate.

I had been born in New York just after the turn of the century took to wheels and engines. But I was leaving the country. There was another place and I was migrating there. They spoke a throaty English in that country. They had numerous accents and they were a tall people, too. It was a big land, sprawling over a huge map of Oceania, yet it had but seven million people. It looked like our once-great Far West in its western plains. It looked like Florida, New Mexico and Texas. It has oceans on its eastern and western shores. A sea was on its northern tier, a bight on its southern tip . . . and I was migrating to that country.

It was June 1946, and the summer was bursting outside my large window. The single ginkgo tree in the stone courtyard had managed well through the winter snow, the spring drought and New York's natural carbon monoxide poisoning. It was a tree for a stony wasteland, said my Chinese neighbor, who had planted the tree a year before. It was a million years old on earth, and, romantically, it was called a Maiden Hair tree. It was the lone survivor of the ages of man, stone, and nature of another time. In China it grew near the temples and was, once, a sacred tree. It had grown fruit that tasted unpleasant. But it was a delicate shade tree and I used to sit under it . . . and now I was kissing good-bye to the leaves that reached my window. A dog, an hour ago, had used the tree like a dog.

I was preparing to go to Australia, to settle in another frontier also a continent wide. I had been there many times during the war. It was a rough, crude country outside of the five major cities. The land had not yet been sacrificed, nor polluted. There were, as yet, no American totemic gods in Australia—and it would develop differently.

And there was elusive Laura, who had not been able to join me in New York. We had agreed to marry one overly sentimental afternoon, at war-grim Brett's Wharf, just before the gray transport sailed from war-time Brisbane with the wounded, the dead, and the dying soldiers, airmen and sailors—all of us who had been to Leyte one day during October 1944.

Laura had made the in-and-out war possible for me when I had been in and out of Australia as a second officer on U.S. Army Transport tankers. I had gone everywhere in the South Pacific, especially up to New Guinea on the short-lived, combustible, exploding tankers as we ferried high octane and diesel oil. We

moved on a war-borne schedule for death. In Sydney, with
Laura, I overdid my fear fantasies. Laura was a bosom. Laura
was a week of love. Laura was not a ship. Sailing again, we
supplied the advanced Fifth Air Force bases for the coming
invasion of the Philippines. We helped to make strange places,
with stranger names, fortified islands. We turned New Guinea's
jungles, coves and razor-backed mountains into man-hacked military depots and tent cities. The bulldozers and the spam changed
the architecture over the kunai grass and the swamps, but not
the heat and the rains. The green hell was always there. You
could see the slashed-down kunai grass leaping up on the hour,
so that it was, once again, five feet tall between the closing and
opening of your sleep-ridden, red-shot, atabrine-yellow eyes. . . .

And there was radiantly random Laura, with whom I had, in
some lesser seasons of private terror—suddenly away from the
war—finished 290 bottles of wine and whiskey at her enchanting
Elizabeth Bay House flat, in Sydney. Whenever I came, I stayed
a few weeks. I went on again, waiting out some private infinity of
time on the tanker's murderous errands. We would hide away—
the Japanese planes came for the tankers, for the airfields, for
the invasion force's mechanical and octane-laden heart. One day
it would be in a cove at Langamach, Dobadurra, Brothel Beach,
Lae or Milne Bay; the next, at sea, we would push toward
Madang at seven knots, on a ferryboat that was not a ferry, on
the blacked-out tanker that was a floating Mt. Vesuvius awaiting a
marauding plane. In Sydney, when we docked at the Wooloo-
mooloo Docks, where the whores waited for the sailors, I was
soon with Laura, lovely tall Laura, Laura of the Bottled Passions,
Laura of the Blond Depths, Blue Eyes and the Fair Skin, with
the soft lyrical voice that remained soft despite her love for
whiskey. Yet she was never drunk. She was always the lady, in
love, using the bottle because it made love easier, her language
more graceful, her body more giving. And we were young
enough, or old enough, to believe that everything we did was
inflamed poetry.

We called it anything during the war. It was love. It ranged
through some fine fancies and little of the dying. The expected
had not happened, though my ship was blown up and I had a
short swim in the water before I was hauled out, off the Western
Carolines, en route to Leyte Gulf.

A mine had hit us up forward. The oil spilled into the sea like a gushing whale spouting black, congealing liquid. My shoulder was broken. A few days earlier, I had come down with malaria. Between my broken shoulder, the raging malaria, and the swim in the oily sea, I was on my way to hell.

But death was not that time and it was not tomorrow. To-morrow was still the dancing and singing time for poetry. And always Laura to help me booze through the war's hallucinations. It was always there, with skeletons dancing before me, a coffin ready, or a tarpaulin and the captain's prayer—a sermon that I would never hear. In the rafts and the lifeboats we heard each other's howling hearts shouting in panic, the oil scuttling us beyond any kind of recognition. And some of the men were call-ing for their mothers, using token words to mother them at their dying. It was the way some men went.

That was in 1944. Now it was postwar—1946—and I, formerly a maritime officer, had become a journalist—the end-all of the impatient poet without a heavenly residence. It was just another profession for arranging and rearranging the world as we tried altering, almost immediately, some of the new cosmic miseries that we soon inherited as the victors of the war. But no matter what we thought we were, we were, basically, all humanistic undertakers.

Europe and Asia had their millions of graves tidily accounted for. The dead had been adequately indexed, though the reasons for their dying were still being argued. In two countries, both under our military occupation, some war criminals were awaiting trial. In other countries millions of refugees were camping out as they awaited visas to humanity and another try at civilization.

For me, too, it was a time to grub out a new career in another country. Australia, anxious to populate its wastes, would give me new roots on the last frontier left to Western man. Australia would soon be gathering up the questing millions under its Antipodean stars. The huddled masses, in their camps, hovels and tenements around the jettisoned world, would come. And I, from a New York apartment.

I loved Australia enough to settle there—with Laura. I needed a home, which I had not had since the Depression's little terrors of rentless, foodless time—the uprooted young man of the Thirties, waiting for everything. We were all going to hell until the WPA changed our direction at $23 a week. Then I had a flat, some furniture, some Purcell and Palestrina records, a few hundred books, some paintings given to me by artists—and there I was, for nine rooted years.

But where were my roots after the war? Once they had been on Cherry Street, where I was born. It was demolishing itself like New York and my roots were in my head. Streets, people and houses, all had gone. I was left with a tight phrase—*in memory lie your roots.* The street of my memory had gone to the bulldozers and the jack drills.

To live, or grub, after the war between 1945 and 1946 I wrote zany articles about the Pacific, questing reviews on literary matters, impolite poems for fashion magazines. I was contributing to the literary quarterlies much as if I were a professor, to *The New York Times* as a non-professor, and to *The New Leader,* a catch-all social democratic weekly concerned with world politics, Stalin, and the cosmic qualities of kitsch literature. Or, as some acid-toned critics had it, the literature of amateur politicians and the egotistical politics of litterateurs.

It was that kind of a novel, inventive and undersubscribed newspaper. Many of *The New Leader's* politest contributors were no longer socialists, Marxists, anarchists, free-lovers, vegetarians —or even liberals. They were now in between their vegetarianism and their vegetating. They were turning anti-liberal because they had discovered some strangely conditioned relapses regarding Comrade Stalin's methods in taking over, with troops and bullets, most of Eastern Europe. Or so said other adventurous contributors over whiskey, coffee, tea, ketchup, 7up and Vat 69 —before they went on to other impolite matters dealing with trade union corruption, John L. Lewis, vertical versus horizontal unionism, United Nations bafflement regarding the self-determination of captive nations, the poetry of e.e. cummings, the indelicacy of the atom bomb—and back to Stalin again.

Some of the weekly's more perceptive writers, like Arthur Koestler, Max Eastman, Sidney Hook and James Burnham—now going through themselves with intellectual bombs—wrote for *The New Leader* because they had once been sentimental Marxists, socialists, Trotskyists and vague revolutionaries. They gave *The New Leader* their weekly disenchantments on how to make socialism, if not Marxism, more human. They got no money—

only some fifteen thousand universal readers, including Second Avenue cafeteria-sitters, corporation lawyers, bad actresses, and State Department socialists (then hardly concerned with the Cold War about to burst on us), and over the same whiskies and beer we said they were the cleverest and the most morally discerning intellectuals in politics—and we went back to talk about Stalin again.

Eventually some of their less adventurous but more career-bound colleagues, who had also sucked at the large left tit of Marxism, went on to the mixed ranks of *The Establishment*, circa 1967. But in 1946, to quote Sol Levitas, the editor of *The New Leader*, "They were the worst trombernicks and shleppers outside of the Café Royale. Some socialists! A few years ago some of them were finely paid Stalinists; this year they're opportunists. Now they are also specialists on Dostoyevsky, Henry James and Melville's white whale. Now they are Zionists! They go from Marxism to gefulte fish without missing the tzimmes. Next year they'll be experts on the schwartzes in Harlem. What are they not experts on—ask me, Herschel? They would like to write for *The Saturday Evening Post* and *Collier's*, but they settle for *The Partisan Review*, for *Commentary* and *The New Leader*. What do I pay them? Exactly nothing, Roskolenko. How much will I pay you for your articles? A little bit more . . ." and Levitas paused to raise his glasses to his nineteenth century forehead, as if to study my financial needs like a good civil servant. He had been that, too, in Simbirsk, in 1918, as the Menshevik against the Bolsheviks, the assistant mayor of that Siberian town until Lenin chased him back to New York.

"You're a poet so you must need money—no? But do you know why those trombernicks really give me their work—because they write in *The New Leader* as they please, or almost. . . ."

One day I phoned the managing editor of *The New Leader*, Liston Oak, to write an article as I pleased. The Soviet Union's iron curtain had closed off Yugoslavia, Hungary, Bulgaria, Romania, Czechoslovakia, Poland, and other countries . . . and it was Churchill's "Cold War" about to become a reality.

"What is your piece all about?" asked amiable Liston Oak, an old friend of the equally embattled Trotskyist Thirties.

"How to force the Russians back to Russia without firing a shot," I answered modestly. It was easy to say this on the telephone.

"I don't get it, Roskolenko. What are you proposing?"

"Atomic blackmail! My article will inform Stalin of the following: if he does not pull his troops out of those countries within
a stated time, we'll threaten to atomize an unpopulated area of
Siberia. And if he still persists in occupying these countries
beyond our deadline, some inhabited Siberian wastes will be
scorched. After that, Moscow. Liston, it's either that or Stalin
will pick us off piecemeal."

God, what a plotter I was! Another dime and we had Stalin.

"What do you think, Liston?" I asked.

"A damned interesting article, Roskolenko."

"Damned or interesting?"

"Both. When can I get it?"

"It's written—tomorrow. I'm sure that I'll be called a sonofabitch for it, at least."

"Not by me. I won't be that modest, Roskolenko."

By the time I reached the post office, I got over Liston's back-
hand flattery. Anybody in 1946 who did not love "Good old
Uncle Joe"—Roosevelt's engaging wartime image—had another
vision in his mind regarding Stalin's political affections. After all,
Uncle Joseph Stalin patted children's heads. He smoked a corncob pipe. He wore a peasant's white tunic. He looked grand-
fatherly. But he killed. It was, therefore, easy to drop the
article into the chute at the post office—and be damned for it
later.

(As for Liston Oak, we had worked together on a book exposing Stalin's murders. It was a work of hate and love for us. We
had done an outline, a hundred pages of preliminary text, and
we had a publisher. We had worked patiently. But we also had,
alas, a fellow-writer listening in most quietly the night we
planned the book on Stalin. Our fellow-writer, then employed
as a Stalin expert for the New York *World-Telegram*, scooped
our ideas and outline—and he was not as patient as we were. He
also hated Stalin. He wrote it in a few months. On publication
date, Oak and I, easily shocked by the obvious stealth, could only
cuss out our speedier friend; but, by then, with certain liberals
and radicals, it was considered a normal theft. In any event,
Stalin's murders had been vigorously portrayed for popular con-
sumers—and I went on to more poetic thoughts.)

As I left the post office, I had a drink of two-bit whiskey. Then
more, from an occasionally used bottle at home. I spent the

night without fear and trembling; that is, I slept between echoes. Below me, in the basement apartment, a couple were at it again.

They were at it every night. A man and his wife and their voices were at it, cursing, battling and banging. Doors kicked; then her voice, getting fouler, rose with the early morning birds on the ginkgo tree.

The birds dashed off and the woman was slapped again. And I, unable to sleep, worrying about what Stalin would say to my proposition, went back to the whiskey to kill the bottle.

I had never liked whiskey, in quantity, even with Laura. Drinking, under my father's calculated religious guidance, was, to quote him most correctly, for "shickera goyem." I drank on nevertheless, feeling very moral about all things—all except the woman being beaten, if mildly now.

Stalin not only beat people—he killed. The bottle killed too and I had killed the bottle. My article, I knew, would cause talk and discussion; and somebody in Washington might get a thought. It would lead to other thoughts; then perhaps later a published declaration to Stalin. It was Either/Or. It was not another Hiroshima, of course, or Liston Oak would have hung up on me and called me a murdering bastard. Liston was a kind, thoughtful man. He hated violence like a preacher did. He loved nature, as well. He had a quaint house in the woods of New Jersey. There were birds, flowers, a swimming pool nearby, women who liked politics and other arts—and I liked to rough it there for a talking weekend in the woods. As for Hiroshima, I had contempt for Truman's real act of murder.

A week later I had a phone call. It was Sol Levitas, the editor, saying angrily, in Yiddish, "Herschel, are you completely mad? Do you think that you are reviewing Ezra Pound's *Pisan Cantos?* Do you think that I'm going to publish your insane article? You're a warmonger, Herschel. Peasant that you are! There are other ways of stopping Stalin's power megalomania!"

"Which way, Levitas. . . ?" And we both hung up.

During my preparations for migrating to Australia, Levitas had made me *The New Leader*'s Far Eastern correspondent—with little pay.

There was no question but that I would take root in Australia. I loved Australia like I loved Laura. But, suppose there were no

roots for me—and no Laura? In war, men created fantasies—to
live. Suppose Down Under was a strange place? Even the Australians had it upside down. But that was a joke for foreigners,
who were, after all, *up above people.* Laura was a nation. . . .

I had laughed at some small irony dealing with the nature of
love and the ways a man missed a woman. The way a man missed
a woman I knew. I knew what the two years away from Laura
had done to me. The beginning of the day and the end of the
night . . . dreams of Laura laughing, dancing, showering, talking,
singing to the birds—Laura so sober, then. What if it was all
my fantasies within her fancies and there were no Laura? And
what if there were no sky? What if there were no trees, pigeons,
brooks, laughter?

But if there were no Laura then what? Then I would go back
to New Guinea. I would go to the Philippines, Japan, China,
Indochina, then on to Europe. In Indochina the communist Ho
Chi Minh was pretending to be a Nationalist with his Viet
Minh; in the Philippines it was the Hukbalahap at the same
game; in China it was Mao Tse-tung. It was a time for cold, hot
and lukewarm games. In America some of Mao's liberal sponsors
called him an agrarian reformer, a Nationalist—never a communist. They would sponsor the devil and call the devil the
prince of peace; it was in the nature of our shoddy thinking and
the way we masked and glossed over reality.

It was a moral vendetta if you cared enough. My father had
known czarism—and now another little father was in Red Square.
Hitler's prisons and extermination camps had Stalin's smaller
counterparts. I had been schooled from 1926 to know both the
fascist and the communist mind, heart—and methodology. I had
been brutally beaten by both. I had been stomped on in Hamburg and in New York. Their mutual philosophy of action was all
over my body. My testicles, once, in 1932, in New York, had the
"Internationale" played over them as I lay, flattened and bleed-
ing—and the communists, over me, were kicking me into insensi-
bility. Soon after that the poet in me went over the hill. The
poems had been kicked out of my testicles.

The honorable lovers of lyrical indifference could have poetry.
Communism was a gun, a rope, a foot, a firing squad, a brilliant
leadership—and another country was lost. And having spent
years, later, within the certified ambiance of the goodwill liberals

(and some of my worst friends were still liberals), I knew their pretenses, their softness and their sobbing tearoom manners. They were a hopeless mob of hapless dreamers, always used by the communists. Wherever they were, no matter in what country, they soon landed in some communist jail when their country, most liberally, went over to the communists.

"*Merde!*" André Gide replied to a howling pack of Parisian communists when he came back from Russia, in the Thirties, to report that Stalin had committed a million crimes against the Russian masses.

In preparation to take roots, I had done a study on Australian migration. I was about to become a migrant—most privately. I had interviewed, among others, Arthur Calwell, the Australian Minister of Immigration, when he had come to New York. I took issue, most publicly, about who makes a good immigrant. That article, too, went to Sol Levitas' lean hands at *The New Leader*.

He was no longer the angry editor trying to tame a poet. He said, appearing to be contrite, which was hard to fathom in his mellowing eyes, "That blackmail article, Herschel, I wish that we had run it. But you, a small boychik from the East Side, why do you fuss with big atom bombs? Leave it to James Burnham— to historians, not to poets. What kind of people are going to Australia? You are going to live with kangaroos or menchen? So, who is going to Australia?"

"Some English, Irish, Welsh, Italians, Poles, ex-Nazi Germans —and a few sad Jews."

"Why only a few sad Jews?"

At that moment James Baldwin came in with a review and we were introduced with Yiddish and Russian Levitical accents. I had read Baldwin's sharp essays and reviews. He, as he said, specialized in books about Negroes because "the color of my skin made me automatically an expert." He was living off reviews and fellowships, and waiting on tables, "to be the honest man and a good writer. . . ." Short, bulging of eye, shy in a rapid-fire way that grounded me, he was a machine gun of nerve ends. He was a socialist then, hardly ready to burn up the white world. He was bookish, literary, a natural essayist, his flaming rhetoric born in Harlem's gathering terror and horror. He was not yet frozen, with angers, social ugliness and homosexuality as a theme, though poverty was a natural enough theme, as well as civil

rights. He had a caustic style in his emotive reactions. He liked
poetry, not picket lines. Shortly he would be in Paris to write
Go Tell It on the Mountain, which he was climbing then.

Shyly, over coffee, he said, "I'm applying to the Rosenwald
Foundation for a fellowship. We Jews and Negroes have many
things that are basic—our fears. . . ." And I lost the rest of his
social indictments. A bleating taxi had just hit an old woman on
Fourteenth Street.

I was leaving this city of multi-racial ghettoes. I had packed like
a refugee, taking some intimate things: addresses of old friends;
a 1906 photograph of my parents, my two sisters, and my two
brothers grouped for the sentimental family album. In the picture
my mother, so Russian and blonde, had two arms. A few years
later she had one. The right arm had been amputated when she
was forty. A truck had run her down. After that her right sleeve
was pinned back and the socket of the arm showed emptiness.
My father, his goatee still black, was smiling fatherly, looking
ahead, directly at the photographer. My sister, Esther, who was
so pretty at fifteen, was no longer on Cherry Street at sixteen.
Another truck. She was dead one afternoon on Lafayette Street.
My two brothers in the photograph, two children in curls—
babies still, had been bribed with chocolates to keep them still
long enough for the photographer's blast.

I packed my legal papers, including the discharge from the
Army Transport Service. I took my second mate's ticket, now
run out, as well as all the odd things that made me legally an
American, if somewhat dispossessed, in 1946. It was the way one
left New York.

Below my apartment, on West Ninetieth Street, off Riverside
Drive, the couple were at it again. The woman was lamenting
again. She was a big bitch, said her husband nightly. That's how
they called each other, at two in the morning, when he came
home from tending a bar on Columbus Avenue. He always
wanted to fornicate—and he went for her like a young bull.

"You're killing me, you bastard! Get a whore from your bar!
Get some animal that likes what you like. Take it out! Cut it off!
Get two whores! Didn't the doctor say that I'm not to be fucked
for another six months? That I'm getting cancer, didn't he? You

little bastard! You whoremaster! Get it out! One night, when you're snoring, I'll cut your balls off."

I had often passed her in the hall, an enormous woman, all breasts, buttocks, voice. She had thin legs and a round face. She was in bed more than she was out—and the delivery boys were often laughing when they left her apartment. Her husband never laughed. Cursing her was easier. He was cursing her now, as he sailed in, tearing at her clothes, mounting her, slapping her into tears, then yelling out, "Whom were you fucking with while I was at the bar? How much did you make, you whore?"

His agitations were the same and her reactions were the same. It was a scheduled affair and eventually included a neighbor, from across the courtyard, who would usually call out, "Why don't you let your wife alone? What again? Why don't you stop abusing your wife—jerk!"

The voice across the courtyard finally challenged the bartending husband at three A.M. one morning. They met under the lamp post at West End Avenue and Ninetieth Street. Four other distressed neighbors attended. The battle was brief, brutal—and galling for the little man.

He came back to his wife with a split lip, a black eye and a kick in his groin that made him inoperative for a few weeks. But now he was at it again. . . .

I put on the radio. I heard an early morning concert. Bach's B Minor Mass, the chords rising above the bitch's lament, above the bastard's language, going towards Jesus Christ. The foul night was encased in another lament, two thousand years older. I was leaving all of it in a few hours, to drive across the United States, to board the S.S. *Flyaway* in San Francisco, sans bitches and bastards, to other expectations, challenges, transitions—and a woman named Laura, in Australia.

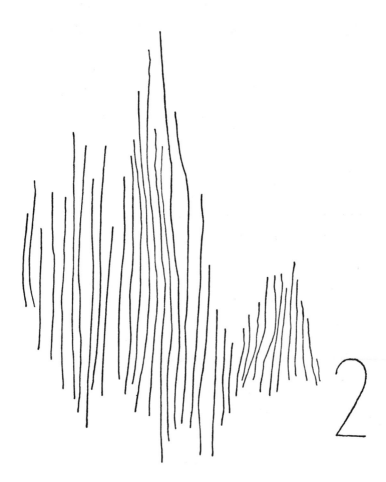

A PRIVATE STATISTIC

FOR A MAN who had never owned a car, the Dantean nature of its awesome mechanics hardly made me feel lyrical. In three hours it broke down three times. By noon I was still in Manhattan. I was just across the George Washington Bridge, at another garage, at two in the afternoon. The car had been sold to me in a hurry by a radical friend of mine, who had shined it up like an energetic car salesman getting rid of his last model— and I was the smiling buyer, paying two hundred dollars for this epic. He was talking about maps, about main gears, about tires, and the road going due west. By four in the afternoon, the last mechanic got another fifteen dollars and I drove towards Buffalo, humbled by gears, awaiting exploding tires, startled by the jabbing lights of the night, and definitely on my way to Australia.

I was not alone. I had a companion-driver, a dancer, on her way home to Seattle. We had been friends, once. Lovers of our own arts, sharing words and physical movements. We had shared the tail ends of ourselves, giving just so much away. We were both waiting, in the interim's drive across the continent, to say good-bye to words and physical movements—and we were making natural observations, especially about nature, to match each other's final indifference to each other.

In the late moon, Lake Cayuga looked like a postcard mailed from a vacation. It had the haunting quality of the not-very-high mountains of New York State, going north; it gave off little dreams of what it had once been. It folded into my eyes the memory of another century, when farms were everywhere, with horses instead of cars, and people walked towards wherever they were going, or they took trains to wherever they had to go.

All you need is gasoline, oil and money, and the world is yours, we used to say. The unconscious American myth of the symbolic roads had made me, in my youth, the eternal wanderer. We had gone as whalers to all the waters. We had once had iron men on wooden ships. On a wartime Pacific atoll, I had seen that solemn yet boastful sense of the American vista, in humor, "Ithaca, 8,000 miles from here," and an arrow pointed to some vaguely conceived Northwest. It was a direction away from the war going to Melville's Pacific and the white whale. It was myself as a sentimental American without an adequate history trying through gears and wheels to find some adequacy in the mechanical wilderness. I went on dreaming, driving, thinking of another Ithaca—where Odysseus had once lived.

In my youth, as a sailor, wanderer, hobo, labor organizer and forced traveler, I had loved the sea-smells and cold winds. Pine needles were my pennies as a boy, the snow my dimes, and the sea my dollars. I had lived in tenements in between my vast journeys—but I loved deserts and the lonely places. I was the poet trying to catch some of the last natural images before our deluge under the gears and the pollutions spreading over the enormous land.

We passed through Buffalo.

Like Buffalo, so went Chicago. I had spent six weeks there

when I was a boy bumming around America. It was a winter of
cold, rain, hunger, and hard for a boy of fifteen . . . soon there
were only prairies and mountains . . . now the prairies were
green. Now the mountains were without ice and snow—and the
freight trains were for other wanderers.

The dancer was driving, talking about Martha Graham's contributions to the American dance. I saw a sign—Madison, Wisconsin. I was thinking back, forgetting about the modern dance,
hardly listening to the modern dancer. (Besides, I preferred the
reactionary ballet.) The dancer was saying, "The ballet is mostly
still in the nineteenth century—and this is 1946. . . ."

I was pointing to the sign; "Let's go there for a small visit."
The dancer took the left turn.

Sixteen years before, in 1930, I had lived in Madison for a
month. I was the one-month college student taking courses with
Professor William Ellery Leonard, which meant literature; with
Professor Selig Pearlman, which meant economics, labor problems and Marxism; with a pale young man, a friend of Ezra
Pound, and the pale young man meant poetry. He looked like
the poet, his pallor almost gothic, his voice disappearing when
he lectured—as if he was really more ghost than man, though he
had created a school of poetry called Objectivism. It was equally
ghostly, dispossessed of body and blood, but possessed of ob-
scurantism and Poundian undercurrents of scholarship, social
credit, illusions of history, and the pale reflections that lived on
and off literary quotations.

In the end it was a game of quotes, though I had really gone
to all the classes not to learn quotations, but to be near a girl.
I had gone via freights to be near her because, one day in New
York, in 1929, she had said, "You need a classical education.
You've only learned things on the run. Come and visit me in
Madison. Live with me and learn from the professors. . . ."

She talked of Neitzsche and I talked of Marx. She spoke of
D. H. Lawrence and I spoke of Melville. Our minds went on
like that to baffle neither of us. When I was there she was about
to become a Doctor of Letters—the youngest on the North
American continent, including Canada. She quoted on, outdoing
the pale poet and many professors.

I quoted back from Lenin's *Empirio-Criticism* to prove my
basic materialism: "To the mouse no beast is stronger than the

cat." To which she replied, metaphysically, from Bergson: "There is at least one reality which we all seize from within, by intuition and not by simple analysis. . . ." After that she became more pragmatic. She quoted William James—*"Does the man go round the squirrel or not?* He goes round the tree, sure enough, and the squirrel is on the tree; but does he go around the squirrel?"

The youngest Doctor of Letters on the North American continent helped me, every evening, to develop some normal eroticism without quotations. She was an opportunist when it came to sex. Marxism, to her, was a terrible philosophy, making man mechanical, "and robbing the spirit and murdering the personality." D. H. Lawrence restored all things to her, soon enough.

I was the Marxist, believing in socialism. I was her lover for a month. I was installed as a part-time scholar, reading five books a day. I was, too hurriedly, stuffing my head with unequal doses of idealistic philosophy, going from class to class. I met her for lunch and then back I went to another class to fill in the vast need. I had to be able to do more than quote the obvious quotations that established you as less than ignorant and less than the scholar. I was very much in between words and meanings, the meanings that a university had, the classical meaning and not the fragmentary one. But I was too full of bizarre fragments, fragments that included the youngest Doctor of Letters in her big wide bed where I was no longer the avid scholar filling up on books.

I was, she said then, the emerging poet. We went to bed with T. S. Eliot's sad, lofty, English-American scene—the nothingness of the heart. But we went on to Neitzsche and the mystical rites of the *ubermensch;* for Marxism died in bed, when I undressed her. The class war almost stopped when her middle-class past wanted my proletarian majesty and arrogance. Then love had a kind voice. Then love had a lovely young face. It laughed the way a girl does on a boat. And love was certainly sexual then— but with poetry, in Madison, that winter of 1930.

Now I was back in Madison, a sixth of a century later, at the end of June 1946. Marxism had changed the world. And the Doctor of Letters had turned Marxist, to lecture as a liberal. It went with the rest of her opportunism. When Israel was established, she became a Zionist, to lecture at Hadassah clubs. I began to forget her, as I walked the streets of Madison, vintage 1946.

A mechanic greased the car. Everything had turned Coca-Cola in Madison. The lake that I loved no longer looked lovable. The streets had crowded up in sixteen years. It was another city, soon to be forgotten, gone with the men who had built it, I thought, as I paid the mechanic. Destruction and construction was the American way of change even at a university town, and it hardly looked scholarly. I had seen the earth, the trees, the lake, and I drove away from the Great American Void into the place names of America still on the Western horizon. We went over the mountains. In a few days we were in the Badlands of North Dakota.

It was a barren fantasia in the geological age of America, a sunken valley through which some other Mississippi had rolled on and through. There were signs that almost read, "Take a bit of ancient America back with you for one dollar." The old guide, as aged as the samples of rock he was selling, told us everything in telescoped comments . . . "Every year more of this place flows down to the Gulf of Mexico. One day all of America will wash down to the Gulf."

I bought some of his rocks, wrapped them in a pair of socks and drove to the West.

The mountains raced to the clouds and we drove through them, towards the Pacific. Other men had come with horses a hundred years earlier. Now highways ran over the tops of the mountains, cascading and pitching; then they descended in vast sweeps down the gaunt mountains, heading for the sun.

I was on some private pilgrimage, and it was unholy. I was seeing this with some vague feeling that I was an apostate. A passport had been visaed for my exiled mind. . . .

What was there to hold on to? The country had worn itself out in less than 150 years. We had devoured the free land, rooted up every animal. We had killed every vision of America, choking the lungs, dirtying the waters, and drowning the sky in garbage. Our senses, made for natural reactions, were dying amid the smoke, the cars, the housing, the progress. It was an idiot's game in every American direction. And this was America *gonev*, which my mother had called it one day in 1913 as she lectured to me to be an honest boy, not to steal, not to punch other boys, not to bear more than the normal malice, to give twice a day to charity, to take old ladies across the wintry gutters and out of the way of the horsecars . . . and now, laced into a pair of socks was a pound of rock that would, one day, lie behind my glass cabinet. I had taken the land with me, bottled in my heart and labelled it in my brain—*gonev!*

The dancer sulked. Once, she said in Montana, "Let's have an orgy!" I had known her before Laura, in San Francisco, while studying celestial navigation and piloting to "land," said my teachers, the Pacific War on New Guinea's beaches. But I had, while in training, landed in the dancer's bedroom, which over-looked the Embarcadero. I was in uniform and I had all the regal and legal excuses to make her a beachhead in a hurry. And we had talked of marriage and we went folk-dancing. We listened to Bach and to Palestrina records before we went off to bed. It was amazing all the things I said, in bed.

The dancer's green eyes had saluted everything, saying yes to everything I was saying, to the lies I was making into truths, to the truths that I was making into lies. It was love, of course. We never doubted it for six weeks above the Embarcadero, in her high house on Montgomery Street, near the Coit Tower, where we could look down on the transports and the freighters going out to sea and war.

She had fine green eyes, an off nose, an exhausting body. Once she sent me nude photographs of herself to help me wallow through the New Guinea days. She was always writing lewd notes, using classical illusions that sounded as if she were a historian. In one letter, out of which popped a nude of herself in a dance pose, she wrote, "Orgies made Roman culture—not Christianity. How many nurses are you screwing in New Guinea? Stay clean, if not pure. Don't get the clap. It's not heroic any-more."

The dancer and I met again, after the war, in New York. And, with all the patent ironies, we had crossed the country in ten days. It was good-bye again, a postwar farewell said in a car, in the American scenery, in hotels, in sad words and in no words. But we finally said good-bye in her mother's house in Seattle, where I was her most temporary house guest before the S.S. *Flyaway*, in San Francisco, took off for Australia.

I had, only once, been flattered by her. She took her Master's

Degree at New York University, using my "collected works" for
her thesis. Now, with her collected works, she sneaked into my
bedroom at her mother's house. She undressed, stood before the
long mirror and admired her body. She did a few dance turns,
sighed plaintively, admired herself again with Narcissistic awe,
and finally crept into bed.

She was a dancer. She was all body, with the sheet down,
looking at herself, then away. She was staring at the mirror and
insisting that we make love in front of the mirror, that this was
her normal exhibitionism, that she was, in bed, Duse and Dun-
can, that tragedy was related to love by its physical relationship,
that sadness was only a reflex for most women, that men were
natural bastards and women were natural bitches, that even
children, unaware of morals, were at least monsters in their own
right. Then she was before the mirror, dancing and acting,
saying, "I still want to marry you. Why don't you convert to
Christianity? Then my aunt who hates Jews will give me a lot
of money. We could have a house. We could travel."

The mirror was in her eyes like a comet's tail and she was
dancing her last orgy. She was picking things from a garden in
her choreography. I saw roses, bushes, hedges, slugs (she had
stepped on dozens of slugs that morning as they came up on her
mother's lawn . . . it was a damp house right off Lake Washington
—and we had watched the college rowers in their eight-oared
shells . . . and she was saying, "Tonight, let's have an orgy . . .")
and now her dancer's body extended itself in the mirroring, all-
giving, all-inclusive antics of the bedroom.

Later she took me to the railroad station to entrain for San
Francisco and the S.S. *Flyaway*, the ship with the unbelievable
name that was to take me to Australia. I was tired, red-eyed. My
emotions, like my baggage, were labelled for another country.

She ought to marry a lawyer she knew, who had money and
loved hamburgers, I said at the station.

I had nothing to give her. I gave her the car—the token of
everything American.

We kissed as brother and sister.

San Francisco squatted on its fat hills, sitting like a Buddha over
the vast bay. Its fat neck, lost in its stomach, wandered between
steel entrails and waters, amid bridge and sky, out to the Golden

Gate. A few days in San Francisco added up my last picture of America the beautiful and America the *gonev*. I was leaving nothing here either. There was Kenneth Rexroth, now on a diet of milk instead of wine. He was a great cook, he said, as he made spaghetti—the anarchist's food of dissolution. He slept in a sleeping bag on the floor of his house on Madison Street, hungering for the green of the High Sierras. Others I knew were in a holy communion of freewheeling meetings discussing Wilhelm Reich's orgone box and the imperiled female orgasm while dreaming of thousands of unknown girls.

The political and the intellectual citizens of the night were a dubious elite, erecting elastic totems of anarchism as a philosophy for living—or dying. But whatever it was, it was the old past regurgitating over salami and spaghetti, over chicken soup and mustard. Though their wine had soured long ago, they still had Trotsky and Kropotkin, Henry James, James Joyce and Kafka— and themselves, looking for anarchism's rare emblems of joy. It was the past already screwing up the future. . . .

Good-bye, San Francisco!

Good-bye, America!

TERRA AUSTRALIS

> "It had been settled by thieves, murderers, prisoners, free women—England's social scum"—a noble historian on Australia.

THE S.S. FLYAWAY took twelve discordant passengers and thousands of tons of hard cargo to Australia.

We stopped at Apia, Samoa, and there was a cable from Laura. "I never believed you would come. My recent silence was my error and my disbelief. I have married a man who resembles Patrick. I cannot explain except to say that I never believed that you meant all those beautiful things that you said through the war. A letter follows. I am terribly sorry, pet. I was too lonely for too long and you took too long to come back to Australia."

It fell, as if my hand had never held it. It was like a bird suddenly dying between my fingers. It was rock, stone, sea and sky. It convulsed my brain. . . .

A fellow passenger picked it up and got a bottle of Scotch. He said nothing but kept on filling my glass. I felt nothing—nothing but the numbed nothing. The Scotch gave me nothing too. I was nothing at a bottle, nothing at a cable, nothing in my eyes. . . .

Melbourne was eight days from Samoa, via New Zealand and then across the blowsy Tasman Sea, with its buffeting spray, crosscurrents, cold and winds. I was sick of my angers, of Laura's little ghosts.

"When is love not love?" I had asked Laura in 1944, when I sailed, much bandaged, for home.

"When the bottle's bloody empty, pet," Laura had said laughingly.

Two days out of Melbourne, and I was down with an old New Guinea war ailment. I had known them all, from dengue to malaria, which no longer killed a man, they said.

Now rocketing through the Tasman Sea, I burned and I froze. I lay in a small whitened room where whistling steam pipes played imagined dirges from Bach. A table, holding my medicines, crashed against the bulwarks when the ship hit a sudden wave. And I lay, within my own waves, unknowing then, going up and down in my fever, sweating through my underclothes, soaking back to life, washing back to thoughts of dying, listening to my mind telling me that it was finally coming—that the whitened walls were places in heaven, that the blasting steam pipes were places in hell.

I was dying, said the purser. I was dying, said the first mate. I was not dying, said the more learned captain . . . then I heard him say, "If that Jew bastard dies, he'll know more about Jesus Christ than any of us. The poor sonofabitch! I never had a passenger die on me before—and it's got to be a little Jew from New York. Hey, Purser, sit with the Jew bastard for the next hour. He's gonna explode if he goes above 106 degrees, so help me Moses!"

I understood nothing. I was in a far-off country called Malaria. I was being lifted up. I was in a clanging ambulance, leaving

Port Melbourne for the Presbyterian Hospital in East Melbourne.

For the first five days I sweated in gloom. When my fever went down, I read. When it went up, I slept on curtains of clouds and went swimming in languid seas. I was a fish, a white fish, and I sank into my vaporish gloom, watching the hospital room sail away. I heard whispering people sail up to me. When I awoke, I was staring into Tolstoy's *War and Peace.*

A girl, a pianist I knew, had brought the book, whispering, "It may bring some sort of peace to your Russian soul."

Another needle went into my right forearm, and next a hand was stroking me.

It was not Laura's hand. She had heard but she had not come up from Sydney. Instead, a priest had come to inquire whether I was a Catholic. I was not a Catholic, not a Protestant—I was a Jew, said Mr. H., my Australian publisher, who had come in a hurry. The doctor took Mr. H. aside and said that I was dying, not responding. The priest had come to administer the last rites.

"Get a rabbi if you must get a man of God," said Mr. H. "Besides, from what I know of Mr. Roskolenko, he was—or is—not too religious. He used to be a Marxist, chum. But during the war, when he became a convinced pantheist, I published his book of lyrical poems. If he comes out of this bloody hospital alive, we'll publish his war novel. You don't know about Mr. Roskolenko? How terribly crude, Doctor. He's known to five hundred buyers of his book of poems. You don't read poetry? You read medical books? Ah, then you might know what's bothering the bloke. If he dies, we'll have to scatter the type."

Mr. H. had a familiar patter. Mr. H. was a funny man, who long ago had established himself as the *enfant terrible* of Australian letters and publishing . . . I was listening to all the funereal literary services. Then came the rabbi, who was a friend of the willing priest. . . .

I became morbidly impolite and hysterical. I swore through the black and white around me—"Get the hell out of here! Visit some other bastard, not me! Say your last rites over that miserable publisher! Say it over Laura," I went on, kicking at the covers, getting out of bed, looking for my clothes, opening the windows. I wanted air, not rabbinical rituals for the dead.

"God did it, Rabbi. No, mosquitoes did it!" I was given another injection and put back to sleep.

My publishers visited me in two installments, a little fearful that my unknown disease was communicable or that it did not have enough literary romance attached to it for a poet's disease. Mr. H. preferred tuberculosis. His partner, Mr. R., suggested some major mental disorder dealing with a split personality. My publishers were extremely cultured regarding literary diseases.

Mr. H. was interested in what I had brought from America. I had come laden with all my gifts—to spend eternity on Terra Australis. I did not smoke but I had ten cartons of cigarettes. Mr. H. smoked "the tender Virginia leaf and ten cartons make two thousand cigarettes. Thanks, chum. At my rate of eighteen to a day, ten cartons will last . . ." and I was lost in the exhaling humor of Mr. H.'s tobacco mathematics.

Old Australian friends of the Second World War came. They were the transient tigers of the 1943, 1944 and 1945 days—when we all expected to die. They were heralds of the *avant-garde,* but they had grown so fat they no longer knew their *avant's* from their arses. Expecting to attend my funeral, they wanted my blood, cameras, cigarettes, books, shirts, suits, and my self-changing portable record player. And since I was far off in fever, I was charitable to all. The home I had come to build was no longer in Sydney. I was unloading my baggage.

But I was no longer dying. I was convalescing, reading *War and Peace,* the gift from the pianist. She was a pretty girl, buxom in the Australian way, legs and buttocks in the Australian way, feminine in the Australian way, anxious to be accepted in the Australian way, the daughter of a minister of the Church of England—which made her somewhat holy—certainly not the kind of a pianist to be tampered with. She was much too close to God. When she visited me she became all the more confessional. She hoped to marry soon. There was an organist who loved her but who kept her too properly virginal, for an organist. Was that fair for a grown woman of twenty-five? "Women must be loved physically as well as spiritually," she said. "He's kissed me but twice—on my birthdays!"

Other visitors came to welcome me back to Australia—the bohemians, the political people, the literary folk, and some architects who had drafted plans for tea rooms and colorful cafes that would be monuments to culture. One daringly envisioned a skyscraper for a more modern Melbourne. There were visitors who were potters, like the inventive Boyd brothers; Sidney Nolan, the artist, who had painted the life of Ned Kelly, the Jesse James of Australia; the Minister of Immigration, Arthur Calwell, who had managed to get me a visa after I was turned down by Canberra. I was too radical, someone had said. I was a Marxist, another had said. I was once a Trotskyist—so no visa. But Minister Calwell, rejecting all these stories, got me in. It was like old home week, twelve thousand miles from New York's Cherry Street. I had been welcomed back to Australia.

One visitor was an elfin, harassed man named Tunn who resembled his name like a puckish faun. He was always in trouble because he specialized in plagiarism. In the literary circles of Melbourne, the object was to find out the sources of Tunn's many ventures in copying the living and the dead works of others— the foreigners.

Tunn wrote literary reviews, literally copying them from known and unknown American and English magazines. When more adventurous, he would try some French sources at the Melbourne Library, which received the weeklies from all over the world. Tunn had already been discovered plagiarizing reviews from America's *Time,* England's *Observer* and Paris' *Figaro.* When discovered, which had to happen, he qualified everything with a puckish smile that soon grew into a charming grin. The literary circles of Melbourne quickly forgave Mr. Tunn's many licenses with the stolen word. But when Tunn wrote an article accusing Banjo Paterson of having swiped Australia's most holy "Waltzing Matilda" from Tunn, long ago, Mr. Tunn suddenly discovered that he had to pay for his whiskey, beer, coffee, tea and cake, for a month. To accuse the dead Banjo Paterson was too much for even the most liberal-hearted Australians.

Tunn came and brought flowers; Mr. H., the publisher, said Tunn had picked the roses in the Botanical Garden the night before. Tunn came a second time and brought a modest book of his own poems—sources unknown. Disarmingly, he asked, "When you're well again, can you review my delicate poems for *The New York Times* Book Review? My influences? Well, they are mostly from the ancient Chinese. I am studying to become a Buddhist monk, you know. Why? I have this unusual field all to myself— and I can't be accused of borrowing a few choice words and rituals from a very old religion. And since the Chinese in Melbourne are mostly Christians, I shall have to do most of my work among Melbourne's natural mystics. You must meet some of them soon, Mr. Roskolenko. By the way, I am giving a lecture on you. You're the most natural mystic in this hospital. . . ."

The third Tunn visit involved my pocketbook. Tunn, it became apparent, needed a lawyer. He needed some rent, too. He also wanted clothes suitable for a Buddhist monk. When I suggested that he dye a white sheet into a saffron sheet, the kind the bonzes wore in Thailand, Tunn looked sacredly unhappy, and said, "But you don't understand. I am going to work with native Australians, not Thais—and the Australians would never tolerate me in the saffron sheets of a bonze. They'd be quite properly upset, I reckon."

Max Tunn, with the help of Buddha, was a very sweet monk in the making.

I left the hospital, three weeks after the ambulance had picked me up at Port Melbourne. I had migrated to Australia—to find a more open, non-geared world. Politically, I was totally American. My parents, earlier, had migrated to the Lower East Side from the Ukraine. Their reasons—pogroms. The Kishinev pogrom was well remembered . . . my father had not been hurt, but a relative, living in Bessarabia's capital city, had been killed. My father, after twelve years in the Czar's army as a handy batman for an officer, nevertheless had the progromchick's *nagaika*—the cat-of-nine-tails—etched in red, blue and purple across his back. It was a permanent feature running between his shoulders and his lower spine. When he bathed in our kitchen sink, it was there like a cross. He was a Jew—so was I—and there were enough psychopaths about to imagine that we were, in their infantile fantasies, responsible for their sad condition.

But this was all-embracing Australia, happy to have other nations send their wandering sons, their hapless voyagers and their homeless ones. But I was far from any of these sad categories. I just loved this smallest continent, three million square miles, with the population of New York City. It was a city-continent, with half of its people living in the million-headed cities of Sydney and Melbourne. I had lived in both cities, and in Adelaide, still much under a million people. But from my exacting studies of Australian populations and the imagined

migrations, Australia was going nowhere in 1946. It was not prepared for anything. But, if you came and stayed at least two
years, you would be settled where the government needed your
arts, crafts and professional skills. In 1946, in came 1,500 humble
Americans, counting one man named Harry Roskolenko. Most
of them had seen the war from Australia's looming beaches, grim
inns, cheap hotels, jump-off camps and New Guinea's embattled
bivouacks. Four thousand Englishmen also arrived. They saw
their impoverished little island, England, ready to give up its
colonies and die a little bit more.

Australia could—given water to irrigate the Dead Heart and
the sandy wastes that ran through its deep center—house 35
million people. In 1946, the ugly suburbs stretched out into the
bush. Beyond, in the Never-Never, it was empty of all but some
hardy homesteaders, gentle wallabies, tough kangaroos, sheep-
killing dingoes, and the eccentric marsupials of the oldest continent in the world. It also had the oldest second-class citizens in
the world—84,000 aborigines. Like the Americans, who had killed
off Indian aborigines by the thousands, so had the Australians.
In a novel called *The Timeless Land*, by Eleanor Dark, whom
I had met during the war with literary Laura, Mrs. Dark claimed
that there were almost 300,000 aborigines about when Captain
Cook first landed in Botany Bay in 1770. It became England's
first penal colony. And as every Australian hates to remember,
the prisoners became the initial propulsion for the future settle-
ment of Australia. To colonize the shores of the Pacific, as well as
the bush, the aborigines were slaughtered.

In 1946, the aborigines were kept to the outback or they
worked at miserable wages on sheep stations. They were aimless
in time and place, fear-encrusted, and still more naked than
dressed. Near the cities, for the tourists, they had their boom-
erang acts. When fed up with white Australian civilization, they
wandered off on their *walkabouts*, moving between the Australian Bight, on the Southern Ocean, and Arnhem Land; through
thousands of miles of the unfertile wastes of the Dead Heart. This
was my Australia.

I came with mixed expectations. Politically, racially, every
Australian politician followed the White Australia Policy. It was,
often innocently, a prime example of exclusionism if you were
yellow, black or misceginated. But as an American, I had all the

freewheeling opportunities to join in and build Australia. Melbourne needed everything American—but how much of gadgeted, crowded, superficial American-do-build-grab could Melbourne stand? From my view—very little. I had not come to bring hamburger stands, traffic jams and tabloid values.

But Australia desperately wanted massive migrations settling in a hurry. It was selective immigration, and Britain was first choice. It was as Anglo-Saxon and as Aryan as Hitler—and all done under the Australian Labor Party. In European camps were 800,000 DPs awaiting new homes. Few of them were Anglo-Saxon enough to fit Australia's specifications for migrating humanity. After the British came the Scandinavians, skilled, blond, blue-eyed. Some headed to open the bushlands outside the six major cities, back of the beyond. Yet, somehow, some people in the DP camps were being insulted, excluded. Had I been an East European Jew, fresh from a Nazi camp, it would have been difficult, then, to waltz on to Australia, though a friend of mine, a social worker in Paris, Rose R., managed to get seven hundred Jews to Australia. I wondered, when she told me about it, whether all of them had become blue-eyed blondes by the time they sailed.

I had once argued this with the Minister of Immigration, Arthur Calwell, in New York. He was embarrassed by the policy—and he was one of the leaders of the Australian Labor Party. But, then, we had done the same during the Oriental Exclusion Act—when The American Federation of Labor pushed through legislation to stem the "perils of the yellow hordes" and to keep the wage line in hand. In London, over a million of the fed-up citizens of England had registered at Australia House—to keep their loyalty to the crown—and become, eventually, New Australians. In Italy, hundreds of thousands registered, including a few members of the Sicilian Mafia, who were later to set up shop in the Australian cities. And then came the Mediterranean inundation, the Greeks, with their classical inner skills and fabulous speech, to add to the mixed moral philosophies of Australia; the Germans, with their outer skills, to add their fabled techniques—when they were not Nazis; the East Europeans, to farm the newly opened lands. All came except the dark people, and the Orientals.

Australia was to be *white* in the minds of every politician, whether he belonged to labor, liberal or the conservative school. In 1946, ninety percent of the population was of British stock. The slogan, however, was Populate or Perish—and perish meant Asiatic inundations.

By 1965, 2,356,569 people, half of them British, found another heartland, and Australia reached eleven and a half million that year. Broken down to national origins, the new arrivals were: 1,232,905 Britishers; 290,002 Italians; 139,204 Dutchmen; 103,911 Germans; 82,274 Poles; 53,935 Yugoslavs; 36,315 Americans; 11,236 Chinese—and 48,394 stateless citizens of the world, many of them, obviously, of Jewish descent. There were, further broken down, 1,279,664 males and 1,076,905 females; and of the total figure, to Australia's inherent greatness, 293,339 were refugees.

It was soon to become another frontier for industry and rapid development. With its Europeans, went the famous Australian work-method, the "Australian crawl," the fifteen-minute time-out for a "cuppa" and a cigarette. This "cuppa," in the past, meant a few beers at the pub and an hour lost. Australian cultural eccentricities, from beer to a "cuppa," were suddenly revolutionized.

With its new populations, Australia, still in the watery masses of the Pacific, "a white island in a brown sea," was also to give up its past dependence on England in matters of economic and military protection. There was another country—the United States, the wartime savior of Australia. The United States began by investing five hundred million dollars in 1946—and many billions by 1966. It was a companion country, sentimental about Australia; a country cousin stemming from another England; a kith and kin from tennis to swimming, and once just as tough when it came to frontiering, gold-rushing, booms, migrations, drinking—the compulsion to crowd a land almost as big as the United States and developing at the same nervous pace.

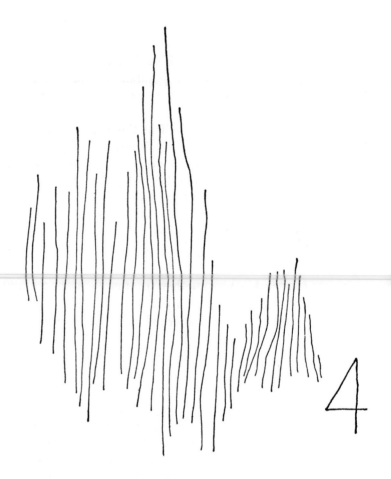

4

ADVANCE AUSTRALIA FAIR

I SETTLED IN a flat near St. Kilda Road. My landlady, who loved
her Americans from the war, only doubled my rent—out of love
for Americans. She left roses every day. She cleaned, when she
thought of it. She invited me up for a "cuppa" once a week. She
was pure Australian down to her speech. She was "properly"
cultured when she went to the pubs. She left newspapers, magazines, suggestions of what to see, what concerts to hear—and
whom to meet, "so as not to be lonely at night. . . ."

I was not lonely. I had a hundred wartime friends—and I had
a job, with my publishers, R. and H., who fell between New
Directions and Grove Press. And I became an editor two days

after leaving my malarial bed. They published poetry and we received, at our King Street address, just off Collins Street, five manuscripts of poetry a week. They published *avant-garde* literature, and we received all sorts of psycological literary adventures, in prose. And since I was the first reader, the second reader, and often all the readers—I made some decisions about the future, if not the past, of Australian letters. We also published a magazine called *Angry Penguins*—and some of the world's elite— cultural, political and *avant-garde*—wrote for it. The magazine went around the world, to shock, by its Antipodean culture lag; but I managed, despite its lag, to get pieces by James T. Farrell, Sidney Hook and Jean-Paul Sartre. Sartre gave us an article about Jewishness—as seen from an existentialist-humanist view. Jewess, a word suggesting rape, was based on the intense femininity of all the six letters spelling out J–E–W–E–S–S.

The two quixotic publishers had various relaxed employees. Some were supported because they were suspected of having betrayed their original talents and because support, part-time— as writers, editors, artists—would, with a bit of money, bring out the better creative man. It worked as a supporting theme, but seldom for the talents expected to develop from this eccentric rendezvous. A man did not burgeon brightly just because someone was paying his literary rent and his creative food bill. But when it worked it did so in a noble fashion. For, alongside of me, as a fellow editor and artist, was Sidney Nolan, who had done a huge series of paintings on Australia's own Jesse James, Ned Kelly, who allegedly robbed the rich to keep the poor—the less poor. It was an earlier anti-poverty program, with a gun. And, collectively, the publishers did not like poverty.

Nolan was an impish type, totally dedicated to art. Ned Kelly, in 1946, was his art. Nolan had painted Kelly the bank robber in a suit of black armor. Actually, it was a headdress to keep Kelly's head from being shot away. Sid Nolan, the artist of the bush and the outback, did more than fifty paintings of the bush-wacker, Kelly, in various stages of his history as an Australian thief, a Robin Hood, a plain hood, a killer, a friend of the poor, a friend of the bush and the hero, uncrowned, of Australia's mayhem history.

When I was not otherwise involved, I wrote for a magazine called *Tomorrow,* also published by this many-sided firm. They were liberal, left, radical—but mostly out to shock the citizens still caught in the center of Australia's alcoholic politics. The magazine, put out in newsprint, was not a thing of beauty. It had cartoons done by Nolan and others. I wrote six articles within a few weeks. I killed off the American cartoon character, Superman, and many fathers and sons wrote in to find out if Superman was actually dead. I wrote about the Ku Klux Klan, crucifying its racist appeals, an unpopular approach in Australia. I wrote about Western Samoa, then under New Zealand as the mandatory power; with it we published a picture of a Polynesian girl stripped down to her ample waist and we got a thousand letters from men in the bush, asking for the address of her thatched hut. We also attacked the Australian Catholics, as well as the Pope, for their collective objection to British socialism, especially after we discovered a reactionary Catholic editing a fascist-minded journal in Australia.

The then leader of Australia's Liberal Party, Robert Gordon Menzies, was always attacked in rhyme by *Tomorrow*'s editor, Jack Bellew. Menzies had allowed, when he was the prewar head of the government, a cargo-load of scrap and pig iron to be sent to Japan. In the war in New Guinea it came back as shrapnel. So every Labor Party sympathizer for years afterwards called Menzies "Pig Iron Bob." We did the same. I recalled that New York had sent the Sixth Avenue El to Japan and a friend of mine got a piece of it in New Guinea, but none of us had called Roosevelt "Sixth Avenue El Roosevelt." Yet, despite the magazine's official line, I had a deep respect for Menzies as the most able, most diplomatic, most statesman-like politician in Australia, a land where the pub is the back room and the politician, usually, was the man with the mostest beers going down his guts. Menzies did not offer up that picture, and he helped to bring Australia up from the lag and into some happier areas of the twentieth century.

Tomorrow had a huge mélange of values, poorly resembling *The Nation, The New Republic, The New Masses*—and *Time*. It was as factual as it could get under this sort of kibitzing editing. It was part pure sewer, part sink, part Australia being natural, all sensational, part sexy. It soon had thirty thousand curious readers in the heartland. It was new, without doubt. It was savage, of course. It was not always honorable. If *To-*

morrow had a father, it was Jack Bellew, who claimed the role. If it had a soul, or some such term to generate its finances, it had the publisher, Mr. R., who warmed up all the cash to keep it going. Mr. R., deeply cultured, managed to practice law and to practice philanthropy—to the arts, to artists, to nudist and sun-bathing organizations, to vegetarian societies and other do-good fraternities—and that's what *Tomorrow* was all about.

Mr. R. was rich and at ease. His law office was a place to receive mail. His big home, in the suburb of Heidelberg, received ballet dancers with six toes, painters with one hand, poets with no poems, and radicals who belonged to the sun. The hand of the amateur was all over Mr. R.'s manifold doings and blessings. He kept a stable of artists, giving them ten pounds a week, sans paint and canvas. He kept a few household males around—to make his ménage more functional, or so the loose gossip had it around the pubs in Melbourne. Nevertheless, *Tomorrow* was a very professional magazine—with Jack Bellew's eccentric pro-Labor slant activating all of us toward greater pains for labor.

Bellew had at least eighteen *noms de plume*, usually forgetting on Tuesday who he was on Monday. Bellew attacked, pipe in mouth, Australian mediocrity—an H. L. Mencken with an Australianese language. Naturally, too, we wanted to be sued by the politicians of the right, by the grafters of the center, by the rich fellow-travelers of the left. But we couldn't even invent a worthy massive insult, to be sued. We wanted publicity for more circulation and we needed a hundred thousand subscribers to break even. It was a challenge to Bellew's quaint professionalism —to make money, not to keep "the rag" going on Mr. R.'s bank balance. And, to increase circulation, we wrote on the increased suicide rate since the end of the war, on rationing, on America's amateur foreign policy, on doing away with the Governor General (Duke of Gloucester), e.g. "We can bloody well run Australia without the Queen's bloody interference here—and we'll save ten thousand bloody quid, in the bargain. . . ."

I sat in the large light room, usually used by Mr. R., who had decided he needed a spiritual sunbathing session on the Barrier Reef. We saw him off and I took over his office. I had carte blanche with the correspondence. Mr. R. was trying to publish Dylan Thomas—and Thomas wanted money, or more money, for his poetry. I suggested sending Thomas a hundred barrels of

Cooper's Ale, "which is splendid stuff," said Bellew. "Make it two hundred barrels and you'll get Thomas to sign. . . ." I offered up the two hundred, but not another word from Dylan Thomas—who was offended, or in the hospital again, by then. There were letters from T. S. Eliot, then at Faber and Faber, regarding an exchange of titles; from Henry Miller, whom we could not publish because of Australian puritanism; from Herbert Read, anarchist, whom we did publish in our magazines; from Thomas Mann, who wanted to know what we were, and from any number of English and American writers who asked about Australia as if the continent had not yet been discovered.

Mornings I was an editor. Afternoons I went opal hunting in Melbourne for a New York dealer, a Mr. Hurzfeld, who offered me ten percent on anything I bought for him. Before my departure from New York, he taught me how to grade opals for depths of veins, for purity of color, to distinguish the deep green, the light green, the green, the deep blue, the blue, the blue-green, the red-green and the milky from the black—the ominous opal with a myth. According to the myth, it meant death to the wearer.

One morning, fed up with the publishers, labor, poets and *Tomorrow*, I started out for the opal mines of Lightning Ridge in New South Wales, a wild three-day drive. I left with a lyrical poet who thought that opals and the mines would inspire him to greater lyricism in praise of Australia's brightness under the oldest earth. He drank as he drove from a private stock of ale and whiskey. He cussed as he drank and drove but he was hardly reaching newer lyrical heights. I saw black opals all over the bush as we careened towards Lightning Ridge. There were ugly villages and towns, uglier pubs and drunks, antique roads, with kangaroos vaulting over our jeep. My poet-friend, Alex, was lost to lyricism during that week, as the bush spread from horizon to horizon. It was salt bush, scraggy bush, gum trees, waterless bush, sheep after sheep. When we saw an Australian he was a swaggy who wanted a ride or a stockman riding herd. To Alex, every man on the track was a "flamin' bang-on coot. Wouldn't he rot you, cobber? He's a bloody friggin' cow of a swaggy, who won't work 'cause it might dirty up his fuckin' hands. My bloody oath! Beauto, pal, let's hit that dingo right on the tail. Here goes, Harry!" And Alex aimed for the poor dog who managed, when I grabbed the wheel, to get down a ravine and away, though Alex would have followed the sheep-killing dingo in the jeep, had I let him.

Lightning Ridge was a nothing of a place 45 miles north of Walgett, which was a nothing of a place. Everything was bush, tents, temporary—in the rough. The mines usually went less than thirty feet into the earth. With pulleys the dedicated miners, weatherized-thin, hauled up stone, dirt, sand and slag to get at the black opals. When they went below, they used candlelight to catch the gleam of the opal. Others worked the surfaces from the sides, usually in teams of twos, to drive down until they eventually wore out the black opal veins at thirty feet. The openings were narrow slits in the earth but wide enough to let a man down. There, more acrobat than miner, a fossicker took up weird physical positions as he chipped away in the semidarkness seeking the precious, beautiful, sparkling gem worth, on one occasion, over $250 a carat.

We tried the local amenities—old Sydney trams turned into single and double rooms. An outdoor shower made it plushier. A mile from Lightning Ridge were the boreheads. Artesian baths steamed up over the wierd mining landscape dotted with humpies, slag hills, and fossickers searching through the mullock heaps for bits and pieces of opal-laden stone.

Alex searched on his own. He was like a madman on a mullock hill, bare-handed, digging in, shunting aside slag, seeking opalesque images as he muttered on, drank on, bottle-laden. If the jeep had anything, it had boxes of beer. We were always stopping, picking up bottles, hardly any food, not until I demanded some tinned meats, bread and steaks. We had one decent meal, at last, camping out before we got to Walgett.

Alex, who was as thin as a miner, finally gave up his fossicking furies, cussed out the slag hill, and decided, right then, "Let's go and have a Japanese bath in one of those bloody bubbles . . ." and off we went again, to bubble in an artesian bath, with Alex still drinking away from the bottles of beer now strewn all over the bath. Soon, when he was drunker than a coot, I left him to find a miner with black opals for sale.

The miners were a wierd lot, wierder than the desolate landscape. Primitive men, loners hoping for "the strike." One miner, George Trough, was the ancient man of Lightning Ridge, having become a fossicker during the Depression of the Thirties. When I came to his shack he grinned, his thin face marked like the slag, his eyes sparkling like an opal. When he handed me a hot bottle of beer he asked, "Are you looking for a bag of blacks? You should have come yesterday, Yank. A bloke came up from Sydney and took all I had. But my cobber, Bluey, he's got all you want. . . ."

We went to Bluey's humpy—a shack built from castaway tin, broken crates, tar paper, and fieldstone. It made up two rooms. Bluey, red of hair, very fat, all from the beer, sat in the center of his domain like a squire of the diggings.

When Trough said that I was buying opals for a New York importer on a letter of credit from the Bank of New South Wales, Bluey took out some plush bags. He opened one. The dazzling, sparkling black opals lit up like mounds of fire.

"Look at this lot, too . . ." and he opened another bag. Each bag weighed ten ounces. Soon he had dozens of bags opened, each bag graded in price. I spent all day arguing and bargaining, pushing the deadly opals about. Each time I messed up the gradings Bluey swore—and soon he had the opals back where they belonged. I sweated, bag after bag, beer after beer, wondering what sort of a damn fool I must appear to Bluey. When Bluey asked a hundred dollars for a carat, I usually said ten. He laughed and asked if it was true what was said about Yankee traders.

"I ought to know. My great-grandfather came here from Boston, via the California gold rush. So I'm part Yankee, Yank," said Bluey, looking patiently grim.

Very late at night, over many burnt-out candles and empty beer bottles, I finally quit. Five hundred ounces had been selected—worth twenty thousand dollars. We were leaving for Sydney the next day in Alex's jeep. In Sydney, the Bank of New South Wales cabled Mr. Hurzfeld for a twenty thousand-dollar letter of credit, and the opals were locked in the bank's safe until the letter of credit arrived.

When it came, three days later, with Alex locked in Menzies Hotel with a whore, I was ready to go back to Melbourne—tired, feeling outfoxed by a red-haired Yank-Australian fossicker, assured that I had been outbargained. When the ominous opals went off by insured airmail I was ready to retire, rich in human percentages, if only I could get Alex, still drunk with his sheila, to get me back to Melbourne.

At Menzies, Alex was still too drunk to drive. I went for a swim to Rose Bay, where Laura and I used to go during the war. She was a natural athlete, she said. She was a great swimmer, she said. She went two strokes and almost drowned. I had to fetch her out of the pool. Now I was recalling Laura, when she was not swimming, when Laura talked beautiful poetic nonsense, Laura of the tall sensuality and her eyes sparkling like blue opals.

The swim did me no good. I left the pool and walked towards Elizabeth Bay to look at Laura's old house. I might run into her. I might phone her. I might see her without apparitions. Instead, I sat at the little park watching the small sailing boats bobbing on the darkening water. I turned every few minutes to stare at the old Macquarie Mansion, turned into flats, where Laura still lived. Laura, much-married, Laura who used to whistle at the birds in the trees outside of her large windows, who could make all the sounds of birds. I whistled to myself. I was all crows, magpies and hawks.

I must hurry back to Menzies Hotel to get Alex. As I headed for Kings Cross to take the tram, I passed by Laura's house. There were party sounds coming from the first floor. A cocktail party was on. I heard sounds from my memory. There was Reginald, the editor; Dobell, the artist; and Friend, the artist. Laughter on laughter came from an open window. When, finally, with a burst of sentiment, I looked up, I saw Reginald, fat, wobbly Reginald who hoarded tins and bottles during the war. Whenever Laura needed sardines, she'd bludge a tin from Reginald, or a canned ham. For Reginald had closets full, a private grocery on which he'd spent a few thousand dollars, the gourmet's hoard, so he'd get fatter and wobble a bit more. Reginald, who pretended that he was more English than the English, had been hiding the fact that he was an Arab, an anglicized Arab sent out from England, disgraced for having taken after little boys. It was better to go to Australia than to jail. But he was no longer the homosexual in Australia. Now he liked little girls. He was a mishmash of a man, unable to understand his own drives. But he knew how to hoard. He'd been Laura's best hoarding friend, ready to bring over a bottle or a tin of beef when her war-rationed hunger for exotic food was too much. And the only thing that Reginald wanted in return, since Laura was not a small girl, but a very tall girl, was a good feel of her bottom. She suffered that, on occasion, for a tin and a bottle.

I wanted to call up, "Hey, you fat-assed Reginald, what are you hoarding now, you bastard?" Instead, unseen, I walked away slowly. As I walked, I stared back. There was Laura by the window. A tall man holding a glass was by her and there was a wobbly Reginald laughing like a band playing a military march. The three were drinking, laughing and swearing, and I marched away, lost in my digressions. I was sad. My eyes were wet. I was wondering about the nature of love.

Returning to Melbourne, the ride was still wilder; we blew two tires. There was Alex, embattled with bottles, trying to fix two flats. Not drinking, I was the better mechanic. Alex oozed beer over the cold patches, thinking that beer was adhesive enough to hold in thirty pounds of tire pressure. It only held Alex, now so drunk that I drove on, without a license. In Melbourne I turned the wheel back to Alex, praised him for his scatological images, his beer capacity, his future book of poetry, and the fact that I was still alive. The next day I dug back into my normal literary affairs with Sidney Nolan, then doing a drawing of a bearded, prophetic Jew for Sartre's article, "Portrait of the Anti-Semite," that we were about to publish. Along with Sartre, we published Charles Peguy's two brilliant essays on Jewish unrest—the driven proletarian Jew in all of his hungers, horrors and grace.

Nolan's drawing of the prophetic Jew was extraordinary. You felt biblical in its presence, holy, ancient, pained, throbbing with its universal sadness. I stood by, awed by its misery and mastery. The Jew made noble, the Jew crucified, the Jew all tears, the Jew lamenting for his history, the Jew on his cosmic cross baring his perplexed anxieties to the Christian world.

We were discussing the drawing and Sartre's article, where to place it. The drawing, eventually, went on the cover, the article was the lead piece in the issue. Then we heard a knock.

Nolan went to the front door. Two post office inspectors stood there. One said to Nolan, "Do you know where a Mr. Harry Roskolenko is?"

Nolan saw it all immediately. He didn't really know where I was.

"He's gone up to New Guinea to do a piece on the bloody old

war! What do you want him for? Has he committed some crime?"

"Not a crime, really. He's merely sent a book to himself posted to this address."

"Well, what sort of a book?" asked Nolan.

"Well, a very much banned book, sir."

"What is the name of this very much banned book?"

"A book by a bloke named Edmund Wilson. It's called, if I pronounce it rightly, HECK-ate County—and awful dirty it is. All about some sheilas at a dance hall in New York. Filthy, sir! When I read it, I wondered what sort of a degenerate could write a book like that. Have you read it, sir?"

"I'd like to," said Nolan, smiling slyly. "Can you leave it with me so that I can give it to Mr. Roskolenko when he gets back? No? Oh, too bad. When will he be back? He might not if you intend to arrest him. What, you're going to burn the dirty book? For shame, gentlemen!"

"It's already been burned, sir," went the talking postal inspector. "We know that he sent over a hundred books here— intending to settle in. Would you know the names of some of those books? Are there more HECK-ate books in the lot?"

"I wouldn't rightly know, Mr. Inspector. However, if it will make you feel better, he did have books on prosody, on philosophy, on natural history, on the Australian language—and Tom Collin's novel about old Australia."

"I never heard of the lot, chum," went the inspector, saying good-bye and closing the door.

"You almost had it, Harry," said Nolan. "They'd have kicked you out in a day."

"We're opening the new Contemporary Art Show in two weeks," said Nolan the next morning. "You're to make the opening speech. What do you want to talk about, Mr. HECK-ate County?"

I had talked a lot—lectures at the Australian P.E.N. Club on Faulkner and Hemingway, and there were enough Hemingways about, between the bush and the tight cities, to enrich the parched Australian earth suffering from various forms of drought.

"How about murals? How about a talk on Diego Rivera, Siqueros and Orozco?" I asked.

"They'll hang you, but go ahead. Who wants murals in Australia?"

It was my own cultural lag. The ex-Marxist was coming back

for one solitary lecture on murals—to be used for social-minded art. I suggested that the new Australian artists paint the Australian myths, for its own reality was ever-present. After all, Nolan was doing it—on easels—a portrait of a country. Beginning with Ned Kelly, Nolan was eventually to travel all over Australia and on to Antarctica, to get the feeling of the enormous mystical spaces. He was, years later, to illustrate Alan Moorehead's *Cooper's Creek*, the history of the first trek to the Dead Heart of the Australian continent. And though Nolan was to emerge as the great national artist, he moved to London, to New York, to Greece, to get away "from the wowsers running the bloody country."

I opened a "bloody show"—for the Contemporaries. Prior to making my address on mural painting, I made three fifteen-minute broadcasts on the A.B.C.—to sell the show, to sell abstract impressionism, to sell Australia "covered over with murals." The average Australian had a deeper interest in beer and swimming. Anything more than calendar art was a challenge to his manhood. So I challenged the land. "No art or country can truly prosper unless it has a national art, for that's the only thing left over after the money is counted and the goods distributed—for posterity." Also, to dig a bit deeper, I mentioned ancient Greece —and two Greeks in the audience applauded. I mentioned Italy, and no one applauded. I did the same for ancient Egypt, and a Syrian migrant applauded.

Later, to make my on-the-spot suggestions applicable, I suggested revamping St. Kilda Road, "To make it more imposing than Champs Elysées. It's the finest street in the Southwest Pacific. But what does it have—rooming houses, some mansions, a tram line, a statue to some general of the First World War, and the decadent crap brought over from England. And you can do the same with Collins Street. What does Collins Street have besides shops, office buildings, some pubs and hotels? And as for Flinders Street, it has Young and Jackson's pub, with a great big pig of a nude painting—Cloe—sitting over the bar like a barmaid ready to serve you from her tits. For that matter, to get closer to home, what does my Fifth Avenue, New York's Golden Mile, now have? I know of one restaurant on 43rd and Fifth Avenue that has a mural, a commercial hack job showing ye olde New York. What cultural *merde!*"

Melbourne's major art critic, a Mr. Turnbull, yawned in my face—then winked. I closed, most mightily, saying, "The Australian artist needs the walls of the cities, an audience, a public receptive to the germinating essence of the new forms created in art. It is far too easy to create the stencil-like minimum of the gum tree school, to have wallabies and kangaroos sitting with their canvassed arses on your walls. And since art must constantly challenge to find new frontiers, the innovator, the intrepid experimentalist, is forced to combat the Australian philistine forever. Rather a man with a mug of beer on the sidewalk during the six o'clock swill than another calendar of the sainted wallaby on your walls. A society arrests the course of progress if it stultifies the artist and abandons him and it dies without an Elgin Marble in its back yards or avenues. . . ."

The major art critic, Mr. Turnbull, yawned again and everybody got up to view the show. Mr. Turnbull, said Nolan later, "took exactly ten minutes to view the hundred paintings—and he is an advocate of your 'intrepid newness'—and out he went." Sixty-one artists had been represented, men like Paul Haefliger, Albert Tucker, William Dobell, William Constable, Arthur Boyd, Sidney Nolan, and others and at least four of them were to become universal as artists within the next cultural decade, in and out of Australia.

A few days later, when I ran into Mr. Turnbull at lunch, at Mario's engaging cosmopolitan restaurant off Collins Street, he said puckishly, as he offered me a cognac, "Oh, you opened the flaming show, Mr. Roskolenko . . ." and twelve cognacs later, to even things out between the head and the heart, as I staggered off, never having known a head like this before, all I could say was, "Yes, Mr. Turnbull, and you closed the bloody show. . . ."

I was settled-in like a literary stock-drover, awaiting Australian revelations—past and present. Whenever you saw a wandering aborigine, you saw man's historical inhumanity. A few aborigines, like Albert Namatjira, and his son, Oscar, became bush artists. They were mission-trained to do polite, picturesque, calendar-like renderings of their mystic past. They were, according to some anthropologists, related to the Dravidians of southern India, to the fuzzy-wuzzies of Papua—but not to Canberra, where policy was made. By 1946 they had decreased by seventy percent since the settling of Australia and they were, by the natural pushing-them-back process, awaiting extinction, or *alcheringa*, the heaven of the aborigine. In a double irony, the Australians used aborigine names for many of their towns, plains, mountains, lakes and rivers—from which the aborigines had been pushed away. Today there are magical place-names over the land, like Maralinga, "the field of thunder," where Australia and England would perform their atom bomb magic. There are lovely names like Buldania, Balladonia, Cocklebiddy, Moonera, Bunabie, Albala, Koonalda, Guinewarra and Yangoonabie. Some were pure aborigine; others were bastardized like the Older Australians of 1946.

Whatever they were, they were not first-class citizens, new or old. Their pay, as domestics or farm laborers, was two shillings a week for pocket money, with three shillings held back as a trust fund. Some of them lived in the slums of Melbourne's Fitzroy, as *lumpens*. With Australia ever union-conscious, none were admitted into the unions. As for Federal pensions and the social services, it did not involve a dark, spindle-legged man called an *abo*—by even the most liberal-hearted Australians.

Twenty-five hundred of them had served in the Australian forces in Europe and the Pacific, and only one had been commissioned a lieutenant.

The aborigine in 1946 could, in the cities, where he was a hopeless minority of nothing, attend school. But in the bush and the country towns the third grade was as far as he could go. And no matter how much miscegination had taken place, he was always the *abo* according to the "Act," which the aborigine called all the laws passed regarding his status. The pub, the measure of Australian mateship, was closed to him. He was taboo everywhere—the *blackfeller* who had once owned all of Australia. Up north, around Cape York, he had often been enslaved to the Chinese, the Malays and the Japanese, who ran the *bêche-de-mer* and trochus luggers, and to the missionaries, who often ran their own jails for trespassing aborigines. For a natural infraction, like going off on a *walkabout* (back to his native place), he had, on occasion, been sent off to Palm Island, a penal colony in northern Queensland.

By 1966, when the laws had eased up greatly, Australia had 175,000,000 sheep and 19,000,000 head of cattle, but only 40,000 aborigine citizens between Perth, Darwin, Cape York,

Townsville and Adelaide. Time's genocide had done yeoman work. The land, Down Under, was coming of age on the last frontier of the white man's Pacific heartland—Australasia.

I, the New Australian, was very much at home. It was just another war—post-war. For poets and novelists it is always a war. Some were still involved with New Guinea, where the Australians had fought—especially Osmar White, author of *Green Armor*, a fine study of the New Guinea campaigns. I had seen some of the hellish greenery of death there. But whatever they were writing about, they were drinking much harder at the six o'clock swill. You found a pub you liked. You met the crowd you liked. You came there regularly—and you were introduced about. Soon all your old friends knew where to find you, to bludge a drink or to borrow a "few quid" until payday. It was like that at the pubs among the spigot-shooting, all-embracing, foul-fulminating, beer-soaked cobbers. And the writers were not much better, from language to largesse.

The poets I knew were mostly dour, when not drunk. One had an ulcer and a Russian wife, and he fellow-traveled about for the Russians. He inspired you to total nothingness in five minutes. He wanted communism, flat, in one "flat-out minute." When he made a house party, it was to invite possible converts—and he served tea, Russian style. He put out a national magazine, Australian style. He was seeking a viable homogenized Nationalism and he specialized in pretentious anthropological material embracing the disappearing aborigine—for even the name of his magazine was aborigine. Unfortunately, he was not dark enough to pass. He was blond, of Scandinavian origin, born in dull Brisbane, educated there, had been to America, and he hated America—because you had to—as a communist. He was the perfect ulcer man, from his breath to his vision—a gashouse of a human being, without love, looking like his sad condition. At his parties, however, when taking women's coats and cloaks, he managed to get his hand on their arses, allegedly by accident, and all he got was a sudden stare back—and nothing much more.

It was a literary life and to "hell with it," as some American had written after expatriating himself to Paris. One of Australia's dullest—and most famous—writers had written about a dog. He was pleasantly dull. But Frank Dalby Davison had gifts, for sheepdog purling and psychiatry. There was also Gavin Casey, whom I had known in New York when he was head of the Australian Information Bureau. Gavin loved his grog and the Irish state of inner and outer affairs and he wrote with great Australian flavors. Basically, he was a fine short story writer, with two books of classical stories—*It's Harder For Girls* and *Downhill It's Easier*. And with Gavin and a bottle, the talk was easier. He was, in some ways, a younger version of James T. Farrell, whom he later met through me, "because, if there was any fucking reason to be in New York, it was to meet that bloke, Farrell, who influenced me with his first fucking novel, *Studs Lonigan. . . .*" Gavin had his language—pure Western Australian.

The poets were having a hard time finding their language. Brought up on earlier attempts at an Australian national literature, they took to men like Christopher Brennan, a friend of Mallarmé. Yet, with the temptation to go all-hog Aussie, with the strains of "Waltzing Matilda" embarrassing the more sophisticated poets, it became a carnival of poetic styles. In Adelaide, earlier, I had met Rex Ingamells, who edited *Jindyworobak,* a magazine totally dedicated to primitivism in the arts. Ingamells was even more sold on going back to the *abo* for themes, sounds, language—and the future of Australia. One day, while going back, he was killed in a car accident and I mourned this wonderful *whitefella* who'd had another vision of Australia to be. Yet there were fine poets, like A. D. Hope, Max Harris, Judith Wright, Geoffrey Dutton, James McAuley, and Kenneth Slessor who had, like Rimbaud, quit while he was full of visions to be.

Australia to be, as I went all-Australian, meant many curious things. It was an outdoor country from its weather to its inner events. Whatever England had done or was doing, Australia was not to follow anymore. It was still provincial, without a whimper. It lived off overseas mail and magazines. There was no boldness about it except with the immigration race. It was cricket, football, horse racing, beer. . . .

I met a few psychiatrists, without much of a well-healed practice. Unlike the United States, there were fewer paying neurotics and psychotics about. The psychiatrists, overly bored, were not wealthy and some of them, to even things out in their social psyches, joined organizations like The Rationalists, who met on alternate Saturday afternoons at pubs like Phairs or The Mitre where they free-thought and free-associated their way through the Australian miasma.

The Rationalists cussed out Foreign Minister Evatt, at the United Nations, who was not champion enough for all their free-associations. They were for labor but against the endless strikes. The trams stopped. The gas was turned off just as you were about to boil water for tea. The bakers struck as you were about to buy bread. The newspapers did the same and everybody, naturally, during the year, was on some strike or other. This, of course, was not properly rational for The Rationalists, who were also fighting nature—the terrible droughts that emasculated the Australian land. They favored dams, of course, and were anti the White Australia Policy "to bring in more than our native intelligence." They discussed, with professional pride, the condition of Australia's railroads, which had been built, state by state, of different track gauges, so that a train going from the state of Queensland, to New South Wales, to Victoria, to South Australia, to Western Australia, had its passengers change many times. And the same with the freight. Imagine going from New York to Chicago—and being forced to change trains in New Jersey, Pennsylvania, Ohio, and Indiana before reaching Union Station. The Rationalists, which I had joined for the malarkey, meant an occasional Saturday afternoon given over to technical Australian digressions and transgressions.

It was a kibitzer's paradise for the doctors, lawyers, justices of peace and the dentists of The Rationalists. It had an air of innocuous middle-class rebellion carried over into middle age. The men were successful professionals still playing at radicalism. Some were fellow-travelers with private maps. Others were normal Australians who wanted to get away from their oppressive lives and wives "on a Saturday." They stood for "decency" at all times and their never-to-be-forgotten own good and welfare. They ate like gourmets, drank like troopers, leched like Don Juans and were properly liberal 24 hours a day. It was, without doubt, a club to belong to if you were a New Australian. And if you liked tinned lamb, the national dish, The Rationalists gave it to you conversationally—with a can opener.

It was a Never-Ever Land in every human direction. It was a conspiracy of geography, so far from Europe, and nature. But events at *Tomorrow*, "the outspoken monthly," were soon to

make another migrant out of me. Everybody there was quarreling with everybody there and everybody not there, and especially with Mr. R., about to return from his sunning session on the
Great Barrier Reef. He was withdrawing his various subsidies—
from men and magazines. He was going broke, he said to Nolan
in a letter.

"We're folding," said Sidney Nolan. "Australia does not want
to support us. What will you do, Harry?"

"What about all those ads we were getting from the unions?"

"We're not getting any. Bellew's tried them all. It's no go,
chum." Neither the Australian Labor Party, which we sponsored,
nor the unions it controlled, would take an inch of an ad.

Mr. H., the imaginative editor of some of the firm's other
magazine ventures, was packing up to get back to Adelaide,
taking the title of ownership in his bags. Mr. Bellew was retiring
to Ballarat to become a country gentleman again. Mr. Nolan was
retiring to Heidelberg to paint the mystical Australian scene.
Others, unnamed, were out looking for uncanny jobs. The firm
was folding up. Journalism, art, poetry—everything the firm
stood for—were through, and most of the artists Mr. R. had supported were soon to leave. It was to be an exodus out of Australia, taking Nolan and William Constable to England, Albert
Tucker to Paris, Roy Dalgarno to India. And many years later,
some of them were to return, the expatriates come home, ac-
ceptable in their own country. But 1946–1947 was their year of
decision—to get the hell out of Australia!

I made no decision. I was content to stay on and free-lance. I
could always give talks on the A.B.C. on America. I lectured
without end at the Chamber of Commerce and The Fellowship
of Australian Writers. But talking to an Australian audience of
poets and novelists, with their merciless animations and towering
envies, was like going onto a modern battlefield in your jockey
underwear. I had already spoken on Hemingway, Faulkner,
Melville, Edgar Lee Masters and Sandburg—on the influences of
the influenced. My last talk was on the patronage of the temporarily dispossessed—the Writers Project of the WPA—from our
own benevolent Thirties. It was 48 States worth of patronage, a
Roman Circus straight from Washington, a Democratic welfare
state. I talked for two hours about my own contributions to a
skiing guide to New York State, a maritime history of New York

City, a hiker's guide to Staten Island (there were farms there then), and I told them that from Staten Island one got an unusual view of the backside of the Statue of Liberty—a tall, stately, sainted, marble welcoming woman.

It had been an unusual time in the United States then, I said. We were practicing a form of low-class socialism. We got the bread but not the cake. The icing was in Washington along with the Scotch. But, no matter our gutter socialism, it had been "creative" in the arts. It had rebuilt America "from promises" made since the Civil War. For me, too, it had meant my first book of poetry, called *Sequence On Violence*. Naturally, I being then most revolutionary as a Trotskyist, its violence was aimed at the "ruling class." Lewis Mumford, a literary friend, wrote the introduction. Most of the poems dealt with the City of New York—

> The new houses amid franchised orations
> number one tenth of one per cent of one hundred.
> In a thousand years your cautious ghost will dwell
> in a streamlined stucco den . . .

I was allowed, I said to my Australian poets and novelists, to stay at home, later, government-sponsored to write the book. Richard Wright, equally sponsored, was at home writing his much-admired novel, *Native Son*. My point—and I must have had at least one—was that the United States was paying for all this. It was as if they had told Lenin, temporarily turned poet, to come and get his pay every two weeks—and to write a book called *State and Revolution*. For we were, in our own modest way, damning the State and calling for a revolution.

There were a lot of communists at the lecture at the Fellowship of Australian Writers. They wore wide red ties, blue work shirts, and were tweedy-seedy in their pragmatic pretenses toward looking proletarian, reminding me of the first expert in the field of proletarian sartorialism, Dwight Macdonald during the engaged Thirties. They argued like they looked—dialectical. One of them, Max Brown, a communist organizer, asked, "How proletarian was your writing on the Project? You supported the Democratic Party did you not?" I did not, I said. Mr Brown turned redder, then asked, "Were you a Trotskyist then?" I was,

COLLEGE OF THE SEQUOIAS
LIBRARY

I said. I also had breathed. Did that make me a collaborator with others who did the same in the Democratic Party?

Mr. Frank Dalby Davison, the dog writer, dognapped throughout the evening. I did not have a word to say about sheepdogs versus gutter socialism. Mr. Tunn, the poet who had visited me in the hospital, and Melbourne's favorite plagiarist, beamed happily. I know his beamish face would, after the lecture, cost me what I would get from the Fellowship as a fee. Mr. Albert Tucker, a soon-to-be great artist, asked, "Where has all the bloody art gone to from the Art Project? I've heard that more than one hundred thousand paintings and murals were executed. Who has them?"

I talked for another two hours. Some of the art had gone to federal and state buildings. Toilets, once without art, now had great paintings over their urinals. It was just as important to look at art then as at any other natural time. There was WPA art in the post offices of the Western prairies. "Even the Rocky Mountain states got their share of murals and easel paintings. How much of the stuff is worth anything? Who knows! But we painted up America, once bleak and hungry, unhoused and ill— and every one of us sonsofbitches got fed, gentlemen. If that's capitalism, then I've just, tonight, at this lecture, become a supporter of capitalism!"

Mr. Frank Dalby Davison awoke, to applaud something. Mr. Tunn applauded everything. Mr. Brown invited me out for a drink and/or a fight. Later, at an after-hours literary club on Collins Street, no one threw a punch. Everybody got drunk— some to celebrate themselves, like Walt Whitman.

My private and public disenchantments in Melbourne were growing daily. I had not even unpacked my library of books and pictures. I was an enforced bachelor in another country, not about to take another job—nor caring. A job now meant permanence in Australia and I was finding its flaws too easily. Yet I loved the look of the land. I could, when I went into the bush on weekends, stare dreamily at the gum trees, at the gaunt, bare, skeletal splendor of the white, pale, purpling bark. The bush and the outback bled into my lonely desires. You looked and saw a poem standing—then the little animals of poetry. And when I turned back after the weekend, there was Melbourne and the city-bred sensuality among the girls.

In spite of Laura and loving Laura, I found the girls who were easy to find. They were handsome, lovely women, red of hair, blonde of hair, swimmers on Sunday, tennis players on Wednesday, drinking companions at the pub, walkers into the bush, living with ease, at home in all vexing situations, always giving, easily comforted when pregnant. They were the kind of girls who took off on "work vacations" and went abroad, working at everything, living in all countries, seeking a tougher world than Australia's, and then settling down to make the family of man another quarrelsome Australian statistic. It was an old view, and D. H. Lawrence had seen it with all its ragged terrors after six months in Australia. It dominated the Australian domestic scene. You saw it in the pinched, married, male faces. You heard it in the married feminine whine. It resembled the American face in another country.

The women I met were an admixture, proudly Australian, partially at odds with the "cultural lag," and it always came up with the bookish ones, or those who kept up with the foreign trends and tendencies in art. At the pubs, as they adventured among their male companions in the world of terse dialogues, you felt the "lag" in every serious expression. And their dress, literally years behind—for men and women alike. Publisher H., as computor of values, reckoned that Australia was at least twenty years behind. When H. talked about jazz, he managed, since we had put out a special issue on jazz, to say as an amalgam, "Jazz is Negro. Jazz is New Orleans. Jazz is Jewish. Jazz is slavery. Jazz is miscegenated. Jazz laments like the Jews do in their synagogues. Jazz is a mishmash. Jazz is aboriginal—straight off the Dead Heart. . . ."

H., when drunk, which was hardly ever, talked bits of Yiddish. When normally sober, he was pure South Australian, with aborigine words thrown in for flare and confusion. After ten beers, he developed some inner honesty and we talked Yiddish, which he said he had learned from a Jewish aborigine. After fifteen beers he was almost ready to join the Haganah to fight the Arabs. He said too at times that he was of German descent, though without beer all of his attempts to hide his Jewish background became grotesque and he covered up his language, his antecedents, "the lot," as Laura used to say during the war.

My Australian friends were leaving Australia, and I was locked within a comedy of unequal ironies—to stay or not to stay. Lacking a total decision, I decided on a two-month assignment to New Guinea. I joined the Royal Australian Air Force Searcher Party—as its historian.

Our mission—the still missing Australian Air Force personnel who had crash-landed or parachuted behind the Japanese lines. There were always rumors—native rumors—that many Australians thought lost during the war were still alive. They had been seen by Papuans in swamps or in razorback mountain villages. They were alleged to be living with native women, lost in geography and time. If the war was over they had not learned of it; and the Searcher Party, about to complete more than a year's long search, asked me to write a definitive report. The search involved Australians, Dutch, Indonesians as well as Americans—literally every country that had fought the Japanese in New Guinea.

Returning to New Guinea meant isolation. It was like going back to the war, being on ships without women. And now, about to leave for New Guinea's jungled isolation, I planned a minor orgy in Melbourne—to celebrate my arrival, my departure, the ocean that had brought me—and Laura's ghost. The cultural lag could go to hell. Mother Australia was my willing mistress.

I ate to fornicate. I rested to fornicate. All my senses between sleep and waking were dedicated to fornication. It was an Australian *Götterdämmerung*.

To drown out our laments for love, or whatever we were offering to each other, I played Bach's mighty organ notes. One night it would be a woman who talked endlessly and left you with a fear for your sanity; another night, repetitions, variations, other sexual inventions, delight and insight, the woman in the woman, the man in the man, another night of a self-imposed orgy. I was, when I thought it through, going through a purge. There were monsters and gargoyles, women who looked pretty until they were naked, who insisted that all the lights go out, who moaned about love as if they were about to die, having just met you an hour before, a stranger with a stranger, two bodies, unacquainted, yet merging, suddenly acquainted, merged in some dry offering to love; women who liked Americans because Americans were generous, Americans took them to dinner, to a show, to the beach and it was easy to make love with an American because he wanted sex, more sex, endless sex, much as if Sex and God were related, blessing your house, anointing your body, and giving you a bastard to take home and hurrah for "The Star-Spangled Banner."

Emily came along in time to save me—if not herself. I had met Emily during the war, when Laura had taken me to Emily's home in Hawthorne. We had gone to tea. Emily had worn a long red gown. Nude photos of her were on her piano and I thought that she was very handsome in her red gown, in the way she moved in her Middle Eastern ways. She had lived in Cairo once. She had lived in Paris once. She had known the world of extremes, as an editor, wanderer, expatriate, and she had come back to Australia as the war was breaking out. Now she raised dogs and published a literary magazine. Now she rode horses out into the bush, "to get the feel of the Egyptian desert . . ." and she took photographs of herself, in the nude, along the shore, in the sand, feeling like a primitive. She had said, "I'd rather be a Dinka in the Sudd than an Australian. They go naked and show off their beauty. Here they'd arrest you for being beautiful. . . ." On that afternoon of the war she had talked of Verlaine and Rimbaud, who'd taken off on a trek. Rimbaud had beaten up Verlaine . . . and then, said Emily, feeling even more primitive, "Rimbaud took off for Aden and Ethiopia to become a gun-runner for Menelek. What a poet! What a strange man! He trusted no man, none of his Somali wives, and he carried fifty pounds of gold around his waist. Ah, Rimbaud!"

Remembering so many exotic details about Emily, I telephoned and started to explain for her own recollections who I was. I mentioned Rimbaud, to help, Verlaine, to help a bit more, the Egyptian desert, to get closer to Emily, and she burst out:

"Oh, Roskolenko! What are you doing in Australia?"

I explained that in five minutes. Somehow, Laura came back into the conversation, and all Emily would say was, "Oh, that bitch! What a way to treat a healthy man. Are you all right now?"

"I am tired," I said. "May I see you? When? Tonight. . . ." She
was flattered, she said.

"By what?" I asked.

"That you recall me," she said. "You didn't stay very long."

"There was a war on—and we were heading for the Philippines
in the morning," I said, becoming heroic about the war.

"Oh, yes, the Philippines. Were you hurt?"

"My ship was hit by a floating mine. . . ."

"I remember Laura writing about your lost tanker. Where are
you living now, where do I meet you?"

"I have a flat, with flowers, with Bach records, with whiskey,
and myself off Saint Kilda Road . . ." and I gave her the number.

"Will eight o'clock be all right?"

"Any hour," I said, "even after midnight. . . ."

There was still an hour before she would arrive. I took out
a Blanche Thebom recording, Purcell's "Love Sickness." Its Elizabethan airs echoed through my large, flowery living room. Piles
of roses had been put into three vases by the landlady. I was
surrounded by Purcell, beautiful Blanche Thebom and my landlady's floating rose garden. It was a place for Emily's conceits,
nature, the panic of love's bewilderments, a plot to circumnavi-
gate within myself.

The record ended. I went on to the Gregorian Chants sung by
the Barcelona Boys Choir, a record I had copied because it was
impossible to obtain. No one had bothered to make new press-
ings. The young chorus welled up, going between heaven and
hell in a pageant of my own purgatory. I was entering the mon-
astery of myself, taking the awful pressure of the chants, raging
sounds, booming voices, ecstatic Godliness—and then the terror
of all the meanings of Christ, the Jew.

The doorbell rang. I shook. It might be the landlady complaining about my missing a few "cuppas," or the welling music up-
setting the fawning arabesques of her mind. But I could see
through the glass door Emily's regal red gown worn as if she
were the queen of Egypt, Isis at Thebes and Luxor.

The sacred glass door was opening. In walked Emily, red-
gowned, hardly the queen, yet very much an austere woman,
looking like Isis at Thebes . . . as if a rose were about to burst
from her navel.

As I took her coat, she said, "Of course, it was your eyes. Do you always stare at women? I heard the music. I breed dogs but I prefer to play the piano. Do you have any Mozart piano pieces? Why do I breed dogs? So that poets can remember me. And how is Saul? He's famous now, no? A Pulitzer Prize winner for poesy. Yes, that book that he wrote about me. How flattering! Of course, since I was the publisher of it, I should have printed more, for it's a collector's rare item. Whatever Saul called it, it was badly named since it replaced love for neither of us. Oh, what the war did to some men!"

"Scotch, sherry or beer?" I asked, more than bewildered.

"Not sherry, thank you. Scotch. And nothing more about dogs. Do you know the difference between a setter and a poodle? Both have four legs and tails, so I'll say nothing more about dogs except that I win prizes. . . ."

I handed her the Scotch. She sipped, winced, then said, "A bit more soda, please . . ." and as I added the soda, I looked at her fully—fleshy, full-armed, strong-legged. A lady dog fancier! Yet there was the fox and the cat about her. The eyes and mouth, however, were Parisian with knowledge. The body was Egyptian. I expected to see the Sacred Boat of Isis come crashing through the floor—Isis, reconstituted.

I asked her about the magazine she edited, *Art and Literature*. It had woodcuts, French translations, Italian translations, and some Australians, soon to be famous.

"It's not for Australia. They prefer *The Bulletin*, or *Truth*, for all the lies about how good the whites are. Bastardized facts! And further, how interesting is it to read that one out of every four Australian girls is slightly preggo before her wedding night? More American influences no doubt."

"No doubt, Emily. More Scotch?"

"No. More music. Mozart."

"The Magic Flute?"

"You came from America with that?"

"With that and more, for the last frontier. Mozart would even make a jungle possible. Even this place," I said defensively.

"Not bloody likely, chum. You won't settle here, Harry, with or without Mozart."

"I won't?"

"You won't. You're still too liberal. You believe in magic and there's none here," said Emily, as I put on *The Magic Flute*.

"We'll end up like your country, but much worse. You know, the Asiatic world outside? That dark-yellow world the politicians are frightening us all with? What muck!"

"Who is the conquering liberal now?" I asked. "Would you like to conquer China, to remove the yellow peril? Ask us to do it for you, Emily."

"We would, if it were not for two other things that keep us endlessly occupied—sports and beer. That's our *Drang nach Osten*, Mr. Roskolenko. We're the eternal athletes. Youth forever! Excelsior! Beer! Tennis! *Merde!* Weren't you an athlete once?"

She was studying me as if I were two totemic elements, sports and beer, of the Australian male. I was drinking Scotch not beer and I had not been very much of an athlete since I stopped chasing Paavo Nurmi around the track at Madison Square Garden.

"Let me see the rest of this quaint flat." As she stood up, she patted the record player, remarking, "Mozart makes me lewd I'm afraid. There's something indecently over-magical!" Whatever she meant, I found her walking toward the bedroom, adding laughingly, "It's so large for one man. Do you sleep alone? Do you bring sheilas in? Are you moral? Are you amoral? Have you made any girls preggo yet? Will you really become a New Australian? Do you think that you can stand us forever? Do you like the racial meaning of the miserable pun by Minister of Immigration Arthur Calwell, who said recently regarding possible Chinese immigrants, 'Two Wongs don't make a White.' "

Emily was sitting on the bed and asking, "And how much do you pay for this flower-laden flat?"

"Six pounds . . ." and I went back to the living room to cut down the overpowering Mozart opera. I felt just as lewd and it would end up as another night.

It did not, that night.

"I only came to look at you and now I must go back to my dogs, sir . . ." she said, her mouth going hard.

"Dinner at Mario's on Saturday?"

She was reserved, I was not. At the door, I kissed her. Her mouth remained closed and hard. I had been turned down, forcefully-gently. We had talked about the yellow peril, Australian athletes, American vulgarity, America the endless winner. And Mozart.

"Eight, at Mario's, Saturday."

Saturday night after Mario's was another time. Emily was married, but separated for two years. In three more years, under Victorian laws, she would get her divorce. As for the Great American Poet, Saul, who had been in Australia during the war, he had wanted to marry Emily then. He had written a book to show his love but when we talked about her recent past Emily said, "I never believed Saul. Poets! Wars! Dogs! They are all related in their fashion. Saul left a beautiful girl behind in Baltimore, so that's his success story. A great poet, no? I'm sure you liked his work. Why are poets so different? You, for instance, are not, I gather. You seem to be half honest with yourself, or at least one quarter honest. Am I wrong? . . . . Please, let's listen to *The Magic Flute* again. I did not hear the end. I like the way it completes itself!"

I set the record where she wanted it. We were kissing, standing against each other, mouthing each other, talking of love, talking of what it must mean again.

I was undressing her. Nothing planned was happening. We were happily going to each other and she was saying, naked, up against the bedroom door, "I want a child from this, please. The doctors say that I'm barren and I want to be pregnant. I'm a woman. I need a child. I need a baby's endless voice. I want a child. . . ."

"My child or will anybody do?"

"I haven't been with a man since I separated. Your child, please! Get me pregnant, please! Fill me up with a baby. Fill me up!"

"Look, this is very serious," I said, lecturing her. I was being decently sociological for a minute, then clinical. The doctors were right, the laws were right, bastards needed fathers and mothers, I was going to New Guinea, I was not settling in Australia, I was having my sexual fling, I was kissing her, my caution gone, my morals on the bed, and floating words about love coming from Emily, from me, from memory, from Laura, from every need I had ever known to father away my loneliness. I was fathering away another world.

The record had finished. It was scratching at the end. . . .

We met three times a week. We were in love, we said. As for her possible pregnancy, she was not pregnant. She made a humorous sally about that evening. "I must have been awfully filthy with what I said or did, yes?" She wanted me to photograph her and one day I went out to her house in the suburbs. It was bush country, tree country, horse country, Australia still so wild outside of the cities. It was not Parisian or Egyptian and she showed me photographs of herself, those that I had seen before, and she was always nude, a proper nude, proud of her strong body, her greening eyes, her soft blonde falling hair, age 33, a statue of pride, made of flesh, arranged by nature, wanting a child and we were in love, we said.

The purge had ended. There was Emily. And New Guinea.

"How long will you be gone? Will you return? If I'm preggo—?"

"I'll return. . . ."

"You'll return?"

"Yes."

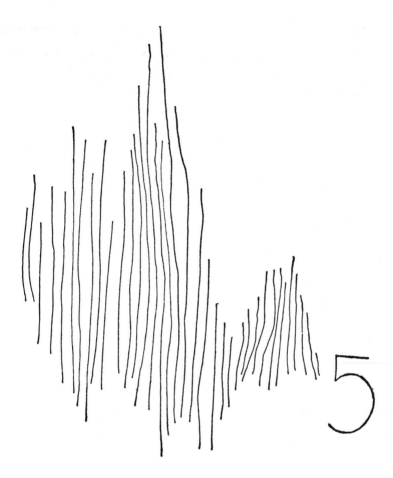

GREEN HELL—NEW GUINEA REVISITED

UNDER THE ASSUMED temporary rank of lieutenant colonel, and uniformed similarly, I was suddenly in the Australian Army—on a humane mission in New Guinea.

I journeyed back into history to the green-on-green war years. We had turned the last primitive bastion in New Guinea into a vast military depot. Plantations, rude villages, dirt tracks, forest trails, jungled savannahs had been altered into two-lane coral roads and landing fields. It was our Western magic via the bull-dozer's might. Inlets, coves—any place to hide our ships and boats—soon made up our transformed naval hideaways. Our tools were hammers, engines—and guns. We had come to kill.

61

It was quiet now. No armies, no bombs dropping—just the returning planters, grazers, gold miners and traders from Australia. They had increased threefold, to exploit the island's inner wealth. It grew tangled. It looked like money after the sweat. It came up from grass, swamps, plateaus, mountains—ready for the engines of peace and the banks. The tangled green idiocy was to be my war re-visited for two months as I saw the past, slogged through the present, discovering the dog tags and the ways of death with the Royal Australian Air Force Searcher Party.

We flew to Townsville, in Queensland, en route to New Guinea. The airstrip, almost totally deserted, had its war reminders—signs faded, signs still recognizable, signs meaning nothing. One sign stuck out—U.S. ARMY REPORT HERE. It was Townsville dead, the gateway to New Guinea dead. Once strident with American voices, it was Australian again. We had sung "Waltzing Matilda" with our nasal voices over a million mugs of beer. What was left of the Officers' Mess, where the drinking bar was open, was a stopover for the RAAF courier service running to occupied Japan, where General MacArthur was the proconsul.

We took off again, swooped over Townsville in the overheated dawn, and headed through a break in the Barrier Reef, to cross the China Straits. I recalled other trips to New Guinea, when we had fighter escorts and destroyers trailing us. Now we saw only the blue sea, coral islands and atolls, with an occasional fishing boat coming back from the trolling areas. The cruisers that once studded these waters no longer broke through, sprayed by sharp forward dives. I thought of the 28 officers who had drowned here in 1943, when a Japanese sub had sunk their ship. Schoolmates of mine, they had been on their way to replace other men at Gili-Gili, in Milne Bay.

The plane landed at Jackson Field, Port Moresby, on a billowing airstrip. Half of it was dangerous and closed off with empty oil drums. Nature burrowed away and rain had washed out what had once been well-paved and taken care of. Only a dozen men were operating the airstrip now. Two years ago, thousands. The barracks looked rotted, the mosquito wiring stove in and broken.

"It's all gone bung," said a thin flight sergeant. On the six-mile trip to Port Moresby in a jeep, he added, "You'll recognize precious little in town now. The planters are back and up to the neck in government muck." I observed military encampments without campers, tents without occupants, everything caved in. Ela Beach could no longer be called Brothel Beach, for now there were no crash boats rushing by. In *lakatoi's* (native craft) big-breasted, almost nude Papuan women smiled their always astonishing joy as they paddled their boats by.

In the center of Port Moresby, stuck up like a totem pole, was the wooden Papuan Hotel, once the planters' paradise. Alongside of it, in poured concrete, a cinema was going up. A summer resort was envisioned, a miniature Southwest Pacific Miami Beach—yachts, water sports, gambling, girls, and sentimental visits to the nearby battlefields. It was an idyllic blueprint for banks, shipping companies, air lines—but not for the Minister of External Territories, Edward Ward. He had told me one day over a few beers, "New Guinea is to be developed for the benefit of the natives and some returning ex-servicemen, with the future of the natives coming first. This is not going to become another bloody colony, mate—neither for the God-awful planters, the bank managers, nor the messing-about missionaries, nor any bloody body else. . . ."

Later, at Port Moresby, I heard a similar view, but with less proletarian splendor, from Colonel John Keith Murray, the administrator, and ex-professor of agriculture at Queensland University. He agreed with the Minister of External Territories—but in the Queen's English. Colonialism had had its day. The two-year contract that the natives signed to work—which literally indentured them—was out. "The ruddy, bloody planters! You'd think this was below the Mason-Dixon Line, circa 1859!" I'd heard it from liberals and conservatives. It was another time. New Guinea was to be transformed into a kindergarten of arts and crafts, with new industries coming in from Australia that were especially geared to native skills. Headhunting had, until a few years ago, been one of their more skillful arts.

As I was leaving, Administrator Murray picked up a brown folder. On it was printed, "Telephone Directory, APO 929, Restricted." And, as he handed it to me, he said, "You might like another souvenir of the war—General MacArthur's phone book folder."

I took it, pride mixed with sarcasm, uncertain of the gift's meaning. Like too many others in the South Pacific, I'd had

various feelings about General MacArthur. Every time he walked
ashore after a bombardment, surging through the Pacific surf, we
remembered what was said—"There, but for the grace of Mac-
Arthur, goes God. . . ."

The radio nerve center of the war, 9PA Radio Moresby, was
no longer a guarded grove to tell the world about the war in the
jungles. A hundred war correspondents had camped here when
General MacArthur had planned each stage of the invasion from
nearby Government House. And I was told by Mr. Vane, who
now ran 9PA Radio Moresby on civil service efficiency, that I
was about to make a half-hour broadcast. "Your subject is what
is it like for an American, who spilled his blood here during the
war, to come back again. . . ."

Radio-culture spread throughout the islands to all the police
posts and medical stations. Local gossip, medical advice, how to
cook cabbage soup, everything, went on the air. For weeks I
kept hearing about "the sentimental Yank who's come back."

The natives had taken over the U.S. Army bivouacks, the tents,
the corrugated buildings, the outhouses, the grass-thatched
churches, the synagogues and everything else we had left behind.
As for Port Moresby itself, it now had fifteen hundred whites
instead of the prewar three hundred. The new population, the
ex-soldiers, had returned like homesteaders to claim their blood-
stained acres, government-granted, in a fellowship offering them
a realizable future with the Papuan on the endlessly green-grow-
ing earth.

The courier plane bound for Finchhafen stopped at Lae for fuel.
Coming through the Kokoda Gap, through the terrifying Owen
Stanley Mountains and titanic cliffs was my single Douglas
where once hundreds of planes had fought. I was still bound in
by the peculiarities of this natural silence, a visitor, familiar and
yet not familiar. For I had only known Lae as a noisy replace-
ment depot. Now there were only razorback mountains and
brown-green splendor.

At Base "F," Finchhafen, were thirteen kid-Americans, part of
the thinned-out, spread-out Fifth Air Force, guarding a ware-
house, the contents of which would soon be shipped to China and
the Indies for other wars. The same billowing strips, cavernous,

surrealist, paraded their unbroken doing over by nature—rain. I remembered how the planes landed right behind the U.S. Coast Guard Station, at Dobadurra, which the Royal Australian Navy now ran. We had built it up into a rushed resort, with the living quarters over the inlet looking like summer shacks in the Adirondacks. I walked away from the destruction, down to where the Liberty and Victory ships used to dock at nearby Langamach. But the docks and the approaches were toppling. Wood tangled on wood, grotesque—yet grand. Burned-out hulks lay in the water. Ships without men, ships for fish swimming through the hulks.

I remembered when I was on a wartime tanker servicing the hidden Dobadurra oil wells. We were signalled to come in and dock, to discharge our explosive high-octane. When we approached the oil dock, a huge wave of fire and smoke rose out of the jungle, where the oil wells were. The Navy Station kept signalling us to dock. I refused to come in with the ship and ordered her out to midstream. Soon we could see the fire above the trees. All of Langamach was shrouded in billowing smoke, making our exit from the harbor acutely hazardous but instinctively essential. I remembered the incident as I looked at the remains of the petroleum dock at Dobadurra, now half submerged. Had we come in, we would have exploded. . . .

The two-lane highway at Finch, on which, it was said, "you can walk knee-deep in mud, after one of those great rains, and still get dust in your eyes," had lost its warring look. The chapel on South Eleventh Street, Finchhafen, where the soldiers used to sell each other their crude arts and crafts made from aluminum, lay on its oblique side. A crude crucifix had been propped up by some religious native as a memento. It was Christ in bamboo. Half-blurred humorous signs pointed to every city in the world. "New York, 10,000 miles this way" was stuck on a post, though the direction was downward rather than to the east. At Song River, as soft as its minstrel name, I met a few of the kid-soldiers on their way back from a crocodile hunt. They were an odd lot now. In no war, watching warehouses, they were the superintendents over grass.

At Butaweng Creek and Mape River, the steel bridges built by Army engineers were half destroyed. In their skeletal remains, they careened dangerously. At these bridges, there had always been a traffic jam—vehicles on vehicles, ready to be loaded, ready for the invasion of the Philippines, ready for the soldiers and the ships. And, whenever I had an errand there, I used to put a wet handkerchief over my face to keep the coral dust, always rising like a red wind, from clogging my eyes and nostrils. But now, at the bridges, were contractors from Australia, Indonesia and other Asian countries. They were buying up the metal, everything considered used up, having no future in New Guinea. It was "bunged"—as the Australians said about everything that the kunai grass took back. They were buying everything labelled "Made in America." Old rubber tires made shoes in China. Old tents made sails on Chinese junks. Aluminum made a metal world of trinkets for Asia's skilled craftsmen. Only the green hell, unexportable, remained.

A few passing natives grinned at me, at my camera, as I snapped them, walking half-dressed in Army clothes worn more for decoration than need in this ferment of heat and rain. I laughed when I saw a three-year-old native boy waddling by, wearing a huge Army raincoat, with an Australian digger's hat for an umbrella. The half million soldiers once here had left their khaki trappings to the flora, fauna and Melanesian man. Progress meant removing these symbols of the past—war and death. The natives, though curiously involved in the war, had not lost more than they had gained. They were still free. They had been invaded by the East and the West. What had been left behind was too odd, too ridiculous, for what they needed.

The whole scene was a *Walpurgisnacht* of memory and emotion. Nearby was the American Cemetery with the bodies of 12,000 troops, guarded by the 33 teen-age American soldiers only three months in the postwar Army. An irony of transplantation, it was a dull time for them as the caretakers of the green-khaki dead.

In the recreation hall, in little gunnysacks, were a dozen bodies the Australians of the Searcher Party had shipped to the American Cemetery at Finchhafen. The history of one: he had bombed Lae when it was held by the Japanese in June 1942. "Reported Missing," his body was now in a sack, recovered only a few weeks ago from a sago swamp behind the Lae airstrip.

Two of the kid-soldiers came from Brooklyn. The fact that I lived in New York, and had come back to New Guinea to write articles baffled them. Why should anyone visit this miserable place? When the lieutenant jokingly said that I was from *Life* magazine, the platoon dragged out their best uniforms, lined up in front of the broken-down chapel and gaped endlessly into my snapping Leica. When would it appear in *Life?* "Or in *Death?*" asked another. With all the death about them, their postwar picnic in the massive military cemetery was strangely human. This was their war. Two years earlier, many of them would have been under grass.

At the Army Transport Service docks, where occasionally my ship would put in for extra supplies, the offices were open and empty, the floors filled with once-sacred official forms. Searching, I found an OUT form signed with my name, for something I had borrowed and had never returned. I put that into my wallet, along with the dust, feeling the kinship of things lost, things found—an eerie world discovered in my brooding blood.

Corrugated steel wiring, deep in rust, resembled the jungle in some peculiar facet of the weaving imagination. I left, going down the road, past the armored tanks left behind, the grass growing right through their metal hearts. I kept thinking of Carl Sandburg's phrase, "I am the grass—let me work!"

I finished with Finch and I returned to Lae to continue compiling the story of the search for the dead and the missing. I met Father Bodger, the English missionary. He had once toured the United States to explain the war of the jungles to the women's clubs of America. He was a big man who knew his relationships as a missionary in the bush. He was a scholar, hardened by God, not made soft by transgressions, given to planning, concerned with the soul, and also with the native's belly. He showed me an honorary medal that President Roosevelt had given him for his lectures in America. He had energy—and God. That was enough in the jungle world he inhabited. One of his boys, "Little Wooly," used to help me during the war, falling all over himself as he loaded my jeep with ship supplies. Now "Little Wooly" was a grown man. He was all muscle. He was a Christian convert now —still calling me *Tabauda*, "Master." He was still smiling his majestic grin and smile at one and the same time. He was all white teeth, round of face and serious about his reading, he said. "I read the Bible all the time, *Tabauda*. . . ." In his hands he carried a copy of *Life* magazine. "Little Wooly" had come of age in New Guinea.

Near Lae was bloody Buna's "Scarlet Beach." The Australians had named it after their blood. A pile of rubble, hacked from planes, lay on the road running down to the beach. Even this rubble had a buyer's name over it. The natives were using the strips of aluminum for lacing the top of their thatched huts, for armbands, for toy creations to make them look like some other people.

Nearby was "Intersect," where a few hundred WACs used to live. It was called, in GI terminology, "Intersex"—and a hundred dollars got you a WAC. They had used the bushes, the beaches, the massive huts.

The road from Buna to Oro Bay now waved like a kunai grass wheat field. On this road, one afternoon, I had seen an Army captain killed by an amphibious duck as he stepped out of his command car. Now it was all kunai grass. Below it, ten feet, was the ragged road. Once, too, there had been an airstrip at this "intersectional point," but the strip had vanished under the grass.

Lae, a great depot for men at war, and once the leading town on the prewar New Guinea frontier, was like an old woman— toothless. The Japanese freighter, which we'd sunk in 1942, was still positioned in the same way. Its bridge above the Huon Gulf told you where the bombs had hit the ship. Now the birds were nesting on the cresting, leafy, nameless hulk.

But Lae had a gold miners' odyssey. A track, running for 26 miles into the jungle, led to Wau's gold fields. It took a week to walk in, but it had only taken a few hours for some quick Australians to walk out with the gold. A million dollars worth of gold was stolen as the Japanese were approaching the Wau-Bololo Gold Mining Company's cache.

The dead were everywhere. Headstones, graves, crosses, names, Stars of David. One stuck out. A Japanese soldier killed in 1943 still remained, waiting to be claimed. Over him was some resemblance to a Japanese headstone, but with no name.

Nadzab, with its many miles of bays for hiding the thousand planes that once lay there, was a spectacle of waste, spoilage, decay and destruction. The broken, twisted planes made an aluminum forest and plain. From the tattooed control tower below nearby Wine Mountain, still yellow and green in camouflage, the scattered masses of metal were Daliesque, backed by the green scrub beyond. The bombers, lacking the military sanitation of wholeness, lay there, stripped of their engines and instruments.

I returned to my jeep, and drove across the immense Nadzab strip until I reached the center of this area of dread and memory. There, the B-24s, B-25s, the Thunderbolts and Lightnings, all the crafts in the deluge of death, still stood, poised, in their wallowing madness, waiting for time to disintegrate them. Crippled, burned, with props at all angles, they added to the gutted aluminum addition lying over miles of ground. It was Western man's machine-made arts disintegrating. Belts of "amo" lay rusted among bomb releases, as neat as ever, ready for the lever's movement. The nude decorations on these partial planes awaiting the junkman were copies of Varga, insinuating sex and death.

I had strayed from the taxiing road, lost in the bays, trying to find my way back to the main road going back to Lae. We had come in over the kunai grass that covered most of the visible roads, but now it was impossible to discern the pattern of difference. We looped from road to road, meeting another jeep containing three men from the Australian Civil Administration. They were floundering about as we were in this high kunai sea of grass. Merging our confusions, we raced around. But we remained, despite all our movements, within the same circle of grass—unable to find an exit. The native with us kept saying, "Savvy this fella, kiss-em," meaning, in Pidgin, try this road, but it did not kiss the road we wanted. Hours later, lost in many seas of the mind and place, we spied a break in the kunai grass and found our way back to Lae.

The Searcher Party, led by Squadron Leader Keith Rundle, was a massive search through New Guinea's swamps, razorback mountains, awesomely primitive villages. We were looking for dog tags—the bodies became part of the grass within one season. It was natural tragedy in the fecund jungles from sudden explosions and men parachuting into nowhere. The dog tags were the end-all of Rundle's year-long search on an island that was a permanent battleground of nature.

Squadron Leader Keith Rundle was tall and thin—a face-creased, eyes-sunken image of a leader. In his New Guinea year, forty pounds had dripped off him like jungle salad dressing. A career officer, coming up from the prewar ranks, he had been through the whirlwind of the war. Now, in the peace of the Casualty Section, he was seeking bodies to put into gunnysacks.

His second in command was Flying Officer J. D. Coape-Smith, from Sydney, formerly a prisoner of war in Roumania. The third man was Flying Officer L. S. Cogswell, who had done the war in New Guinea as a defense officer. Then came Warrant Officer D. Bingley, Sergeant Tom Henderson, Warrant Officer Standen, a former missionary who had spent many years in Daru, New Guinea—and he was the linguist of the party. A trawler, piloted by Warrant Officer F. C. Coleman, made possible the sea-search in the coves and nearby islands. In all, they were the leaders who led the split-up parties, with native porters, mapping their operations, questioning thousands of natives, walking up towering razorbacks, then down again into a valley and a swamp. When lucky, they found a dog tag. Then one lost airman's history was accounted for in the humanizing record of the war.

It was a picnic in purgatory for some of the men. To Rundle, who was half saint, it meant getting a letter from a stranger in Melbourne: "My son, James, was reported lost in March 1942 on a flight from Darwin to New Guinea. I would like to join your party. I can pay my own expenses. I know that my son, Flying Officer James R. Rose, is alive. He must be alive. He must be living in some native village. He's probably crippled, but he's alive. My wife constantly has dreams about him—begging me to come to New Guinea, to greet him at the entrance to this village. From my wife's dreams, we feel it's in the vicinity of a sago swamp before you reach Nadzab. Have you tried that swamp? Yes, I've studied the terrain from afar—but every time I ask the RAAF to let me help, they say that it's up to you. I can come within the month. I may be too old, but I'm also tough enough to take the heat. Please expect me. . . ."

Rundle did not drink. Among all the other things he'd gotten on the search was an ulcer, and yaws, which wrecked his handsome face, and malaria, which had put him into the hospital for weeks, and dengue, which did not put him into the hospital. He had, too, an intensity of major proportions regarding "the mission."

Beginning at Madang in November 1945, the Searcher Party had sailed around New Britain, calling in Tawui Point, Massaua Bay, Lolabau Island, Cape Koas, Bangular Bay, Bakota, Cape Hoskins, Megigi Plantation, Mai, San Remo, Talasea, Willaumez Peninsula, Borgans Bay, Cape Gloucester, Lagoon Point, Sag Sag, Arawe, Gasmata, Lindenhafen, Jacquinot Bay and Rabaul. As exhaustive as all these ports of call were, so were the minute, colorful interrogations of the natives. More often they received the wrong information, or a native invented when he did not exaggerate. A plane had been seen. It flew away. The bird came back. The bird exploded. An angel was seen winging down—if the native had been missionary-bred—and the angel, in khaki, walked away. The angel had a gun. The angel had a big bag over his head—a parachute. The angel lay on the ground as the angel of death. . . . And the native, schooled from mission to God, talked on in Pidgin or Krangit, or he made signs on the ground describing the exploding plane. It was an art, as abstract as it was impressionist. But they knew the fire, the explosion, the angel, if not the meaning of the dog tag—the final identification of the fallen angel of the RAAF.

Gasmata, one of the major areas for the Searcher Party, is an island on the south coast of New Britain. It conceals a beautiful harbor much used by the Japanese for hiding their freighters. The island was ringed with revetments. Swamps and crocodiles added to the war furnishings. The shores were mined. An airstrip made Gasmata a "must" target for Allied aircraft, and we had lost a lot of planes there. At Gasmata the famous Australian airman, Group Captain J. Lerew, had been shot down, and he was the only survivor of a crew of four. Rundle had gone in, stayed in, combed all of Gasmata—and found the dog tags that identified Captain Lerew's colleagues, Flying Officer Watts and Sergeants McDonald and Henry.

At Jacquinot Bay, in March 1946, Rundle's party was out to find a Beaufort bomber shot down in 1944. The natives knew of it. It was near Tokai, fifteen miles away, they said. It turned out to be a Japanese flying boat—and Rundle started his interrogations over again. This time, a native chieftain recalled seeing four Australian airmen coming down from the mountains. When they reached Jacquinot Bay, out came the Japanese, who took them to Rabaul. As for the Beaufort bomber, it was stuck up on a mountain—and the chief pointed to a peak six thousand feet high, miles off through the jungle. Rundle climbed that mountain, and there was no Beaufort. At the village of Ram, the story was confirmed. The natives had seen the Beaufort bomber crash, then four Australians crawling out of the wreckage. But it was on another mountain peak, and they pointed in the opposite direction, miles away, through more jungled valleys.

Days later, when exhaustion had become as natural as having a beer, Rundle came across his "Beaufort" bomber—an American Flying Fortress shot down by Japanese fighters as it was returning from Rabaul. Yet whether Beaufort or Flying Fortress, enough of the story and the clues were accurate. Four men had been on the plane. Rundle found the remains of three dead men, who were bagged and carried by his native carriers back to Finch. The fourth, Staff Sergeant J. Lascio, captured by the Japanese, had been taken to Japan. After the war, he had told the story of his terror, his broken body, his comrades dead, and the natives unable to help him. There had been no medicine, no whiskey, no gun for suicide—just the shattering sequences of a Flying Fortress that would no longer fly with its crew. When the Searcher Party finally cleared through New Britain, they found the remains of 60 men and 28 planes, American and Australian . . . an odyssey of dog-tagged death.

In order to ascertain time and seasons, as well as the possible hour of the crash, the natives were queried about winds, rains, the sun, the moon—to register some kind of impossible accuracy on a timeless island—before they enlisted the natives, who loved these *walkabouts*—and loved the inevitable gifts. It meant unusual food—spam, the staple of the Searcher Party. It meant leftover American tinned rations, chocolates and cigarettes. Often a native would have three cigarettes in his mouth at one time, each one smaller than the other. He would puff away, emperor of a tin, lord of a *walkabout*, inventing as he went, seeing planes on every mountain, missing men in every valley—cigarettes everywhere else.

Christmas, when it came, meant no bush sing-sing for the searchers. They had a Christmas dinner of bully beef, rice and biscuits. Somebody had forgotten to lug in the beer or the rum. Then the party split up, their Christmas over, and one group headed for the area north of Madang, in the Aitape region. Flying Officer Cogswell led his team through the immense jungles of the Ramu Valley to an old police post at Annenberg. Then for days they went by native canoes down the flooding Ramu River to the coast. They covered, when they finally arrived back at Aitape, 300 miles on foot, which meant swamps, torrential streams, kunai grass plains, and 147 miles via native canoe. They found the bones of eleven airmen and six American aircraft, growing, as Flying Officer Cogswell related it to me, "roses out of the bloody aluminum wings."

It was an endlessly enveloping saga on foot and by boat. Cogswell's men walked overland from Lae to the east coast of New Guinea—a great trek that found them nothing in flesh, bones or aluminum. There had been survivors. Some had walked on, to rejoin some unit eventually. And, as Rundle said, "Not one of our blokes went native, though one of your chaps did. He should have gotten a medal, not a court-martial, pal."

It was an Australian-American search, though I seldom ran into the Americans, who were always elsewhere, hard to reach, using helicopters for American efficiency in finding the dead. As for Rundle, he had his team and his natives, and each native carried a load of forty pounds, though they ate half as much as the Australians. They had their wages, pegged like a good union agreement. It included bonuses for finds. A dog tag brought ten cigarettes, as well as salt, sticks of tobacco, trench mirrors, cheap combs that the native loved to plow into his fuzzy hair, razor blades, lap-laps. A steel axe was the prize bonus. On occasion, too, when local natives had buried the dead airmen, Rundle told them that the next of kin would cry forever until the bodies were found—and they were found.

Back at Lae, I met Mr. Rose, a man over fifty. He was a boss carpenter in Melbourne, physically harder than mulga wood. His son, James, was somewhere. He was dead and unfound, Rundle knew—for he had done the Lae search once before. But to Mr. Rose, carpenter, who had come out from England as a boy, James was a religion of his flesh.

"It's not entirely hopeless, sir," he said to Rundle. "God does not just take away His best worshippers."

"Of course, Mr. Rose. We're breaking up into four parties. And I agree with God, too . . . ," said Rundle quietly.

On the road, as if preparing for a huge jungle patrol, were several hundred natives. The search area was ten miles in depth and equally as long. In it were swamps, sago growths, dense trees, snakes, crocs, every creature that lived in the soggy, screeching semidarkness. The four parties, each led by one of Rundle's year-old trackers, moved off at four oblique angles as they entered the swamp. On their return, they would re-angle their original angle—to make the search an inch-by-inch, exacting march through. I went along with Rundle and fifty natives, each with a machete. It would take a few days and we would live in the swamp. The natives carried our gear—tents, water and rations. We carried pistols—and I had a movie camera.

Rundle led off, compass in hand, going through the beginning scrub, which soon became deep bush, then deeper kunai, then watery, mushy ground. At this point several of the natives took over, and we followed behind their hacking machetes, their singsong plaintive shouts, their discoveries of snakes, which they beheaded and then lifted up on their bloody machetes. For everything made way, kept away, stole away, swam back, took to the trees and the swamp as the natives sang on, pushed on and swept on with their machetes and singing.

Soon we were waist high. The swamp water tasted sour. My camera went above my head when I was not shooting the natives up ahead. It went to the trees, to the water, to the crocs rushing off, frightened of the invading party. Occasionally Rundle would shoot off his pistol and hit one, but it went off just the same, tracking some blood. At one point that day we were almost shoulder high in the water, waltzing through a rain forest.

"We don't have to swim, Harry," said Rundle when he saw me sacking the camera into a rubber-tight container as I readied for swimming. "I know this bit of hell too well. And we won't find Mr. Rose's boy, either. I know, you'd like to see a body."

"I saw three at Finch—in the sacks. That's enough, Keith."

"I sent Mr. Rose along with Warrant Officer Standen, the ex-missionary. They can talk about what God can do and what God can't do. Are you on, mate?"

"I'm on, mate."

"There's no beer, chum."

"If there was, you wouldn't drink it, Keith. You look like hell, man. If you don't take some home leave soon, you'll be ready for a dog tag. . . ."

"I'll go, when this Lae bit ends," said Rundle, sagging. "Would you care to meet my wife and kids when you get back to Melbourne? Will you go back soon?"

"After Mount Hagen," I said. And I talked about the skullcap primitives who lived up in the Central Range. "They may be my Jewish brethren—the very much lost tribes. They are everybody's lost tribes—for we Jews are always one up when we look for ancient ancestors."

"Not bloody likely! You related to them blokes?"

"I'm Jewish, so I'm related to everybody today. . . ."

"Not to them blokes!"

I laughed, for we had not talked religion or race or people before. We had talked war and death. We had seen many Stars of David in New Guinea's war cemeteries. I had photographed them, out of strange pride.

"Well, I'm hardly a man to talk about another man's religion, Harry. Yet Mr. Rose would have driven me blotto, chum. Oh, I've been to church, but have you been to the synagogue recently?"

"On Yom Kippur, for atonement, but not recently."

It was a hell of a conversation in a swamp. We were wet up to our brains. We camped. We had found nothing. We talked over our walkie-talkies with the other groups. Rundle talked with Mr. Rose—and more humane abstractions went through the walkie-talkie. There was no James Rose, the former flying officer. There was a swamp and all of us were in it with maps, rations, natives and the terrifying vacuum.

It was the same the next day. We were wet all the time, until we camped for the night on dry ground. During the day the natives hacked away and sang. Often some excited shouts brought Rundle up—but it was not a plane. It was not a body. It was nothing but the natives in play, at half play, not always in full seriousness. They would like to find a white body—for a white body brought them white gifts. And two miles away, Mr. Rose was offering a thousand Australian pounds to anyone who found his son. We heard that on the walkie-talkie from Warrant Officer Standen, who agreed to give the money to his former mission. Rundle cursed them both.

That was the way it went in this liquid terror. At night it was worse, though our tents were lit up, safe, mosquito-netted. Yet everything slithered. It was not a place for men. It was abysmal, crowding down, shadowed in permanence, shrieking its natural nightmares for us.

We reached our end of the swamp on the second day—the angle ending for us. We walkie-talked with the other groups to realign, then head back. We headed back, Rundle hardly talking, not anxious to meet Mr. Rose. Two nights later, on the road, back at Lae, we met Mr. Rose, still with Jesus, still with belief. He had faith in a boy named James.

Before I took off for Mt. Hagen, to end my return to New Guinea, Rundle told me that his party had found more than 200 men and dog tags along with the remains of 85 Allied planes. They had gone to every rumor, including the Kokoda Trail. As a farewell gesture, we camped at Roana Falls, near the red buildings of a sapphire mine that once, allegedly, had belonged to the Tasmanian Errol Flynn, who had left much of his earthy youth in Port Moresby before he became a Hollywood hero. Flynn was remembered for other and more local follies, said Rundle.

Roana Falls, tumbling majestically into a gap, was the beginning of the blood-soaked Kokoda Trail, which had knocked out more than 75 percent of the Australian forces in 1942. Malaria, scrub typhus and dengue made another kind of war. At the gap, a monument stood, inscribed: "In memory of the officers, NCOs, and men of the Australian Military Forces who died on the Kokoda Track in June–November 1942." Then a short verse: "To strive, to seek and not to yield." Somewhere, between all those words, the Owen Stanley mountains and the jungles and plains, was dead Flying Officer James Rose. . . .

From Lae to the plateau-highlands of Mt. Hagen was several hundred miles of hazardous, peak-slicing flying with the weekly medical courier plane. The six-seater and incidental cargo-carrier brought in basic medical supplies, including cigarettes and beer, for the primitive Dr. Schweitzer-type hospital, the adjacent leprosarium, and the small police post captained by Jim Goreham, the medical assistant and district officer. Under him were a few natives clad in long, draping, military sweaters: a unique police force that kept some sort of a peace on this isolated plateau, where murder, no longer legal, was hardly punishable, and usually done with the sudden swing of a stone axe. The courier plane was the contact machine for everything. It came and it went. It took back murderers and fresh vegetables.

We took off like an animated air-circus. We skirted over Lae's busted harbor, dipped to salute the dead Japanese freighter, then rose into dark banks of clouds, hoping one of these banks was not a peak. Below I saw the once-dreaded Markham Valley, where we had fought a war of malaria, bullets and man. But it was no longer man at war. Now it threw up its razorback peaks and lofty ranges, great, upshooting, brown, yellow and black peaks thrusting up from the Central Mountain Ranges, the Muller Range, and the Hagen Range. Its middle, Mt. Hagen, was our destination.

To the west, like a locked vault of mountains, swamps and mystery, was West Irian—Dutch New Guinea, soon to be given over to Indonesia by American compliance and United Nations blackmailing. In November 1946, it was a still unknown natural complex, undeveloped, Dutch controlled, with war-torn Hollandia and Merauke as the seats of colonial power. The Dutch, the oldest colonizers, were nervously hanging on to their coffee-bean-cum-democracy politics in transition.

The Australian plane, as we neared Mt. Hagen, took us over Australia's mandated territory. Below were the Chimbu Valley and a few police posts—jungle miles and peaks apart. There, dedicated old army men—all eccentric Australians—policed by horse, by single-seater planes, by *lakatoi's* and on foot the recent headhunters among the Chimbus. Only five years back, the naked, bearded, nose-pierced, skullcapped, cicatrized, totemized Chimbus had head-whacked another tribe a valley away. Every valley had its tribes. Every mountain the same. And they killed like other non-Western and non-Eastern citizens of the world, with pre-historical military equipment: Stone Age bone-pointing —and the *wish*—when a native wished death upon a suddenly disliked member of the tribe. It was a death-psychiatry—and I had seen that in Australia's Nullarbor Desert. But for art and for a living, the natives carved. And soon the white aborigines of the West bought up their arrows, their totemic masks, their wooden idols, their crudely painted shields, their stone axes, their statued penises. It became, by 1950, prior to abstract expressionism, the living-room art of the cultured man of the West.

I saw it now, down below, up above, God-graced, totemic-

split, natives between new religions, green as all life is, dead as
all black must become, gray when it is only noxious, red when
blood must be spread. And when in mourning, after some tribal
battling, a woman of the Chimbus wore her love and hate for
death as a mask. Her face, her arms, her hands were clay-
painted, whitened—and life in mourning then became white.
From her neck hung a mass of beads, her latter-day Judaic-
Christian, mission-led token of status. The more beads, the more
middle-class, like gold bracelets for Indian women, or diamonds
for Arab, Greek, Italian and Jewish women. The Chimbu was as
much Jewish as she was Christian in her wild decor. But she had
not, as yet, found chewing gum. She had not, as yet, discovered
hair curlers. Yet she was a female, barbaric, pagan, animist—
delighting in her old tokens if not her new taboos.

In and about Mt. Hagen and the surrounding Chimbu Valley,
lived 25,000 Stone Age natives. All of the Eastern Highlands,
which covered an area of almost 7,000 square miles, had less than
300,000 naked and semi-naked people. Whoever had discovered
Mt. Hagen had named it, with some Nibelungen mythical in-
sistence, after Hagen, who had murdered Siegfried at Brunhild's
behest. And murder was what I saw, a few minutes after landing
on the small strip.

It took only a swing of a stone axe. The wielder was a male
native who had come to court a sixteen-year-old girl. He had
brought two wild pigs to her, placed the basketed pigs at her
feet, and then, with some mighty shoving, he proceeded to drag
her into the bush. She rejected him, his two basketed pigs and
his demands. He shouted, he threatened, he shoved. The girl
shoved back. She insulted him, and the watching natives, as well
as Jim Goreham, laughed aloud.

With that, most suddenly, the basketed pigs were dropped.
They squealed and grunted. The man in love reached behind
for his stone axe—and he swung. The axe crashed into the girl's
skull. Her brains bashed in and out—she died at once. And the
police officer, with the help of two native assistants, soon had
Mr. Primitive Stone Age Murderer under lock and key, in a jail
of thatched kunai grass next door to the leprosarium. In a few
days he would be flown down to Port Moresby, tried, found
guilty—and sentenced to two years at hard labor, which meant
unloading the ships or working on the bush roads. Murder, with-

out a Nibelungen myth, or Wagner to attend to its sounds, was still a simple non-musical affair at Mt. Hagen.

I was looking about for one of the ten lost or wandering Jewish tribes here. I was the only member of the Roskolenko tribe, lost in myself, adrift on a plateau, and hardly resembling the Mt. Hagen native. He was many things. But, then, so were the Jews. There were black Jews in Ethiopia—the fallashim. They were in Harlem too—as converts to Judaism—and I, looking on, saw this primitive man. He was very short, very muscular, always smiling, and always ready to trade his wild pigs for prized steel axes. His nose was longer than de Gaulle's, and just as hooked. He was, with Shakespeare's Shylock, a ready caricature. He wore a Phoenician beard. On his head, passing for a skullcap, was a feathered *yamalkah* decorated with beads. He looked as pre-Biblical as any myth. Standing and endlessly grinning, waiting for chocolates, beads, old shirts, old khakis, old shoes, they were like Orchard Street peddlers as they shivered in the fifty-degree temperature. They shook and they laughed. The shaking was an exercise to keep them warm. Over their muscled bodies, they had put on pig fat to cloak them against the cold, which went below thirty degrees at night.

It was, I thought, to be only a few hours before we returned to Lae. We took off, rounded Mt. Hagen, swept down towards Goroka, when a mass of black clouds darkened up the entire sky. There was no visibility towards Lae. It was black, with thunder claps and lightning heads cracking through the valleys and razorbacks below. We turned back to Mt. Hagen, overran the short landing strip, and crashed. The right wing was crushed, but we were safe.

Jim Goreham, the Australian medical assistant who ran the leprosarium, delivered babies, curing—and hardly killing any-body—with his brief medical training, was hugely amused as he reached us on the strip—"Don't worry, chums. It's time we enlarged this strip, and about time we got a new courier kite to come in with the iodine and band-aids. Anyhow, you're just on the mo for a beer and a bit of lunch. I'll telegraph Port Moresby to send up a relief kite!"

At lunch, with more beer than food—spam sandwiches—Goreham told a little folktale about a native police boy who owned a motorcycle. One night he parked it outside his hut. In the morning, there was only the chassis left. The nuts, bolts, wheels, handlebar and fuel tank—"the lot"—were being worn by the natives, who had merely added the removable parts to their wild decor. The police boy spent the next two weeks rounding up the parts to reassemble the machine. I wondered, with the courier plane badly damaged, what the natives would remove from that by morning.

I joined Goreham on his daily visit to his hospital.

The patients, mostly women, were naked except for a cloth between their legs, which extended like a tail from their buttocks. They had pneumonia, which came easily to them when the missionaries put dresses on their bodies. They had the traditional yaws—enormous welts, raw, bulging, sickening, looking like syphilis sores. They had, Goreham explained, whatever the white man had brought in, along with the native collection. In the leprosarium, which I refused to enter, they had an old Biblical ailment. Who had brought that in? Goreham did not know. "It just came in with the troops, like gonorrhea, the common cold—and beer, I reckon!" Mt. Hagen had been a temporary rest camp for airmen during the war; and there were some of their miscegenated offsprings, including a boy albino, whom everybody worshipped, bowed to and looked up to. He was a non-pigmented kid-god from afar for their Judaic-Christian-animist religious animations.

In another large hut were the pregnant women, their husbands sitting on makeshift cots alongside of them. Goreham said, "The women used to stay in their villages, where half of them lost their kids to the witch doctors. Here they fare much better and so the population is increasing. Of course, they want their husbands with them, but you ought to see the men going into labor pains. They double up and howl like banshees just before their wives give birth!"

One husband was just beginning to howl. His wife was sweating and pain-writhed. Her thighs were spread open. Her husband was in the same position, half expecting the baby. With that, I left everything to Goreham and his two assistants. Another alleged Semite was about to be born.

"No kite on hand," was Port Moresby's answer to our message. "There will be one in two weeks coming up from Townsville. Please ask Mr. Roskolenko to be patient and to be our guest. Is there enough beer on tap? Tell Mr. Roskolenko that he has a rare

opportunity to study the native culture. Of course, he can ride
out. But we'd hate to suggest that in any sort of emergency. One
of our police officers was recently done in near the Purari River.
Be patient, Mr. Roskolenko."

I was patient, bound down by a plateau and a busted plane.
My food, by the forced Australian amenities and cuisine, was
ever-handy spam instead of steak and eggs. But we had eggs,
small eggs, brought in by the natives who stood outside of Goreham's wooden house holding up miserable-looking chickens that
looked as though they could not possibly have hatched a pebble,
let alone an egg.

Between their eggs and their chickens, the natives began their
trading vigil when the sun came up. Naked, greased with fat,
shaking to keep warm, they smoked bits of mad cigars made
from fresh kunai grass and vintage dung. In the high mountain
air, clearer than in Noah's time, I was constantly aware of the
sudden change of odors—from their dung tobacco. They also
smoked homemade corncob pipes filled with the same dung, as
they stood by shaking in rhythm, waiting for Goreham to wake
up and bargain with them. For eggs, for chickens, for wild pigs,
they wanted most of all steel axes. Axes were money. They
wanted knives for their feuding. A steel axe was better to bash
a head in with—and they shook, smoked, smiled, smelled, naked
except for their weird *yamalkah's*, the shells around their necks,
their earrings, the semicircular shells pinched through their
nostrils, their beaded loin-bags, and the thin beaded belts they
used for stomachers.

I kept a small diary. And I walked. My walks took me to a
nearby village. I headed down towards Goroka, days away, merely
to see the land and its people. I would enter a small village,
crowds would gather, my cigarettes were given out and a small
pig was usually offered for sale. Stone axes went for a shilling,
and I bought several. But Goroka was too far, and I turned back,
hoping the new plane had arrived. But Mt. Hagen, now without beer, without real cigarettes, was a solemn place. Nothing
had arrived, and I talked to Goreham about getting me a horse
to ride out on.

"Ride out of here? You're troppo, man. You wouldn't last a
day! Those bloody coots down below would have you for a lousy
steak by midnight. I won't permit it—my oath!"

I was not permitted. I slept almost comatose, the high air

making me drunk at the same time. At night, in my thatched hut, I heard rats run over the top. Later, they ran in to nibble at whatever I had—and off they went. I slept, enjoined with nature, aloft on a plateau, always half sick, dizzied by the heights, unable to acclimate, fighting for air and doped by pills that Goreham gave me. And I was not the only sick white man. The crew was down, each man on his own. "It takes weeks before you acclimate," said Goreham. "It hits your lungs, your heart, your blood pressure, your eyes—and you just want to die at times. . . ."

When I felt better, and the dizziness was gone, I kept my diary—a rude set of notes to humor me:

Saturday

At seven A.M. the houseboy brought tea. I am now as Australian as the crew—tea, some newly found steak, and eggs. I swear all day, limiting the world to a few dozen wild words, ready to fight the world—if there were just enough beer. Outdoors, at the cookhouse, there is the usual collection of bargaining natives. Pigs are squealing everywhere. They grunt along with the natives so you can't tell the sounds apart. One pig, tied up near a fire, suddenly breaks loose and dashes across the field, with all the loungers chasing him. The women with the bigger tits can't run as well. A small boy eventually catches the pig—and soon the pig is stewing over the fire. . . .

I bargained for four arrows, giving away two old razor blades. My red handkerchief got me a large carved shield that has a head and a penis. It is certainly primitive art in contemporary Freudian symbols. . . .

I have decided to ride out and to take my chances. Austin Tohey, who came in a few days ago from Goroka by horse, said that he'd take me along as he must get back. We'll both take our turns on the horse. No guns, of course. To have one means trouble, said Tohey. When the natives saw that you were unarmed, they trusted you. In any event the trip will take six days, all downhill through the Chimbu Mountains. I told Goreham and he's still dead against it. We said, nevertheless, that we were going. If Tohey could make it up to Mt. Hagen alone, two of us can make it back to Goroka, we reasoned—and we packed for the trip. . . .

We hit the trail, but we had not gone more than a mile, clearing the adjacent sugarcane fields, when we heard a plane above us.

It was a Douglas coming for us, said Goreham to our walkie-talkie. We dashed back and gave all of our food to the cook with the three wives. We thanked Goreham—and we piled into the Douglas. . . .

On the way back to Lae, we flew over Gusap Field—another Nadzab that the Fifth Air Force had used for raiding Wewak. A small rainbow stretched across Markham Valley, as if to bid us welcome—and right into a tropical front we flew. Up we went to fifteen thousand feet. We passed over Yule Island, skirted the coast, and listened to Keith Rundle on the radio talking to us from Lae . . . "Sgt. Tom Henderson went into the Lae bush with a dozen natives. All he carried was a bottle of gin and some lemonade. He says that it's better than my compass—and he found an American Lightning. So hurry in, Harry, for we'll have that farewell party tonight. . . ."

This was New Guinea, revisited during the winter of 1946—an enormous island, smaller than Greenland, fifteen hundred miles long, ready then for nothing, happily lost in time, given to stone axes, cultivating with pre-Biblical tools, animistic and living in another dawn. For it was a savage island, a mountain-valley-swamp. It was nature still being natural, without too many activities of the Western cultivator, the builder, the culture-conscious hero, the engineer—all the humanistic professions of the West.

Now, in the winter of 1966, the coconut plantations, the sponge, pearl and shell fisheries and the stone axes are giving way to Western man's factories, his mills, his wages and the Coca-Cola culture. The forests of sandalwood, ebony and cedar are now ringing with gigantic buzz saws, and the great rivers like the Fly, the Sepik and the Purari are being turned into discolored streams by the lumber industries. A new island had been found. And they are tearing into it, taking away its trees, polluting its streams, killing the air. The natives—Negritos, Papuans and Melanesians—are wearing blue jeans—their nakedness covered, their labor in demand, their superficial contact complete. . . .

Up in Mt. Hagen, the surveyors had come. An industrial installation to process pyrethrum, which had been grown as a flower by the Department of Agriculture, had been built. It was, they said, an insecticide low in toxicity. A cash crop for the natives. It would spray the green-grown world for more "silent springs"—and add up, one day, to a terrible New Guinea irony.

In 1930, 600,000 black people had lived in the "silent spring" and through all the seasons of New Guinea. But today, like the West, there are people on people, noses on noses, asses on asses— and more than two million natives whacking away at newly adopted Western conceits. Fifty million dollars worth of New Guinea's new industries had been exported during 1965. And now, dressed, there is the movie house, the TV set, the inundation of noises, the letter of credit, the bank for the letter of credit, the telephone, the typewriter, the Xerox machine. Rubber and the passion fruit, cocoa, tea, coffee—and pyrethrum—to make a Western pyre of New Guinea in fifty years, or less. It would go like other primitive places, like New York, dead within three hundred years of hacking away.

Lae, Port Moresby, Keravat, Nondugl, Wabag, Banz, Finschha-fen, Wau, Bololo, Goroka, Mt. Hagen—the names are endless and the machine is everywhere in the highlands and the lowlands. A concrete industry at Lae. In 1964, a House of Assembly was created and an election was held.

Democracy and the buzz saw has found another island in transition, coming of age—our age—tomorrow morning's New Guinea.

A LAND CALLED DOZOO

AFTER NEW GUINEA, Melbourne shrank to its pedestrian surfaces of wattle, prattle, beer binges, as we talked about the Labour Party's inner wars—the Catholic wing against the liberal and the left. Soon the Labour Party would split and doom itself for twenty years, with a more conservative Menzies leading Australia to its "promises" of another United-States-in-the-making. And I was, or had been, a refugee of an already over-expanded United States. In less than two hundred years after becoming a sovereign nation, we had polluted the land, the air, the water ways—and our politics. We had an overall genius for making garbage, and I was seeing the beginning of the same thing in Australia, cultural lag or not.

If you wanted to leave a country, the reasons came. The land was foreign, yet most hospitable. Melbourne was not New York, where everything happened. My friend Max was editing an Irgun paper in New York, and I began to write for it. The Irgun, the Stern gang—the extremes of Zionist politics in Palestine—were causing havoc for the British mandators. In Paris, too, other friends were seeking a Third Force and not a liberal accomodation to Stalin. And the Third Force, so possible in 1946 and 1947, arrived like a madam, set up house—and soon it was whoring along Paris style. . . . But in Melbourne, the desert of the Australian mind gave me back nothing. I was in the barrens of art and politics, brooding about my *expatriate* life. It was a word from hell—and I thought of home. It had been New York, after a fashion—rooted to stone, to a mass of friends, involved in the poesy of the times. Melbourne had involved me in nothing. I had come with malaria—and I was leaving without it.

Objectively, I could have done everything—as a writer, editor, businessman—to become the rich New Australian. It was there, easy to pick up, hardly as competitive as New York—rich if that was what you wanted. Come, stay, become a citizen, give the country your talents, work—and you'll be a rich bastard soon enough!

But I was quitting.

I told Emily—and she objected. "Why leave when we have each other? Why are you always racing against yourself? You're the original wanderer—burning up everything in you. Stay! Settle in! Be patient! You can become very important in this barren, bloody country!"

It was cynicism, at best. She lived in Australia, because, "I've got an old Mum to take care of, Harry. I've got those kennels, which give me a good living; and I've got a man whom I'm separated from and who won't give me a divorce. So what do I do after you go—find another wandering bastard?"

"I'm going to Tokyo, Emily," I said six weeks later. We had met constantly. It was love, we said too easily. It was walks into the bush, riding horses over the scrub, my eyes on the gum trees and the Never-Never.

I told Sidney Nolan that I was leaving, and he made a party. With him came Albert Tucker, a fellow artist. And since I was accredited to various newspapers, SCAP in Japan soon accepted me as a visiting correspondent. But there was Albert Tucker, too, who wanted to come along. He was then barely recognized. He was then very bitter about Australia. He was always dissenting, hardly ever selling a painting—and he was asking me to take him along, "so I can get the hell out of this wowser country. Without doubt, you need an artist to illustrate the Japanese Occupation, mate. . . ."

I got Tucker accredited, for he had once been a staff artist on the *Melbourne Argus*—and the night that we departed for Tokyo was very touching. Tunn, the plagiarist, came with a red-blue engraved poem about Australia—the source of which I could never find out. Nolan gave me a drawing of Ned Kelly, the Australian Jesse James. An English liaison officer, who had helped me through the "sticky business at SCAP," gave me a footlocker. And Tucker, who had done a portrait of me, signed it with a flourish. I sent that to New York along with my hundred books —my recent library-in-migration, sans Edmund Wilson's *Hecate County*.

The RAAF crew had come along to buy their way into their future—the Japanese black market. In Laoog, the fuel stop in the Philippines, it meant going to a cigarette distributor, paying GI prices and hauling hundreds of cartons, packed a hundred to a box, back to the plane. On the plane, covered over with parachutes, pennants, footlockers and Australian flags—for patriotic camouflage—their "future" was protected. In Iwakuni, where the Australians had an air base, they also had their cooperating comrades with a handy truck. No sooner had the plane landed when off went the cigarettes and the crew. In town, the Japanese middlemen-receivers were all over with the yen—and a hundred cartons, bought for less than $150 in the Philippines, went for more than $1500 in Iwakuni.

Bert bought fifty cartons and so did I. As for the crew, each of the four members bought six hundred cartons apiece. There was no nonsense about their reasons for "loving the air ferry to a future." Every trip meant, by any kind of mathematics, some seven thousand dollars from their monthly round-trip to Japan.

On their way back from Japan, they secreted art. They secreted cultured pearls—anything they could get away with in Australia. When they sarcastically detailed all of their piratical transactions,

I could only murmur, in blessed moments of disgust and envy, "Man, what an Occupation! How long has this been going on?"

Black market or white market, the crewmen were flying actors. They were men of action living out their sudden answers at the end of 1946. They sought a faith and it became another money faith. They were couriers, birds, male dancers of the skies in a moneyed sky of their own questing. They went from one exotic geography to another, seeing wealth in the aftermath of a war— on the flattened-out terror of the destruction they had helped to bring about. They had destroyed Japan's war machine and its civilian edifice. Now they were the heroes of an eccentric economy via cigarettes—the IBM artificers, black-marketing within the spaces and the people the bombs had left intact. They could not leave their past behind—as if they had no past, no memory, no pain and no killing scores. They had, however, flown planes. They had dropped the bombs and killed the dead Japanese. Their cigarette cosmos was their in-between state. They had shifted their past military polish to some unmanageable awkwardness of the body during the interim between the end of the war, the beginning of the peace—and the political uncertainties of 1946 and 1947. They were like pedestrians caught between the red and the green lights. They wore uniforms that made them officers of the RAAF. They had power but hardly any conscience. It was reality made unreal, an Occupation that was both a daydream and a nightmare. They were, too quickly, verging on wealth—and ecstacy was projecting them into tomorrow morning's world of impermanence. What, they asked, do warriors do without wars? And what do small bankers do with money?

I looked embarrassed at my fifty cartons of cigarettes when the plane landed at Iwakuni. I was an ex-poet owning only fifty cartons. I had envy, I was certain.

I saw a truck being loaded and a crewman, acting for all of his mates, join an Australian driver. I saw the truck go off. The rest of us went into a shack to report our arrival.

It was to be a three-month journey into a contemporary Inferno, but one that Dante would have contempt for. Winter, Spring, but seasons without Japanese artists and flowers. Hunger beyond the belly, and the war-crime trials, with Tojo smiling like a waxed paternal grandfather. It was not hell, not purgatory—just modern man in his newest form of the ridiculous posture. But I was to meet the humble and the elite. They were not always ridiculous, not always assured—just men of the quixotic moment. They would include artists like Foujita, whom I had known in Paris as a boy; a poet called Kitasono, whom Ezra Pound admired; Prince Takimatzu, Emperor Hirohito's second brother; Premier Katayama, the Presbyterian socialist. And, finally, General Mac-Arthur, the real emperor of Japan.

Leaving Iwakuni we were billeted in Hiro, a few miles from Hiroshima. We had a rice-paper house, a huge vat-like tub for communal bathing, a boy of sixteen and a girl of fifteen to cook, wash, make our beds, heat the vat and do all things that made us, temporarily, imported Caucasian gentlemen of Japan.

Hiro was like Hiroshima, but without the Bomb. It was stall upon stall of sudden skeletal buildings—and Japan smelled, but not of rosewater. The odor was ancient—human feces to fertilize the fields. It came by in "honey carts" early in the morning—and they came by wherever we went, from the Inland Sea, still glowing with inconceivable liquid fantasy, to Tokyo, glowing with the black market on the Ginza. They had gone from natural vision to eyeglasses and gold teeth. It was rubble on rubble, plowed up, plowed under, lying in maddening regimentation. It was a woman kneeling on the road to pee in front of you; another culture, another sanitation, another fantasia of 1947. A nation that had learned to do everything Western in a hurry was, temporarily, going back to wooden shacks. In fifty years they had gone from samurai robes to baggy trousers. It was the past confronting the present ruins—Hiroshige and Utamaro, sea scenes and land scenes; ancient Japan never again to know that the wheel for the machine, brought in during the nineteenth century, was the enemy. Japan, too, had violated, by aggressive intent, Western man's vision of the East—"Stay where you are, be what you were, keep to the past. . . ."

Bert sketched Hiroshima. On the walls of my apartment today, are several of his Hiroshima sketches—an unpainted shack, tilted over; a child crying within a tattered tent. Everything was oblique—trees that had not quite burned up and angles that smelled of total death. A sagging poured-concrete bridge not too far from the city hall, where the metal, like some modern sculp-

ture, had become a perpetual image of the alleged moral agony
of President Truman—the first exploder of the Bomb—and of the
American conquest over God.

Destruction and pain glanced back everywhere. Social and
physical wreckage, like the terracing on the nearby mountains,
stared back like a vast Buddha with his belly slit open. The
entrails were Japan's, gutted in the last gutters of mankind.

Improvisation makes a country. Human backs now replaced
cars, trucks, busses and horses. Pantalooned for winter, everybody in coats made from black-marketed khaki blankets carried
burdens—doors, tubs, tables, chairs, old lumber and panes of
glass gotten for family art treasures.

The shacks lining every street in Hiro and Hiroshima, raw
down to their frontier look, made up the commerce. They sold
bits of American black marketing—shoelaces for people without
shoes, chocolate for toothless Japanese—a grab bag of nothing
for two cities that needed the greatest bulldozers and architects
in the world to rebuild every terrible place, every street and
every home. One afternoon in August 1945, 180,000 Japanese had
burned and dissolved here in man's most unique way of death. . . .

We walked every day. We worked to acquaint ourselves with
the saga of a bomb. We refused, politely, to visit the hospitals—
where the living were dying and would die for years. But we
could not hide from them. We saw them in the streets, faces
discolored, skin torn, skin burned, skin no longer skin but some
medical magic; paste on paste in every searing and crippling
distortion; eyes that were no longer eyes, angled differently,
glued to a forehead that made the face something that Dali and
Picasso could not do with paint. Abnormal, unnatural, yet living,
they were breathing some sort of life. We looked, feeling our
own features, as if we expected, by some mystical sin, to change
places with the victims of the Bomb.

Many women were demi-whoring, and every other man was
black-marketing. There was no sort of a shock left for the sons
and daughters of Nippon, the children of other earthquakes and
volcanic explosions. An earth fault, under the Japanese islands,
streamed across the Pacific. We had, on two holy days, added a
heavenly fault—the Bomb.

The Japanese, an admixture of Malays and Mongolians, had
known every religion, beginning with Shinto, then Buddhism,

and Christianity, when St. Francis Xavier came to tell them about
Jesus. Genghis Khan had brought the Mongols in earlier, in 1274,
to tell them something else. Their shoguns and samurais, their
endless wars against China and the acquisition of Chinese culture
and literature, earlier, hardly made them brothers under their
yellow skin. Then came Commodore Matthew Calbraith Perry
to Yedo, in 1854, to "open up Japan" for the West. Then more
wars, to add some Chinese and Russian maritime provinces. And
then we came in 1945.

Every other child was begging. I saw cripples, their eyes
bulging, their eyes like a certain bomb—and hands no longer
hands. The fingers were gone. A small voice had learned a word,
a Romanized word with a slight Japanese lilt. It was "presento"
and you gave the kid a chocolate. You gave everybody sweet
things and they smiled. You gave them nothing and they smiled.
In Kyoto, at the Hongwanji Temple, where a huge hair-rope lay
curled under a glass cage with a poem about faith by Lafcadio
Hearn, they smiled. In the once-greatest arsenal of the world,
along the Inland Sea at Kure, where miles of war engineering
had fitted Japan for the Second World War, the children smiled
at the broken gates. Inside was a dead machine that had made
munitions, guns, ships—and they smiled their little brown greet-
ings, saying, "Arigato" and "Presento." Often it was "Thank you,
Mister American"—and it brought laughter. Chocolates brought
laughter. The Bomb was "chocolado" for yesterday.

In Shimonoseki, where the peace with Russia had been signed in
1905, I was the guest of Mr. Nagabi, a rich man who owned
twelve whaling ships. He was short, stocky and cultured. His
large house was islanded on a lake. Small red bridges crossed to
the island. Birds, ducks, fish, another Japan, Hiroshige's, crossed
my eyes. The house was as traditional as the tea service. Braziers
burned, room separations moved, two daughters appeared.

"Japan needs the whales for food," said Mr. Nagabi. I tried
whale meat with saki. I didn't need whale meat—but outside,
some assistants of Mr. Nagabi were serving, from black market
stocks, ten thousand meals. Men, line on line, with the yen going
to Mr. Nagabi. They got blubber, rice, spam, or whatever was
being stolen by the Australians, the New Zealanders and the
Americans stationed around Shimonoseki.

Mr. Nagabi said that he loved art. After more saki, he turned from whale blubber to old Japanese scrolls, unrolling some original Utamaros. He radiated over a scene of a bird landing on the Inland Sea. His mouth sucked in as he looked at the lovely breasts of nudes. His daughters giggled slightly. In New York, people showed their diamonds. Here, in hungry Shimonoseki, an equally sensitive Mr. Nagabi was showing me his scrolls.

I came away, an expert on whaling, sympathetic to all, alerted by Herman Melville's white whale. I bowed to Mr. Nagabi, ready to board one of his twelve whalers and follow his seven hundred hungry hunters with harpoons.

Japan, which had just reentered the whaling industry, had broken every international convention. They sliced and boiled up every whale they could harpoon, to add a few hundred calories to Japan's starvation diet. In Tokyo, General MacArthur said, when queried, "Japan needs food. Let them whale away...."

Mr. Nagabi's whalers had harpooned two thousand blue whales for his two factory ships. The meat sold at fourteen thousand yen a ton. Outside of his picture-postcard estate, I saw some of the hungry citizens of Shimonoseki with their tin platters—and I thought of Utamaro scrolls and those pink breasts of another time.

Twenty years later, in 1966, there were only six hundred blue whales left in the seas of the world. During the hungrier Thirties, almost fifteen thousand blue whales, many of them one hundred feet long, had cavorted about. It was just another statistic, helped toward its extinction by the whalers of the Soviet Union, Norway —and Mr. Nagabi's killers for food.

From Shimonoseki, I returned to Hiroshima for a last look before going to strident Tokyo. The total wreck, eighteen months old, was being transformed daily. For every Japanese was a donkey for work, a mule for chores, a Trojan for discipline. The pile of rubble grew, hourly, into jerry-built shacks. It was fantasy and reality—a Hollywood set emerging from a Doomsday scene to make up floating streets without names, places of business based on magic; a village, a town, a city emerging from a composite of desolation.

Walking by, often barefoot, often on geta's that klopped like military drums, were some of the former workers of the past war industries, bound for made-up, on the spot, new occupations.

They were salvaging a city in a vacuum. Their women, in rough trousers and old kimonos, were carrying and pushing everything that moved on wheels. These camels of Japanese humanity carried wood for heat, found in the nowhere of Hiroshima, or madly distorted gadgets, gleaned from the mountainous rubble of a city, to make into furniture. And every movement was all-consuming for the finders, foragers, and builders of this hungry maze.

I went through a tunnel built on a former military road that arched along the Inland Sea. Huge boats were being sculled. Women, with babies strapped to their backs, were the scullers. There was more junk in the boats—grass, forage, and things found or stolen. They waved, they laughed, they sculled. Behind them were a dozen fishermen dragging their empty nets. No one had caught anything. Even the fish had died that day, or all that were left already had been caught and eaten.

There was no universal cliché possible about the Atom Bomb. It was, in the end, Armageddon and *Walpurgisnacht*. The final image was the approaches to a bridge, a repaired concrete bridge that once again spanned the river. It sagged like an old man who had no legs or shoulders. In back, now green again, were the little mountains that bowled up—to center the city's flatness, where the Bomb had hit and boomed back, to make, one day, a spineless city. What had escaped destruction was more than mystical—the railway station now used solely by Allied personnel taking one of the three daily trains to Tokyo, 550 miles north. The troops rode the trains like heroes, and the Japanese bundled into boxcars, odd-and-end cars, and rode their way towards another destiny.

We saw the cities, whole and not whole. It was a tour to write and draw. We had schedules made by SCAP. We met trains, jeeps, cars, boats, and we walked, which was what we wanted to do. A few days to write about Atsugi arsenal; a week at Shimonoseki, for whales; and time for what the Allied soldiers did, at every one of their normal and illicit occupations.

"They screw everything in a skirt," said Bert.

Kure took another week—to examine the docks, the destruction of enemy shipping and enemy military equipment. Thirty-eight Australian soldiers, all experts in bomb and ordnance disposal, were supervising the destruction of Japan's past war potential. The job, begun a year before by the American Eighth Army when it occupied the vast ring of arsenals on the southern tip of Honshu Island, would end in two months. But it was more than a job of wrecking guns. The planning included the basis for Japan's future peace industries—metal, to be transformed into plowshares of future Honda motorcycles. DEE, the Destruction of Enemy Equipment unit, was supervising and reselling the metal to the Japanese Home Ministry. During the 1960's, DEE's devotion to salvage came back purified, ready for American Woolworth stores. Japan became the third highest producing country, just behind the United States and the Soviet Union.

We saw two-ton bombs divested of their TNT. One day the metal would make a wheel, a camera, a hand tool for Japanese gardening. In the greatest military junkyard in the world, at Kure, the recent Japanese war might was being put to torch. On a day in June, in 1945, the yards had employed 115,000 Japanese. In July 1945, several thousand American planes had blown up the blast furnaces, the armories, the rolling mills, the massive conglomerations for the host of Mars. On one spot, on a few square feet of turf and concrete, 450 bodies were still buried. There had been nothing to dig up and rebury.

The victor, on occasion, is the purist Christian, given to charity and hope. With an eye towards some kinder Japanese future, we had not bombed the dry docks. Today the Japanese are building the world's largest tankers there. As Lieutenant Commander Raleigh (USN) said to me, "Many a Bronx junk dealer would give his soul for this junk. Here is the new Japan, rising like a slant-eyed phoenix. . . ."

It was a spectacle of terrifying grandeur to stand on a huge crane and see the leftovers of the Japanese Navy being put to torch. The ships that had invaded the Philippines and gone through the two Coral Sea battles were there. The hell-ship *Haruna* was there. The wreckers, all Japanese workers, many without homes, had built their transitional homes within cornices of this maddened, metal-strewn, liquid-laced agony under the torch.

7

THE SONS OF HEAVEN

THE GI WAS the Son of another Heaven on Tokyo's strident Ginza.
Across a nearby moat was Emperor Hirohito. At SCAP, past the
moat, was General MacArthur. It was Tokyo, February 1947,
eighteen months after World War II.

The new Son of Heaven, in his khaki robes, had every sort of
moral, political and physical mandate. He was the conqueror.
The PX was his palace of fine art. He traveled everywhere on
leave. He was a tourist in between his soldiering duties and his
princely arrogance—an American samurai from another hinter-
land of Western man. On the Ginza he traded his PX materials,
his Woolworth store world and his Pepsi-Cola mannerisms. The

Americans, as we all know, are the most generous of peoples
when it does not involve Negroes, Orientals, American Indians
or others not completely Caucasian. In Japan, lost in an ancient
social system, the GI, unless tutored to regard the ancient nation
he occupied with some esteem, was, too often, a loud-mouthed
boasting brat abroad. Yet, from his khaki kingdom, he soon discovered that the Japanese played baseball—and that mellowed
him for a moment. When he discovered Japanese pearls, girls,
porcelain, cloisonné, Satsuma, gardens, the Noh and Kabuki
dramas, he took some of the bits and pieces and pasted Japan
together into his own private puzzle. But whatever warrant he
found adrift in Japan, he was a boy ballplayer with a loser known
in advance. He was, nevertheless, the remarkable political and
social engineer from America come to put Japan together again.

Tokyo, with few bombings, was basically intact. Large buildings, taken by the Allied staffs, loomed up with their carnivals in
khaki. Tokyo was policed by 125,000 Allied troops, mostly
American, and 15,000 civilians, most Americans. They brought
in the civil service engineering to make Japan obey, to make her
become materially solvent, learn civil rights, learn new industries,
and unlearn old industries. The silk industry was to be replaced
by a new one—rayon. The "honey carts," too, would have to go—
chemical fertilizers were healthier. We were agriculturally pro-
fessorial with our advice, and industrially professional. We were
advising the Japanese for their material and social progress. It
was a teacher-to-pupil relationship welcoming the new learner.
We led, and the stolid, adaptable Japanese followed. But General
MacArthur, despite the Allied military representatives who
dutifully attended the monthly Allied Council meetings, did
what he wanted to as the first American Imperator of Japan,
with the Russian, General Derevyanko, constantly saying *niet*.

I lived at the Press Club at No. 1 Shimbun Alley. There a Japanese could be invited legally for a needed drink and a meal. The
meal was our most democratic method of enlarging on our facts,
learning Japanese, refurbishing our historical nuances and main-
taining any sort of journalistic decency with our beaten Japanese
colleagues. The Press Club, more dubious than saintly, was run
by Richard Hughes, an Australian who wore a pince-nez, which
no proper Australian ever wore, drunk or sober. Hughes, a friend

of Jack Bellew's from Melbourne, soon had me sharing a room at
his tightly run Press Club. My eighteen dollars a week also got
me three American meals daily, put together by pandemonium,
gas, Japanese waitresses, and an imported chef. My temporary
roommate, Robert Martin of the New York *Post*, had just been
given twelve hours to leave Japan. We were protesting, like old
trade unionists, Martin's momentary expulsion.

Hughes had turned himself into a restaurateur-correspondent—
a new profession. Dedicated, floridly gracious, posing an odd
sobriety for an Australian, his high-pitched voice accenting both
his flavors and Press Club favors, he was drafting a reply to
Colonel Eccles, the American PRO who had decided to expel
Robert Martin.

The incident involved PRO protocol. It was full of fury and
sudden peace, particularly when Colonel Eccles confessed, after
our protest, that an error had been made. Martin could stay on
forever. Martin had come to Tokyo when Dixie Tighe, the New
York *Post*'s correspondent, died suddenly. Martin, coming in
from China, was taking care of her personal effects after handling
her funeral. He was filing stories—"nasty stories," said SCAP.
After our mass meeting nobody was expelled.

Life, American-Japanese style, was put together for us at the
Press Club's small bar in the back. The bar was sacrosanct, offering you moments of nobility amid furious promises. Often, sitting
over two stools, was a fat intellectual Englishman, a scholar who
spoke Japanese, who wrote hokku poems, who talked quietly for
a reporter, and who had lived in Japan before the war. There was
a great *Time-Life* photographer, and Joe Frome, a skillful writer
from *U.S. News and World Report*. Frome ran the Saturday night
dances, hoping to balance off our moral meanderings, our token
offerings to grace and probity—and our American ways of life
amid the wreckage.

We were democrats, republicans, socialists and liberals. But
most of us acted like philosophical anarchists. We fed our Japanese guests for under sixty cents. One drink made them drunk, and
then we picked their *dozoo* brains apart. What had happened at
the Diet? What was happening here, there, everywhere? As for
the labor unions, they were mushrooming like the CIO of the
Thirties, with similar trade unions competing in organizing the
workers. General MacArthur, we had just learned, had forbidden

a national strike, and the strike leaders wept in public. Disgraced, they lost face, but no one committed suicide. A leftist leader, too, had just been beaten up. Was not Japan a democracy now? Over American roast beef, we asked proper and improper questions. We asked about Emperor Hirohito—was he collecting butterflies or collecting face? The New Constitution, Japan disarmed, women's rights? Would the newly franchised wives vote like their husbands?

Our Japanese guests wore old clothes, third-handed down. We gave them our clothes and little things for their families—PX items, in exchange for their minds. When we were not charitable, it meant hunger. When we were, it sickened us. Our American souls, so victorious, were at ease amid the universalisms and the values of 1947, en masse, in all countries. At the Press Club we were politically civil, and often outrageously decent—trying to lift an Oriental veil where there was none. In three more years, many of these Americans would be dead—when the Korean War killed them. But in 1947, the Press Club was a modern opera for a comically sensitized parade of infants and careerists, of journalists and photographers, of specialists and pretenders—ready for every nuance for tomorrow morning's magazine, radio, book and newspaper.

The Russian delegation to the Allied Council lived directly in back of the Press Club. Windows locked, blinds drawn, Russians within Russians, they were hardly Churchill's enigma to us. They spied, all of us knew. They created havoc at the meetings of the Allied Council. Japan was not like Korea, already preparing to split apart. China was like Korea, but MacArthur, in Japan, went his way. He was tough, liberal and heralded, preparing the country for its own eventual determination. The trials and purges were not like the de-Nazification purges. The Japanese had not gone in for genocide. Japan had not quite been a fascist state— just a militaristic one. But, now, in the cleansing process, suddenly a cabinet minister would find his bad past published in *Asahi Shimbun* or *Mainichi*—and out of the cabinet he went. Who had not collaborated? Everybody, it was agreed, had been devoted to his country. And now, the moral and political equivalent for soap and water was washing through Japan's public institutions. It was a day of lament, eternal hunger and frustration. To cope, to cleanse, to live, to eat, to ride the broken-down transportation systems was a profane adventure daily. Suicides, always high, went higher. In 1947 it was easier to die than to live.

Into this political stew went everything. The first Yoshida government of Liberals had not been liberal. It had been SCAP's elected answer to the massive social problems. Japan needed stability, via its new democracy. We gave it stability via our Military Government's blueprint for the times. And since, too often, we could not tell a socialist from a communist, we helped to brew the stew along with many honorable Japanese—only we did not have to eat it.

The night before the Diet convened—and it was to be the last session before the new constitution went into effect—I interviewed the executive committee of the Japanese Social Democratic Party. It took place in a bare caucus room at the Diet. It was stripped down to chairs, smoke, socialist leaders, and panic. It had been a year of crisis for the Yoshida cabinet. No one dared go against MacArthur's no-strike demand. There was no strike. But a new election, requested by MacArthur, was heralded by the chairman of the executive committee, a chubby, soft-voiced, intellectual and Episcopalian Tetsu Katayama. He said, over many cups of tea, "It is time to test our people again—to see what they have learned. We have organized one and one-half million workers into the Japan Federation of Labor. They must have a voice. Our weekly paper, *Shakai Shimbun,* which now has one hundred thousand readers, will soon become a daily. We are for the nationalization of the coal and the fertilizer industries. Today we have ninety-nine seats in the Diet. All of the other five parties have three hundred forty-seven seats. We can win in a coalition with the Liberals and Progressives. There is inflation, hunger and a black market—and no country can make an honorable start under such miserable conditions. Also, since eighty percent of the government bonds are held by the banks, we must cease paying them interest. That is our platform. . . ."

It was socialism, Japanese style. They'd had no contact, as yet, with the reconstituted Second International. Karl Marx was a socialist's name—but not to Tetsu Katayama. I was almost about to ask if he had recently read Marx. It was apparent that Social Democratic thinking had been too long in the underground for a literature and a criticism to develop, Western style. Katayama's faith was Christian in piety and semi-demi socialist in economics. The communists had polled over two million votes in the prior election. A left wing within the Social Democratic Party, led by Kanju Kato and his wife, the former Baroness Ishi, was collaborating with the communists. And Katayama, a right-wing socialist, was under constant attack by his leftist colleagues. Wages, less than a dollar a day, helped the left. Living costs had gone up fifty percent in two months. On the Ginza, the left paraded. They wore red neckerchiefs, white handkerchiefs—and shouted like communists. Life and politics were all-engulfing.

The next day, April 25, the Social Democrats won the election and formed a government. Tetsu Katayama became the premier of Japan.

I was to know dozens of poets, composers and painters. They'd heard that an American poet was at the Press Club, and they came, scores in hand, books of poems in briefcases and with paintings under their arms.

The Japanese-American, Hirato, a representative of *Time* magazine, started it over a drink. The next day, we fed lunch to sad-faced Inakuma, once a Parisian, and anxious to be one again. He was the School of Paris in Tokyo. His art, still impressionist, was Right Bank scenery of the Butte and Montparnasse in the morning—little islands of Pascin, and Cezanne fusing into careful, Japanese craftsmanship.

Inakuma did a drawing of me to break into my mind. He was sick—ulcers, hunger, anguish. He was lost in his own Japan. He preferred to be lost in Paris on the Left Bank. Mr. Inakuma objected to *Romaji*—the Romanized alphabet begun eighty years earlier by Hepburn. "We must change it. We pronounce words like *till, tip* and *tin—chill, chip* and *chin.*" The letter *c* bothered Inakuma. He was also bothered by Buddhism—currently in disfavor. It had been, with some aspect of Zen, the religion of the contemporary samurai.

It was easier to talk of Paris—of Soutine, Chirico, Roualt and Picasso. Inakuma, who had simple ways of expressing his likes and dislikes, would say, when he liked an artist, "This is good. That is bad."

Hunger had its own vulgarity and unusual features. No one, or few among the Allied hosts, wanted to buy art—or even trade for it. The artists and writers, in no habitable world, were wanted by few and fed by fewer. They were lost completely among the businessmen of the West, then arranging every sort of commercial continuity. Each man, whether or not with the Military Government, found his Japanese counterpart to deal his way into the future of Japan. I knew textile experts, film people, publishers, importers, all ready to commercially profane the present and the future. It was simple to buy into a company that had no cash for expansion or cash for daily production. And with American knowhow, those infamous words, they became brothers in greedy, seedy operations. I preferred the poets, the writers, the painters, who had the basic impurity of their immediate hunger. I fed those I could from what I could get. In return, I wanted to write about their work, to edit an anthology of Japanese poetry, to arrange exhibitions—and to reintroduce them to New York's many nuances of contemporary Madison Avenue art.

There was Kazu Wakita, who painted boys and girls lyrically, much as if he were always painting himself. Small, cherubic, thirty-five, he had lived briefly in Germany, and German became the language we used. Wakita, shy, bombed out many times, now lived in a wreck of a house in the country. He visited Tokyo to meet others in misery, while waiting for something to develop. As a founder of the New Work Society, he opposed the academic "government art," as he called it. He did occasional drawings for the press—to get some rice and saki. In 1949, he mailed many of his paintings of children to me to sell in New York. Most of them were lost in transit, but by 1960 he was to become one of Japan's leading abstract impressionists, better than our own Franz Kline, who had calligraphied in black his American-made Japanese image of the sundered, brittle, aggravating half century we had finally given up.

There was Santa, even sadder, who wanted sweets for his morbid children and his wife. It was a condition of chemistry that starved the healthier emotions. We had met at a party to honor my interest in painting. Inakuma had arranged it, saying, "Opposite Radio Tokyo is little French restaurant. You come seven o'clock P.M., Wednesday, yes?"

White tables, beer and wine, with gallant attempts to please my eyes, my stomach and my floating thoughts. The owners of the French restaurant were Japanese who knew the PX peddlers. Sardines, crackers, olives, peanuts—it was party-planned. With the French steak came a soya sauce and Nipponese invention. Lacking French flavors, there was Japanese courage to spice its way. It had cost the dozen artists too much, but it was their means of reaching out to a once-fellow poet.

Santa had been a war artist with the Japanese forces in Rabaul and New Guinea. When I said that I had been there during the war, he shook with pain and mixed reflections. In his carrying case were five water colors, war scenes of my own New Guinea memories. I insisted on buying them and he insisted on giving them to me. Now they hang in my flat, New Guinea endlessly revisited. It was a bizarre party, with sadness sitting like a dethroned emperor before the faces of all of us.

Foujita was in Tokyo. I had seen him last when I was a boy, bumming about Paris, in 1922. A quarter of a century later, I was jeeping to his house on Kataecho Street, in Itabashiku, a suburb of Tokyo. Mrs. Okamura, an editor of the Japanese edition of *The Reader's Digest,* had arranged the interview.

It was raining. It was cold. We splashed through deep puddles. Streets once paved were now mired country roads.

When we arrived, Foujita was outside. His famous Parisian bangs were still there. Puckish, smiling, wiry, he had recently married his fifth wife. He purred like his celebrated cats. He looked at me, then said, "You have grown many years since Le Dôme."

When he left Paris, much before the war, he had told the French newspapers, "I do not love Paris anymore." He had, like all of the celebrated foreigners, come to Paris before the First World War. He had grown with Renoir, Picasso, Rouault, Pascin, Vlaminck and Soutine. They were friends and companions. A Renoir drawing of Foujita hung above a mantel. And the living room, warmed by a brazier and much green tea, was a gallery of intimates.

He had suffered much, he said. "I have sold only three paintings to the Americans. They do not know of me. They do not come and so I am hungry. I want to leave. Can you get me a visa to America? Can you get me a big exhibition? Ah, yes, I introduce you to Kiki long time ago!"

During the war Foujita had gone with the Japanese Imperial Army to various countries, arranging exhibitions in the occupied areas. Had he collaborated? "Was art collaboration?" he answered whimsically. "I exhibited cats, dogs, foxes—all ready to bite the enemy!" and he laughed. "But no one was eaten. They have the war trials, but they do not want me. I am not Tojo—yes? I am Foujita—no?"

Yes, he was Foujita. After all, he had taught soldiers how to paint. When they painted they did not fire bullets. And art softened the heart, we agreed. Now Foujita was asking me into his small studio, packed to the ceilings with gay canvases of his feline world.

But they were more than his hairline cats, dogs and foxes. Paris roofs, streets, cafés and people. There was Le Dôme, the Butte and Rue Ordener, where Foujita still owned a studio—pictures of a city that had made Foujita the first Japanese artist gone Western of the twentieth century.

A great draftsman, as Parisian in style as he was Japanese, he pulled out his paintings. When I paused too long and remained silent, he would put the painting to the right. When I murmured, "I like that very much," over to the left it went. When I looked at a piece of Rodin sculpture—given to Foujita by Rodin in 1916, a copy of the "Man with Broken Nose"—the painting he was holding was put on the liked sector of the studio. I wondered why he was dividing them. Was there a right and a left to his art?

Soon came a huge study of Mrs. Foujita—more cat than woman—then views of Okinawa, when the Japanese held it before the American Navy took it over. And the cathedral at Hanoi, and Mexican peons, Indochinese boys, Malayan women and Peruvians—peasant women and llamas.

Then came two huge screens that folded up like an accordion, six panels to each. The screens had cats, dogs and foxes leaping about in every motion and mood imaginable. To this, too, I said, "I like it very much, Mr. Foujita. . . ."

The exhibition was over. The rain had stopped. We started back, then stopped to shake Foujita's hand. At the door, he said, "Mr. Roskolenko, you are not taking those paintings?"

"Which paintings?"

"Those!" He pointed to the left.

"Those are yours, Mr. Foujita."

"No, they are yours—please!"

"It is impossible. Why, that little cat alone would cost me five hundred dollars."

"No, only five dollars. No one wants these paintings. No one comes. You remember me from Paris, so you come. You are a sentimental boy. Please! If you have no money, then you pay when you have—when you get back to New York. If you have a few hundred dollars now, that is enough. I paint very fast. In a month I will have more than those . . ." and he counted out the fifty paintings in the pile on the left. "But if you buy them, I must ask one thing—will you exhibit them in New York? I would like, Mr. Roskolenko, to have another exhibition. My last one was at the Reinhardt Gallery. Oh, so long ago! *Dozoo!* Maybe 1930? You can arrange it for me, please?"

I drove back in a well-packaged jeep, worth over a hundred thousand dollars for its art collection. And I did what Foujita asked of me—an exhibition at the Kennedy Gallery later that year and a visa for him to enter the United States, the first one for a postwar Japanese. I had become a forced collector of fifty Foujita paintings and a dedicated man.

A day later Emily phoned me from Australia. "Darling, I'm pregnant. No, I will not have an abortion. No, I can't come to Japan to marry you. You forget, I am separated from my husband. No, it takes five years for a divorce. Yes, I want the baby more than I want you. No, I don't mean that at all. I do want you—but how? I can't leave Australia because I can't leave my old Mum. I also have those dogs—five hundred in kennels. What, you want to come back to Melbourne? You hated it, darling. You love me—how wonderful! But you love Laura. I am writing you directly—everything. It will not be a bastard child—please! Will I be able to use your name? Thank you, darling. You are the father and I am the mother. The baby was conceived over Purcell's *Dido and Aeneas.*"

It was amoral, I knew. Our musical evenings had been fleshy fiestas. Bach and Purcell had helped. But Emily wanted a child, in the end, not me. She was a mother—and I never became the father, by her impossible situation and by her own conceits. My letters, for months, did not alter Emily's conception. It was the way it was to be—a proxy arrangement, like the Japanese girls made pregnant by the occupation troops. Suddenly there were blue-eyed babies. Suddenly there were bastards all over Japan. The children were given over to orphanages. Twenty years later, when fully grown and matured, they were the lost people— other hairy Anus, who though lighter of skin, were "despised and rejected" by Japanese Christians, Shintoists and Buddhists. An old Japanese folk song said it better:

> The full moon in the East,
> Saburu, the star, in the West—
> And my beloved is between . . .

When Emily rang off, I celebrated my private fatherhood-to-be.

Now the scattered and tattered poets and novelists came to tell me their truths about the war. One poet, who had gone with the troops, a beatnik before his time, long-haired and bearded like a prophet, said what I was to hear from many Japanese war correspondents: "We lost the war after the second Coral Sea battle. Prince Kono tried, with the Swedish diplomat, Count Folke Bernadotte, to get us out of this stupid war. Would you like to read the verses that I wrote about the Coral Sea battles . . . ?"

Literature went with the planes, bombs, soldiers and expansionism during 1935 to 1945. It followed, thematically, wherever the ruling parties sent their soldiers after the invasion of Manchuria. Poetry, prose and political criticism were Japanese toys to the generals and the samurai-politicians. Books were paste and words on paper—to march as books, and make, in its strident relationship, Japan's drive towards the new land masses of China, Malaya and New Guinea easier. Art was a bullet aimed at the brain. It was as Hitlerian as it was Stalinesque, totally rhetorical and grotesque with its seizure of the mind. It was Max Eastman's *Artists in Uniform*, though the uniform was baggier. Everything in opposition was forbidden and assassins were hardly new in Japan's drive towards new frontiers.

The P.E.N. Club, made dormant by this spiritual death, was just reorganizing. I met its organizer, Haruwo Mizusshima, the editor of *World Culture*—and the world was always within view, for he had just published an article by André Gide, "Who Will Save the World?" SCAP saw nothing wrong and allowed such peaceful thoughts, said Mr. Misusshima. "When the peace treaty is finally signed, then we can really be critical. Today we must obey. . . ."

I lectured at P.E.N. I talked of the Thirties: Hemingway, Dos Passos, Steinbeck, Faulkner—names of another past known to some, yet unknown to others of the two hundred writers who crowded into a hall.

A day later I was repeating the same lecture at the office of *Asahi*, the leading newspaper. Before the lecture I saw them put together a newspaper that was all Gilbert and Sullivan. A man like a bull sergeant was barking out to small boys who chased for the Japanese characters from font to font. Each boy was in charge of so many characters, to feed the typesetting tables almost a block-length away. Something happened and a paper came out. Somehow thousands of separate characters, fetched by little boys, found their way to the tables. There, makeup men, editors, writers and little boys got it together and *Asahi* was on the streets.

After the lecture, over saki and tea at a nearby café, I met one of the more avid listeners, Saneatsu Mushakoji, a Tolstoyian who had founded a cooperative colony called New Village at the southern end of Kyushu. He was Tolstoyian from beard to smock. He wrote with a feather. He bound his own books. Alongside of him was piquant Fumiko Hayashi who had gone with the Japanese armies to Java and Singapore as a correspondent. She giggled, as if to apologize for what she had written—"I was a very bad correspondent. I walked very slow. There was no car for me. I wrote letters to friends. I ate Army rations. But during the Sino-Japanese War it was even worse. I was always a slow walker, so that some of the male correspondents had to carry me, which kept them from writing good stories. They were too tired by the time we reached Hankow to write about the sacking of the city. I am, as you see, not very political. I am just natural, without politics, but is that possible today?"

Another novelist, Yoziro Ishizaka, compared himself to Gide. Was he as frank, I was about to ask, when he distilled other associations? He wrote, in a style called *Shimpen Shosetsu*, books about his private and intimate life. The author was always the subject. "In that way, one wears many faces," said Mr. Ishizaka. "In Japan, where we must save face, a poem about a long nose can be insulting. A novel that says things straight out could get your literary throat cut. We did our own censoring. We had natural taboos. Even before the war we could not go in for human evaluations of soldiers and sailors—what their real feelings were about shooting and killing. Yes, some of our men raped. There was Nanking, of course—but did we report it? We could not. For that matter, we could not even write about human love, the simple feelings—or about getting drunk. Men, especially soldiers, had to be described lyrically. They were robots of Nippon. The best example of an author-soldier was Sergeant Ashihei Hino. What great books did he write? Ah, so! He wrote *Wheat and Soldiers, Mud and Soldiers.* And to complete his rapturous trinity to the Emperor and to the guns, he also wrote *Flowers and Soldiers.*"

One morning, the publisher of *Utopia,* Mitsuru Iwaya, burst into my room. With him were fifteen surrealist poets, including Ezra Pound's Japanese friend, Katue Kitasono. He gleamed with joy. He carried a magazine showing my name. I had once contributed four lines to an international chain-poem before the war—and Kit-Kat, boyish and frenetic, got up on a chair. He read! He declaimed! He postured! He danced! He translated! The four lines became a token of universality—the end of a chain-poem. I was not a stranger, said Kit-Kat. But what was I doing with all those squares at *Asahi* and P.E.N.? A serious writer must be surrealistic or in the *avant-garde* like Ezra Pound. And Kit-Kat flew off the chair.

Another poet took over the same chair. I sat by the window wondering whether Richard Hughes would come to expel them. It was a demonstration for poetry and I was their natural audience, by fiat. They read like Japanese Hamlets. They praised William Carlos Williams and Whitman by the hour, each one ready to vagabond in Paris and "Manahatta." They talked, when they were not reciting, about English and European influences—James Joyce, Kafka, Gide, Louis Aragon, André Breton, and Paul Eluard. They had read everything new and old. To hell with hokku and waka! "Up with William Carlos Williams!" shrieked Kit-Kat. "Down with classicism!" shrieked Takuro Suetsune.

Soon, out came a long piece of rice paper, and sixteen poets wrote out single poems. I was also presented with books, signed and dated, and I was blessed in surrealist folklore. Out they went, dashing down the three flights, shrieking by a dazed Richard Hughes, his pince-nez falling as he elephantined his bulk away from the surrealists charging past him, down Shimbun Alley, on their way to the Ginza—and Paris.

I had seen Japan in between. Kyoto was the ancient palace city of the shoguns, a capital going back to 794. It had cherry trees and the tomb of Japan's feudal hero, Hideyoshi—the military dictator who had ended more than five centuries of internal wars. He had hated Christianity. He had warred against China— and Korea knew him as an invader in the sixteenth century. General Toyotomi Hideyoshi had built temples, palaces, Osaka and Tokyo. He had, in his way, been an earlier Napoleon. And I bowed to a history of another time, when our Pilgrim Fathers were landing on a small rock in Massachusetts. I bowed at Kyoto's Hongwanji Temple, gleaming red. The huge wooden timbers had been put in place by a woven hair-rope. Long ago the women of Japan had given their long black hair to weave a huge rope to lift the tall, heavy timbers. The rope, now under glass, had a poem by Lafcadio Hearn, to celebrate their hair and hearts. It said: "What faith can do in the way of such sacrifice he best knows who has seen the great cables woven of women's hair in the vast Hongwanji in Kyoto."

A jack-o'-lantern city! Gongs, beating sticks, canals, candles in the soft winds and chanting voices praying to Buddha. Someone had saved Kyoto. The fire bombs had not found a target. Our general staffs had been so Christian about some cities. They had sent the planes to three other Japanese cities—and two had disappeared. And I walked, Western-eyed, through an Oriental garden of my mind, through wooden and stone edifices gracing another faith, one more expansionist. It was a tight city, a tight country, a tighter morality. There was the Emperor's summer palace, Nija Castle. Unreal Kyoto! Hallucinated city! I had my own hair ropes, and I wore them as a shirt while in Kyoto.

And I bowed, most clumsily, a few weeks later, when I was ready to leave Japan. It was the formal way to leave. A friend of mine, Roger Rutchik, was interpreting American law for Japan's war criminals. He cited the Kellogg Pact in defense of Tojo. I cited my malaria, gotten in New Guinea, as a result of

Tojo's Pearl Harbor assault. And then Roger, once big in Min-
nesota's farmer-labor politics, remarked, "It's funny that we meet
again. Do you remember the truck drivers' strike in Minneapolis
during the Thirties—and the Dunn brothers?"

The trial of the 26 war criminals had been running a year at
the War Ministry building, as imposing as the men in the dock
were decomposing. They were yellow under yellow, their skin
more parchment than skin, eyes within eyes, voices left to their
lungs and throats. They were men of politics and military machines, men who had made pacts with Hitler—and others. Men
who as yet had not committed hara-kiri, criminals in a world
that preferred flower arrangements, open bathing and the worship of age. They were Japanese, who were the Germans of the
Orient, contemporary samurais who could only yell and not speak
softly. Yet everything in Japan was for flowers, winds, children
and quietude. Its art, suspended, was Zen suspended—the in-
complete gesture of the hand and the eye hairlined to some
subjective infinity.

In the dock, under Kleig lights, sat Sir William Webb, the
hawk-nosed Australian, as the Chief Judge. At the bar later I
heard Sir William say, as I drank with Roger Rutchik, "They are
so brilliantly defended, they may well be shot instead of hung!"
The Geneva Convention—on "how to kill"—had, a few minutes
ago, been under discussion.

"The phrase, 'Greater East Asia Co-Prosperity Sphere' is no
different from Wendell Willkie's 'One World' or the American
cliché, 'Good Neighbor,'" said an American defense lawyer, Mr.
Logan.

After the laughter, Mr. Logan continued: "For example, evidence will be produced showing Russian aggression against
Finland, Italy's expulsion from the League of Nations, Russian
aggression against Manchuria and the British-Russian occupation
of Iran. . . ."

It was this sort of a dialogue every day at the War Ministry.
Legal abstractions became laws. Laws became legal abstractions.
And translators, behind a glass façade, repeated everything for
the telephone that brought the trial in word after word. Everything was typed and printed. It was, at times, so objective it
was impossible to believe that it was not machines but men on
trial.

In time, some did try hara-kiri. Tojo merely wounded himself awkwardly with a bullet. Some went to prison. A Schopenhauerian philosopher, Shumei Okawa, who had once playfully struck Tojo, went mad. And some were executed against a background of cherry blossoms.

I bowed again before I left Japan; once to Prince Takimatsu, Emperor Hirohito's second brother, and once to General MacArthur, who addressed a luncheon at the Tokyo Press Club. It was the second interview he had granted. The first was in Australia, when he had emerged from a submarine after the fall of the Philippines. This time he was heralded fore and aft by MPs, motorcycle escort and the Japanese masses. Lit up for the press of the world, he was photographed in every viable nuance. Shimbun Alley had become God's own acres, sacrosanct and inviolate, barred to the Japanese journalists but open to the 45 Allied press representatives. To General MacArthur it was just another afternoon, for the same sort of heraldry happened daily at his offices. It was a pageant, stiff, policed and restrained. It was as exact as a battle plan.

Inside, lined up like second lieutenants, we waited for MacArthur to reach us. He came, escorted by Richard Hughes and his PRO. He said, with godly tones, as erect as Moses, as splendid as Jesus, "How do you do . . ." and there were 45 such salutations to our ninety eyes. As he walked by like a humanized god, his two eyes encircled a band of men who had, at different times, cut him to little bits during the Pacific War. He had, at times, called on God—to bless us in battle. He was the Christian always, marshalling the Lord of hosts. Laura, too, used to make irreligious comments—"What would MacArthur do without God?" I used to say that General Montgomery also called on God—as did the Kaiser in an earlier war. It was a Western prayer before their armies crucified each other. But there was no crucifixion in MacArthur's voice as he spoke about the problems facing Japan.

Strangely, he was very liberal. The United Nations should take over the occupation so that it "would be considered protective rather than repressive—to teach Japan democracy and Christianity." I thought of this years later, when many Japanese spoke of adopting Judaism, the religion of the most defeated people in the world. Defeat created other crucifixions and transitions to grace. And the Japanese, as Jewish converts, were without a basic ethical passion. After much philosophical ambivalence few converted.

On the platform, MacArthur talked about food, calories, a peace treaty and democracy. He was noble and generous to the recent enemy. The egocentric general did not strut. His vanity, on the platform, was a private mirror. He dumbfounded our ninety eyes. MacArthur, a liberal? MacArthur, all too human? MacArthur said about food, "On eleven hundred calories, or less, you die soon enough. We are starving the Japanese. They must be fed. . . ." A month later he was to invite Roger Baldwin over to organize the basis for civil liberties. An epochal man, he was creating his own democratic epic on the platform. He threw his speech away and freewheeled through Japan's human needs and hunger.

The Allied Council, who had expected to run Japan by suggesting useful ideas, had offered up more than one hundred such suggestions to the General. Few, if any, were accepted. He had forbidden a strike, lost face, then saved himself by suggesting new elections. He had recouped so much face and esteem that all the political parties thanked him. On that afternoon at Shimbun Alley, he was ready for the White House, said ten reporters.

From my files I have extracted something that I wrote for *The New Leader* that afternoon: "Obviously, to many, to be against the General is to line up with the Russians. The success of his occupation is usually weighed in this sense. It is, of course, an error, but it persists. There is always the lack of success in Korea with an impending civil war on the list. Measured against Korea and Germany, the element of praise that General MacArthur is receiving is as true as it is false. At least he has not partitioned Japan into four squares of negation. He has measured the pressure of the Japanese people and he is happily accepted as an apostle of American democracy. . . ."

It was another sort of an afternoon with Prince Takimatzu as I sat stiffly while meeting my first prince. Mrs. Okamura, an old friend of Prince Takimatzu, had arranged the visit to Shiba. The dusty, still regal palace was silent. The prince, charitably, had turned over part of the grounds to war widows and orphans. One widow had opened a dress shop, another a café. The prince, detailing his interests, served tea and talked about democracy and monarchism—accepting both. They were compatible, he insisted, but the Japanese now had to create a new cultural synthesis. Their long past, based on Emperor, Nation, People, was over. The Japanese trinity had gone with the defeat. . . .

"Unlike the British royal family," said Prince Takimatzu, "the Japanese royal line has been continuous and has not taken in a foreign elite. And since the Emperor in the past has been looked upon by the people as an *ideal*, the same fact makes it just as British. . . ."

As for democracy, did he prefer the British, French, American, Icelandic or Russian? He laughed, sipped his tea, signed a photograph of himself, and inferred that Japan would develop its own forms, though he privately preferred the American ideal of individual liberty. "But it is too early to notice any sudden burst of enthusiasm on the part of our people. It must, above all, include the concept of individual rights. That, above all, is sacred. . . ."

One of Prince Takimatzu's brothers, believing in individual rights, had been living in a subway to expiate for Japan's condition. He had turned towards Christianity and poverty. Prince Takimatzu, whom Mrs. Okamura said was one of the wealthiest men in Japan, had turned towards charities, European scholarship, and democratic thoughts. But everybody in Japan then was thinking of poverty and democracy. It was an endless searching, from princes to clerks—all interpreting General MacArthur's last biblical words at the Press Club.

I left as I had come, from Iwakuni. A Sunderland took me to Hong Kong. After that, it was to be Kweilin, in China—to see Red armies marching, and China, dying with its civil war.

In a land called *Dozoo* (please), I had learned many token words, including *Presento* (gift), *Ai* (love), *Ashita* (tomorrow), *Awaseru* (to put together), *Atai* (price), *Bakuhatsu* (explosion), *Bunka* (civilization or culture), *Byoo-in* (hospital), *Chika* (underground), *Choosetsu* (adjustment), *Choowa* (harmony), and *Arigato* (thank you).

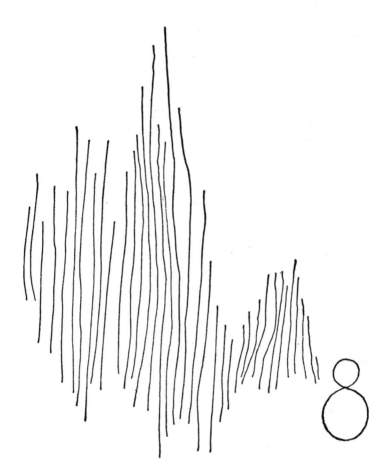

THE TERRORIZED

WEST FROM IWAKUNI was Hong Kong, ten hours on a Sunderland
flying boat. It skimmed over the waters, rose like a buffalo,
shivered like a canoe in a gale. It was the route to the interior of
China and another civil war. Only Japan was at peace. Saigon,
four hours from Hong Kong, was already swamped with civil
war, revolution, anti-French colonialism, and communism badly
disguised as Nationalism by Ho Chi Minh.

From the Sunderland, Hong Kong shone like a smashed dia-
mond. As we moved down to land, the Peak came up—looted,
despoiled, hardly the Victoria Peak that it once was. The day the
Japanese surrendered, the local Chinese population looted all the

homes. They invaded the grand old English mansions, taking doors, windows, roofing, bath fixtures and furniture. They left the mountain itself. Down below was Hong Kong—all sensitized vice and extra-territorialism, a Crown Colony within the Empire's fading economy. And the economy was in the streets.

Sleek cars and narrow lanes, rickshaws and pedicabs, with the coolies whining some objective lament. The streets tumbled out like dice. A mad city, a bargain basement, everybody was in business and trade. It was a social riot waiting for the civil war to come down. In Shanghai, the riots had the communists to move them, by default, towards the bloodied center. In Shantung and Shensi they already had the centers. In Washington, Dean Acheson was preparing a White Paper. No more aid to the Nationalists. In less than two years Chiang Kai-shek would flee to Formosa.

And there was the Hong Kong way to die. At night people died on burlap bags in the streets. Somebody had not given them rice that week. Children curled near their mothers as the rain fell. Sacking-webbing was thrown over them. If they lived through the night, they ransacked the garbage along the narrow streets the next day. Life was always just a day. The men stole, they mugged, they dynamited, they extorted. Others, better off, did it better off. Every bank and jewelry shop had Sikh guards with rifles. Private armies, political panic, but Britannia was still ruling. It was Hong Kong, English since 1842—and due, when the lease ended, to go back to some China in 1997.

In Kowloon, at a RAF billet, I met Lieutenant Jim Hines, whom I had known in Tokyo. He invited me to come along to Kweilin with a load of U.N.R.R.A. staples—rice, dried milk and dried eggs.

We flew over Canton. Pearl River was a mass of boats—junks with humanity. We flew on and landed at Kweilin set between a bowl of mountains. It looked like Hiroshima, with the same terrain bowling up. At the airport were hundreds of soldiers, rifles ready, to keep the hordes of hungry Chinese away from our U.N.R.R.A. food.

They cried! They pointed! They tried rushing—and a few were shot down. They lay like the rice sacks. We cursed! We protested! The soldiers had their own trained indifference. Death was normal. Death was every second. Death was only blood. Death had no eyes.

We refueled, and wondered if we would be next. We took off, and flew over Changsha and Hankow—a yellowed land, empty between the cities and villages—harsh, dry, waiting—mountains that jutted up like Oriental faces in the darkness. We landed on a flared field in the dark. Oddly, it was quieter at the Nanking airfield, with the ragged soldiers of the Nationalist Army quickly unloading the last of our supplies.

We slept in a tent. Two of the crew remained with the flying boxcar, sentries over an empty plane. "We always do it here," said Jim, "or tomorrow there'll be nothing left to fly away with. Nobody trusts anybody. No one cares about this Goddamn war anymore—nobody but us, the United States. Do I care? Like hell I do! Wait'll you see the Reds!"

We flew in from the Yellow Sea. Darien, once Russian, then Japanese, and now Russian again, was to our right, way off in the liquid mist over the brown hills and mountains of the mainland. Shantung, rich, extra-territorialized by England, Germany and Japan, had been the birthplace of Confucius and Mencius. Now the communists had enveloped the entire region, and the Nationalists, weary and out-maneuvered, were watching their own deterioration. We had been pressuring Chiang to enter into a coalition with the communists.

Confucius, in his time, had thought, "A family must first destroy itself before others can destroy it. A kingdom must first smite itself before others can smite it." We were pressuring the Nationalists to death from Washington. The Russians, who were nearer and who had made the Japanese Kwantung Army of 800,000 men surrender to the Chinese communist armies, must have read Confucius along with Lenin.

Jim was participating from above as we circled over the massed communist encampments. "They won't shoot. They know our U.N.R.R.A. markings. Whatever we deliver to the Nationalists will be theirs soon enough. We're just an express service for those Goddamn commies! You know what the Gizmo used to say during 1944, when I was flying around here—'The Japanese are only lice on the body of China, but the communists are a disease of the heart.' I think they're in the Goddamn guts, by now!"

In Canton, later that week, the disease became even more

sickening. An American-Chinese soldier at my hotel, John Lee, had gone up the Pearl River to visit his aged parents. He had left China as a boy to live with his relatives in San Francisco. Now, on leave from his unit in Japan, he had come bearing gifts— packages of food and clothes. He had taken passage up the Pearl River on a boat carrying ten peasants, some wealthy, some not —all heading for their villages two days from Canton. On their first night, the boat was attacked by river pirates and all the passengers were killed. The crew swam off, and so did John Lee.

"They were going to kill me, but then they saw my uniform. To kill an American would be bad—so they just took my packages. They tore my clothes. They beat me, kicked me, and took my money. They threw me into the river. I swam to the bank and walked to a village. I got a ride in a truck to Canton. I saw the American consul, who said he'd help me get back to my unit in Japan. He didn't give me any money. He just put me into this flea-bitten hotel. I said I had to see my parents. The consul said he would arrange for them to come to Canton. But what gifts can I give them? I'll ask the consul for an advance on my army pay. It's been so many years since I saw them, and they're so old. I hate China. I hope it dies! I hope the floods, monsoons and earthquakes eat it up! A dead, stupid, vicious country. . . ."

Everything was sad in Canton, on the Pearl River, on the crowded junks, in the gagging city, in the wallowing streets filled with Nationalist soldiers waiting for the communists to sweep in on them.

From Hong Kong, we flew to Saigon, and another civil war. It was in the frightened streets, in the tense cafés, in the exploding pedicabs. It was in the long foreign faces and in the Annamite round faces. It was April 1947.

I was prepared for nothing. It was an old war by now, four months on the roads of Indochina. Little did I know, that hot afternoon in Saigon, that twenty years later, without end, and stalemated, it would eventually swallow up France. It would kill off a dozen graduating classes of St. Cyr, and many thousands of metropolitan Frenchmen, Annamites, Algerians, Africans, including the stalwarts of the French Foreign Legion.

I was billeted by the RAF at a broken-down hotel opposite the Saigon River. It faced the airless docks, where transports and freighters were unloading the new war. I heard the winches whine through the day into the night. I heard explosions through the night, and grenades going through the windows into French government offices. Then would come the racing French jeeps looking for marauding communist terrorists. In the morning it was just as customary to find a stave somewhere in the market-place—and a head stuck on the top. Below it, as if to signify some pictorial mandate, were written the Viet Minh's reasons. The beheaded one was a French soldier, an Annamite collabora-tor, said the Viet Minh. It was to become the classical twentieth-century war, as anti-colonial as it was Nationalist and communist.

When World War II ended, France found her colonial empire heir to social and political violence, following a pattern that involved every European colonizer. It was happening in India and Indonesia. It was happening with thunder, riots, battles, destruction, raids, proclamations, demonstrations, dis-guises, gallantry, cowardice, confusion, corruption, loyalty. And it went on like every classical distortion after every major war. For France, it meant another dubious reckoning. In Paris there was hardly bread and wine. But France still was the savage colonial power if without the teeth to bite into its old colonial meat.

It had been the magnificent boast of France in 1884 that Tonkin—where Ho Chi Minh's communists began exercising their preamble to power in April 1947—had once been captured and held by only 188 French marines. But now, 63 years later, one hundred thousand marines, foreign legionnaires, reservists and regular army men couldn't hold it. By May, another forty thousand soldiers would arrive from France to try and hold the paddy fields, the cultivated marshes of Laos, the jungles of Annam, and the mountains up north where the primitive Meo and Mois tribes, along with their goats and their mountain sheep, drank fermented milk and stayed mildly drunk for years on end.

The provinces of Laos and Annam were in the middle of the war. And Saigon, on that hot afternoon of my arrival, was no longer a petite French city—despite the buxom, nervous, heat-exhausted French women being pedicabbed about. In the cafés on Rue Catinat, an aperitif often meant an invitation to a

slaughter. It was the way of the oncoming terror—Molotov cock-
tails, grenades, and then some Europeans were dead. There was
arrogance too. The strutting French foreign legionnaires were
bolder with their new taste for another existence. They were a
mob of husky Poles, Czechs and Hungarians. But mostly they
were Germans, former collaborators, who preferred a long enlistment in the French Foreign Legion to long terms in prison or
hunger in their own country. Former fascists were now blood
brothers to republicans and democrats as ideologies mixed
with wine, heat and the bullets. In the interim, before Europe
reorganized for bread and meat, Indochina was a way for an
ex-Nazi to get by on French terms.

The French were again doing their amoral, colonial book-
keeping in East Asia. Japan, after its capitulation in 1945, had
obligingly surrendered Indochina to English bayonets and sea
power. And the Potsdam Conference divided Indochina in behalf
of France. The English, in the interim, policed Indochina until
France could marshal enough troops once again to take over
suzerainty. Commission after commission met to argue against
French colonialism, for Indochinese Nationalism, or for covert
covers for the communists—the Viet Minh, Ho Chi Minh's
amalgamated political party. Finally, on March 6, 1946, France
signed an agreement with Ho Chi Minh for the creation of an
Indochina Federation, within the French Union.

On June 1, 1946, the Republic of Cochin China was officially
born and the tragic comedy began. Pacts followed pacts. Agreements followed agreements. Commissions followed commissions.
Every day there was another solution. The three-cornered communist Viet Minh head used anti-colonialism, Nationalism—and
communism—to initiate, by devious routines, the attempt to
seize power by terror.

The first blow within this cycle was the clash at Haiphong.
On December 6, 1946, the Viet Minh beheaded 296 Annamites
and 8 Europeans. The second incident took place at Langson,
when French troops, while searching a former Japanese charnel
house, were attacked by the Viet Minh. Soon after that the Viet
Minh cut the road between Hanoi and Haiphong and encircled
the capital. On December 19, the Viet Minh attacked Hanoi and
isolated outposts in Tonkin and Annam.

In Paris, Premier Ramadier insisted that the French would

not yield to communist terror. The stalemate now shifted to the United Nations, then to Moscow, then back to Paris. Premier Ramadier sent a new High Commissioner, Monsieur Bollaert, who had been a prisoner of war in Dachau. After all, Bollaert, as a former civil servant, a Radical Socialist, and a man who had suffered in prison just like Ho Chi Minh, knew all about the human approach, as he later told me.

Emperor Bao Dai, playboy, exploiter, alleged whorehouse owner, gambler, a man of many regal talents, was suddenly recalled from Hong Kong to form a national government or a national political whorehouse of his own with France's partnership. In satin and sables, or gowned in uniforms of many colors, wearing dark glasses like a badge of courage, he was disliked by all. He was everything to everybody. From monarchists to Nationalists, he was the head political pimp. In 1954, when the last battle at Dien Bien Phu took France out of Indochina, we came in, with more than the seven hundred million dollars we had given to a France still trying to be an in-hock colonial power in East Asia.

I was the observer with a small camera, a long question, and a tattered notebook as I walked into the terrible night of the civil war. After a month, I was a small expert. There were rendezvous to get more small facts. They came in capsules, in envelopes, in handouts, in letters, in sudden conversations. The facts came from girls, from pedicab drivers, from servants, from politicians, and from street dentists sitting over the Mekong with their spindles and needles. They came from men in *langouti*'s, from East Indians anxious to bribe Westerners for import licenses, from the water boy who filled up my tub.

I met political secretaries, ministers coming up from their political miasma, and press officers enchained. When a Frenchman became rude, I became ruder. But the French, who were at ease within the arrogance of their vested colonial dreams, had a natural authority. They were, too often, more German than some of their ex-Nazis in the Foreign Legion.

One of my first visits was to a French political officer, Jean Ferry, a young historian who had met Ho Chi Minh. He was convinced that Ho Chi Minh was a prisoner of his own propaganda. Monsieur Ferry was also a sad young man, though he smiled fatly with his cheeks puffing up. He was not completely sympathetic with France's attempt to reestablish itself in Indochina. Monsieur Ferry was always weary and he drank too much. He sweated like an uncomfortable Parisian, drifting between French propaganda and some inner reserve that he managed to maintain. After a while I would learn to accept that eccentric, oblique detachment that so many civil servants gave off between words, as they weighed their consciences against what they were there for—France *Outre-Mer*. They looked toxic. Their words were alcoholic and pure in turn. They offered you dubious distillations of value, much as if they were embalming France's republican conceits along with everything else in Saigon's heat and civil war.

At the Press Club, adjacent to Hotel Continental, a French businessman, over a cognac, was showing me photographs of a murder. It had taken place the night before, in Cholon, the all-Chinese town outside of Saigon. A Chinese gambler had been murdered. He had not been robbed. The body was neatly butchered into four equal parts, as if to mystify the French authorities.

"They left every piaster in his pockets—and he had many," said the Frenchman, mopping his forehead. He used three handkerchiefs, going from a blue one to a white one to a green one, and as he mopped, he said, "Who was he? Who knows? But he's dead, I know that. Who was he an agent for? There are four kinds of agents here. There are Chinese and Annamites for Bao Dai; Chinese, Annamites and some crazy Frenchmen working for Ho Chi Minh; Chinese and Annamites cooperating with France. And then, I have been assured there are agents who work for all at the same time. This is, Monsieur Roskolenko, a very corrupt country!"

The next day I had lunch with Le Van Hoach, the Annamite president of Cochin China, who had been an eye specialist prior to entering politics. He looked even sadder, much as if he was betraying his country by accepting his appointment from the French. He was frightened and watched the large wooden door every time a secretary knocked and entered, as if he expected a bullet in his head or a grenade tossed at his desk as he signed a paper or answered the telephone. And not oddly, all the Annamites for the French had the same engraved look of terror.

After demitasse, he said, "Who can we deal with among the Viet Minh? They honor nothing they sign—nor do the French. We can't hold popular elections. Who is ready for that? But there are many things that we can do to help our people, especially the peasants who must borrow money. We can do something about the usurious rate of interest. Today a peasant pays over three hundred percent on loans. We must reduce that to one hundred percent, which is almost revolutionary. We must create a system of social services and improve the condition of the workers and the peasants, or they will go over to Ho Chi Minh. Unfortunately, whether we like it or not, we are not yet ready for total sovereignty. The French, alas, must still provide a big umbrella for us. . . ."

Within a year, Le Van Hoach was dead, assassinated by himself.

I met the French High Commissioner, Monsieur Bollaert. He was spectacled, dumpy and laughing. Dachau had made him more humane, he said over a glass of champagne. Dachau was not like the Commissioner's palace, and he gestured about the sunny room.

"But I will try and set things right," he said, stopping the waiter to get me another glass. "But it will take time, you must understand. I am studying everything carefully. If Ho Chi Minh stopped his terrorism, we could talk again. Yes, we must hold another conference! At least, while we're talking, we're not killing each other. Death! Death! Death! I've seen all I care to see in this world, believe me, Monsieur Roskolenko. All those heads! Here they are just as bestial. Those decapitations! How can you deal with such people? We are sending for more troops. . . ."

The huge drawing room was hot. A few large fans spun uselessly, moving through the heated air, which came in bursts over the champagne. I was pasted to my tropical suit, spinning with the fan, listening to another sad man on a civil errand in Saigon's burgeoning civil war.

To relax, one hot evening, I smoked opium. A French girl had insisted that I go along, with the promise that I would experience many new things. New worlds would appear and others would vanish, she said urgently.

The night before I lay awake into the early hours. The airless room in my RAF billet had a large fan that spun about less than ten times a minute—and I had counted the revolutions of the spinning blade for an hour. When I counted a thousand spins, I quit the game. I thought of the war again—and I quit that, soon enough. I stretched out on the broad windowsill to catch the slender breeze coming off the river. When I finally nodded, almost asleep, I found myself leaning out over the sill—and I went back to the bed. Opium, the girl had said. Opium tomorrow night. The whole idea was sickening.

I had met this buxom French girl on the stairs of the billet. I had seen her on several occasions, mostly when she stopped to quarrel with the drivers of the rickshaw bicycles, making crude scenes when it came to tipping them. After that, she would bounce up the stairs, animated, overly alive in the seducing heat, more Annamite than Parisian. When we met, she asked, "Are you *américain* or *anglais?*" and up the circular stairs she ran.

"Flier, journalist, businessman or politician?" she asked again, perched over the broad bannister.

"I know many Americans from Paris—even here, last year. It was very wild last year when the shooting started. Killings. So many killings!"

We agreed to meet. . . .

I met her outside the billet, at the big wooden door. She was chatting with two French officers, who were laughing as only French can, in registered explosions of Gallic unison. An armed soldier patrolling the entrance stared at the girl.

"Where to?" I asked her.

She did not answer. Instead, my right arm was laced, and she was rushing down Rue Catinat. Soon we turned on a side street and went halfway down. At a broken fence, we entered a backyard. She pounded the first door, first with her knuckles, then with the flat of both hands. Finally her bag was banging against the door, which still did not open.

"Where is that fat Chinaman?" she yelled. "I tell him that I fly back with an American soon. *Canaille!* Big pig, too!"

Then we heard the softness of feet padding toward the door and the door opened. A fat Chinese was grinning at the entrance. He was beckoning and saying anxiously, "Come, come. Many officers from ships. Must fix many many pipes—hurry! Tonight only nine piasters for pipe—yes?"

"Cheat! This afternoon it is only six piasters," she said to the Chinese as he closed the door.

"Six in afternoon, nine at night, Mademoiselle—yes?"

The smokers were grouped on a large bed. Some were detached, furtive, anxiety-ridden, compulsive, waiting for more pipes to come. A tall, thin girl was reciting poetry, bits of Rimbaud that I recognized. She was getting off the bed, coming towards us, putting her arms out and remarking, "You must smoke with me, sir—and together we will find Rimbaud. You like Rimbaud?"

"She's crazy—very crazy," said the girl who had brought me. "She is like the war, dirty and crazy. You like crazy girls?"

"I like the *américain*," said the tall girl, dragging me to the bed. "You do not go with that bitch! She only want your money later. I, I want no money. I work for the government as a statistician. Come, *américain*."

The other girl left, dashing to a back room to smoke alone. I was on the bed with the others, dangling my legs, staring at the French maritime officers squatting alongside of me, hanging onto opium pipes, looking distracted, and waiting for introductions. Instead they heard the tall girl intone more poetry from Rimbaud. She was reciting stray lines, joining Rimbaud's *Alphabet* poem to his *Drunken Boat* poem. Finally, in a burst, she orated—

> Par les soirs bleus d'été, j'irai dans les sentiers,
> Picote par les blés, fouler l'herbe menue:
> Rêveur, j'en sentirai la fraîcheur à mes pieds,
> Je laisserai le vent baigner ma tête nue . . .

The other girl had come back and now she pulled me off the bed to a side room. Soon a pipe was brought in and she puffed away quickly. It came with a deep sucking-in, hurried and panicky. The fat Chinese came back with a second pipe and he handed it to me. I tried but I was disgusted. I held the pipe away from my lips as if it were an explosive about to go off. The girl grabbed it from me, sucking in madly. A moment later she stuck it into my mouth and demanded that I do what she had done. I could not inhale, not even a cigarette, and I finally quit. She finished my pipe, and I took out a cigarette and blew smoke about aimlessly.

I got up to leave. The girl, too, was disgusting me. Her panic was surfacing despite her smoking. If she was a whore, I would know it soon enough. It would come after she was done with the pipes. I went back to the front room to talk to the four officers and Mlle. Rimbaud, as one of the officers called her.

"We brought in American ammunition," said an officer with a badly scarred face. "It's a hell of a war!"

"It's no hell of a war for some Americans," said the officer alongside of him. "It's a war to make money on. Ammunition makes money for you Americans—no?"

"Ammunition kills," said Mlle. Rimbaud. "Poetry makes men live—yes?"

"*Merde! Merde!*" said the officer with the scarred face. "My face, yes, my face—it is like a map of the Alps Maritime, with peaks and valleys."

He looked sad, ugly, contrite. And he sucked away at his new pipe. It gave him other mountains and valleys—and a new face. A minute later he was sobbing and one of the officers was hugging him, saying, "Jean, Jean! It's all right. No one notices your scars. The girl does not notice your scars. The scars are only in your mind, Jean."

Jean sobbed on. Soon he was standing up, going to the toilet, washing his face, trying to make his ugliness sanitary. Mlle. Rimbaud was shaking her head, stroking my arm, and repeating again, "I work for the government as a statistician. I do not need money. Are you a nice man? You like poetry so you must be kind, yes? I am a statistician, Monsieur *américain,* and I can add up everything. . . ."

"More dreams about an opium empire for France overseas? It's all over," I answered, just as sad now.

"Don't go with that girl in the back. She wants money. She can get it from the officers. I do not need any more pipes. Come with me. That other girl is too fat. You come to my apartment, yes? We do not go to your RAF hotel. I know where you stay. My office is across from you, and I see you every day. You are running all the time. You make interviews all the time—yes? And the English girls in your billet, they too are fat. They have fat bosoms and fat ankles. Me, I am thin. That's better for making love. There is no imagination in fat women. They are like pigs."

We took a pedicab, and the driver smiled, as if the turning

wheels turned on his smile. Then I smiled, as if there was something to be happy about.

"He's in the Binh Xuyen—the gangsters," said the girl. "That's
his badge. They run everything that is not nice here in Saigon.
They run that opium place, the brothels between here and
Cholon, and all the smuggling. He smiles so big!" and the girl
laughed.

"He should smile," I said, watching the pedicab driver's face
go round and round. "He's got Bao Dai as well as General Le Van
Viem, the chief of police, behind him. Whom do you have?"

"Ramadier, in Paris. General de Gaulle, out of Paris. André
Malraux, who once lived here. And now I have you for a house
guest—no?"

"Yes. I have President Truman, at home."

"Anybody else? Do you have a wife?"

"No, not a wife."

"A woman here or in New York?"

"Nowhere. There used to be one in Australia. . . ."

"And she is not there now?"

"I'm not there now. I'm with you in a pedicab," I said.

"And you do not know my name. Don't you want my name?"

"What is it?"

"Genevieve Martel, Monsieur *américain*."

"Like the cognac? Is it a real name?"

"Not like the cognac, it is like myself. . . ." She called to the
pedicab driver, "Stop here, please."

It was a red two-story house built like a Cambodian temple.
The roof had green tiles and "S" curves laced and jutted out
from the corners of the roof. Inside, however, it was all French,
overstuffed, with a Pleyel piano and some paintings of Paris.

"Cognac, Martel?" she asked, giving me a humorous kiss.

"Cognac, Genevieve. . . ."

"Tomorrow I do not work. It is Sunday and for sleeping. You
wish to go to church?" she asked, spilling over the cognac
hurriedly.

"Not even to synagogue," I said.

"You are Jewish, no?"

"Yes, Jewish, like Captain Dreyfus."

"I am not Jewish. I am nothing now anymore. Once I was a

Catholic—but not for very long. But perhaps, after tonight, I will become Jewish—no?"

"Why do you want to become Jewish, Genevieve?"

"Because you are Jewish and you like poetry. That is enough, no?"

"Hardly! How do you know I like poetry? Because I know about Rimbaud?"

"Ah, ha! It is because you go with me and not with that fat whore—that is why."

I was following her up the stairs to the bedroom. She was undressing, going towards the bathroom. I heard the shower run and her voice echoing some nonsense music I could not make out. When she came out she was wearing a thin robe and smoking a cigarette. She stood before her dresser and began to fix her hair, to perfume herself, to ask me more questions.

"Do you not take a shower?"

"I had three baths today. I am not dirty and I do not smell, except from that stupid opium," I said nervously.

"I smell from flowers, from orchids. And where do you go from here—and when?"

"To Pnom-Pehn on an armed vessel tomorrow," I said, looking at the unmade bed.

"No, not tomorrow—please!"

"I have an interview with King Sihanouk in two days," I mumbled, starting to undress.

"Oh, that terrible saxophone player! That little fat king!"

"He is still loyal to France, so you mustn't insult Sihanouk, Genevieve."

"He is loyal to himself all the time. Please, get into bed. I am finished with my hair. See how thin I am?" She had taken off her robe.

"You are thin," I said, "but your thin body fills up my hands. . . ."

"And your mouth?"

"And my mouth—and you smoke opium with your mouth. I still smell your opium. Why do you smoke that miserable stuff?"

"Because I am made stupid here. War! Heat! Soldiers! Colonials! It is all very stupid! So I smoke. We all smoke. Maybe in two years, in three years or next month, we will all go away. Let us save ourselves, no? Let the Viet Minh have this stupid land. They are all idiotic anyway. Bao Dai! Binh Xuyen! Viet Minh! Cao Dai! Hoa-Hao! All are very stupid! Please, get into the bed. If you stay here, you smoke. That is how it begins."

"Why don't you go back to Paris?" I asked. "Get married in Paris, Genevieve. Ramadier needs statisticians and married women for babies. You are important, Genevieve."

"I am not so important. As for marriage, would you marry me? I smoke opium and I will always smoke it, even in Paris. Who will marry an addict?"

I was in the bed. And now she was talking about seeing blue scenes everywhere. Her sky was in the room, over the bed, in the bed, in her eyes, and in her opium-sated body, as she spread herself. She was walking over blue grass in large fields. She was climbing trees and swimming in little lakes. She was moving as if she were a houri in a temple of virgins, fusing her motions with her speech-making. They came together—Rimbaud, Cao Dai, Viet Minh and Binh Xuyen. There were the gangsters, emperors, poets, communists, holy men, mystics. . . .

She was another Laura, but Laura of the opium pipes—and I felt strangely related to this strange statistician. There was, too, something beautiful about her instincts despite her opium dreams and her private dramas—the interrelated dreams, the desperate poetic chasms, much as if Rimbaud's subterranean world made up Genevieve's real world in Saigon.

She lay there in the blue ether of her eyes, with the tented mosquito netting framing her bedraggled blonde hair. And she would grab me and mumble, "Stay near me—they are shooting again. They are always shooting at night . . . and tomorrow, you must smoke—you *must!*"

An echo of the civil war broke through the open window, banging against the night like a rifle going off in an alley. I lay near her listening to her and the churning winches on the unloading American freighter, to the terror switching on and off in Genevieve's flickering eyes. Obviously, it was the opium wearing off and Sunday arriving. The dreams were leaving, and reality, like the Catholic church down the street, was banging on her head.

I was to meet her years later, in Paris. She would say that I had made all of this up, that she had never smoked opium, that it was in my mind. After Saigon, she was off to French Equa-

torial Africa, still the colonial statistician. There would be letters
about the weather aging her and that she wanted to be back in
Paris and go to concerts. When I finally met her during the late
1950's, in Paris, she had adopted a child and the child was her
real world along with the Catholic Church. She had never become Jewish, Buddhist, Moslem. She had not married, "for who
wants a drug addict? What do I smoke now? My dreams, as you
said. I still love Rimbaud . . . and the Church is my last
poem. . . ."

The clumsy little steamer would soon pass the Point, turn out of
Saigon at the bend and meet the long winding Mekong, which
ran yellow and endless. A politically disturbing river, it went
through several countries, beginning in the Tangla mountains of
Tibet, passing through China, Burma, Thailand and Indochina.
After several thousand meandering miles, it fell into the peaceful
South China Sea.

From the boat I recognized some French army officers tea-
dancing at the little open-air café suspended above the Point.
They were scarred with an older death, brutalized as self-exiles
in Indochina's new war. They were there daily—and I waved.
They bounced jerkily, unsteadily, somewhat drunk.

Later, to cool their little-war minds, they would smoke opium.
It made them feel less desperate. It calmed the guts along with
the brain. The boat was carrying more than fifty French foreign
legionnaires going to Pnom-Penh for extra-territorial duties, and
they hogged the rails. They were husky men with tight faces—
big men in a still-small war. They had been strangers a year ago.
Now they were intimate friends of the knife, the rifle, the
machine gun. After a while their private histories became apparent—in their accents, their nervous laughter, their inadequate
silences when they were not bantering and haranguing each
other in German, Polish, Czech and French. They stared at the
Mekong winding through the towering swamps and the embattled rice paddies.

The overnight, open-deck steamer had once been a pleasure
boat, but pleasure was no longer its trade. Now it made the
eighteen-hour trip to Pnom-Penh, carrying peasants and businessmen, sailors and legionnaires. The only armament that it had
was a special three-inch gun which almost tore the boat apart

whenever it was fired. The young captain, M. Mallat, cynical and sneering, had an overall contempt for the minor attempts at arming his vessel.

He had a pleasant face, but it had been frightened too long. His thin cheeks contradicted the rest of his bravado, puffing up with fear at every bend in the river. Then his hands clawed away at the rails, tightening with the rhythm of the engines. Yet, despite that, he gave off the image of the young adventurer. He was as tall as General de Gaulle and his hands were just as huge and knotty. He had volunteered as a civilian maritime officer for the pay, which he gambled away in Cholon. He had visions of winning millions of piasters—enough to open a ski lodge in Super Couchervel, near Chamonix.

"I like snow and cold. It is ridiculous, I am always in the heat. In Couchervel, the snow is very deep. I know the right place for the ski lodge," and Captain Mallat looked even younger as he pointed to the right place, which happened to be a series of rushes thrusting up from the banks of the Mekong.

He carried a pistol belted around his khakis, for there was always the possibility of piracy. After all, many of the passengers were Annamites, who had, however, been searched for weapons as they came aboard. It had happened too many times, as though armed Indochinese mermaids were swimming alongside, passing up weapons with their flukes as the boat went through the squirming narrows of the mad river.

From the battered pilot house the captain surveyed the yellow waters. He sneered as he said about his schedule, "One night in Pnom-Penh, one night for the trip, and one night in Cholon at the tables. . . ." Ironically, he added, "Maybe one night in the river and it is all finished. No more ski lodge!"

He spit a mouthful of cognac into the river. He was always drinking straight from a dirty bottle, and he bellowed, as if the river held the real answer, "I want a ski lodge, not this filthy river! I want zero weather, not one hundred ten degrees."

He pointed to a legionnaire, a tall blond man, over thirty, all muscle, sunning himself down to his waist. He said, with more contempt, "*Kaput, alles!*" He spit again, and now the river was the legionnaire, who was more Wotan-like than the mythical god. "*Kaput, alles!*" he repeated. "You know who that man is? He was in the S.S. in Poland. Just a good S.S. man. He says that he has never killed an unarmed person—and not even one Jew! Do I believe him? *Absolument* no!" And the captain spit again, exaggerating his twisted mouth.

The ex-S.S. man was pointing to some dark forms moving through a rice paddy off the river. His automatic rifle began to chase the figures, in hurried bursts of three shots. The figures kept moving, dodging, taking to the paddy—and the river boat passed out of range.

"Viet Minh?" I asked the captain.

"Just ordinary river thieves or it would not be so easy. That German, he still likes to shoot! Now he shoots at a Jew with an Oriental face . . ." and he laughed grimly.

I laughed, equally grim, looking at the passengers on the open deck. Many had hidden behind stanchions, out of the range of river pirates or Viet Minh shooting around the next bend of the Mekong. A few of the passengers made for their hard-to-get staterooms and for more protection. One of them, a fat trader who had a load of dry goods on board, soon bolted from his stateroom, calling out, in Annamite, "It is better to breathe on deck than to die in that airless box," and he made for the stanchions in one dash.

I tried my own dirty stateroom for a nap. With the impossible heat generating on the airless river, I soon rejoined the captain in the pilot house.

"Why don't you get a naval patrol to convoy you?" I asked, watching the blond legionnaire aiming again.

"I cannot wait for them!" he barked. "I have a schedule to keep so that I can get rich by next year!"

The captain glanced at his piloting chart and sneered his special sneer. It made his face all nose and mouth, and he said, "This chart is all wrong, *aussi!* The river has changed many times, but the chart is always the same. *Kaput!*"

"You might find yourself in the Delta and not in Pnom-Penh at the next bend, Captain," I said, looking over a torn section of the old chart. "Take a look at where the juncture is!"

"Who cares where anything is? It is *surréaliste.* You like Paris? You like André Breton? You like French girls?"

"Who doesn't?"

"*Kaput! Kaput!* Lutecia is *fin.* It is broken! It is hungry! No wine, no bread, no work. Nothing!" When the captain tried laughing, it was an insult to his features and his psyche. He looked uncomfortable when he was not sneering.

"André Breton, what a revolutionary theoretician of the arts!" thundered the young captain as if he were writing a manifesto. "What *merde!*"

"I knew him in New York. He was a lot of *merde* then, too, Captain."

"Like this river? Like the world? Like the United States? It is all *merde*. Do not apologize for your country. We all go from one war to another. Like fools! And your country always fights on another country's land."

I left the captain and joined a group of legionnaires lying under a strung tarpaulin for shade. They had taken off their shirts. They were lapping at bottles of beer. A lieutenant made room for me under the tarpaulin, leaving a damp buttock mark on the wooden deck. He was soaking wet, dripping from his face to his stomach.

"Have a warm bottle," he said.

"Thanks, Lieutenant."

"An Englishman?"

"An American," I said, feeling his tense question. "And what are you?" I asked suddenly. He was not blue-eyed. He was dark. His nose was long and bent, and he had not sounded too French.

"Alsatian. Does it not please you?"

"It doesn't matter if you're a dog," I said.

"And now you would like to know if I was a collaborator, wouldn't you?"

"Were you?"

"I was a German first. Which means, sir . . ."

"That you were a great patriot, yes?"

"And, sir, what are you doing here? Did you come for the Cambodian dancing girls? Did you come to steal art from Angor Vat? Do you like smoking opium because it is cheaper here? Or is it, sir, the Khmer exoticism? Here, have another bottle of beer." He pushed one at me so that it hit me in the ribs.

I had offended him intentionally. They were the great patriots of the ego, of the bottle, of the word.

I wanted to sleep. While the tarpaulin shaded me, it cut off the air. I moved out, feeling numbed with fatigue.

"Come back, sir," said the Alsatian. "The sun, it can kill! I know from the desert."

"What desert?" I asked, feeling doped.

"I was with the Afrika Korps. You know, General Rommel?"

At least he had been with Rommel, who had been in on the plot to kill Hitler. Now my Alsatian companion was becoming a dark hero.

He talked about El Alamein and the thunder of the English and Australian advance that eventually kicked Rommel out of the desert. "It was like Wagner playing over the whole desert. And then those terrible guns!

"But it is much worse here," he continued. "Here we have more heat, more rain, more confusion and only half of a war. But which half! I do not like any kind of a war. But I do not like prisons either—so I am here. . . ."

We were here together, with beer to chase everything away. He had not liked two wars. I had not liked one war. Who does like a war? Only madmen. The Alsatian sounded rational, noble, heroic, proud, a bit cynical, friendly, cultured. He had mentioned Wagner. But then, it was like an American saying that he liked Irving Berlin.

"But my conscience is good. I never shot at the French, only at the English," and he smirked apologetically. "I beg your pardon, I shot at the Americans, too."

I turned red and he was apologetic again.

"Every man I killed would have killed me. But I suffer just the same for their dying."

"You're out here suffering?"

"Would you prefer, perhaps, that I be treated as a criminal? I was nothing but a soldier. And you?"

"A sailor, thank you! But you had some moral choice as an Alsatian—not as a German!" I said. "You could have joined the Free-French—not Hitler's hordes?"

"You want morals, political morals, no less? Well, it does not exist any place, sir. Ah, you infantile Americans! You have every answer after the facts."

It was useless arguing. I finished the beer, thanked the lieutenant and took a few turns around the deck. The boat was squirming like a huge snake, and the browish-yellow wake showed all our serpentine movements. Occasionally we barely missed grounding. We hit the shores with our stern whenever the river narrowed. Off we would go, engines revving up and the captain blowing his steam whistle.

On the shore, the tall weeds made the land beyond look even swampier as the setting sun glazed the rice paddies. To add to our terror, we passed black junks, with their torn rattan sails. We billowed by in a hurry. Any one of them could carry dozens of armed river pirates or the Viet Minh. Once the polers on a junk cursed us, for we splashed them as we raced by. One pole was smashed when it caught in our propeller, almost hurling the poler into the water. Our captain, cursing back, started to haul out his pistol when he saw the blond legionnaire aim his submachine gun at the junk.

"Don't you shoot, you German fool!" he yelled. "It was my fault."

After dinner, at a long table put up amidship, I went back to the pilot house. A legionnaire was strumming a Spanish guitar and the Alsatian was humming a French song. I was depressed by all the juxtapositions, the music, the purpose of the trip, the legionnaires, the broken pole, the blond German, the little agonies within the narrowing Mekong. Suddenly the river widened. We could no longer be shot at from the shores. Captain Mallat pointed towards Soai Rieng, a town halfway to Pnom-Penh. There were little lights, hardly making up a town, and he essayed all the contradictions to the fore. . . .

"On the last trip four nights ago, there was a four-second blinker at the entrance to Soai-Rieng—but now, no blinker. Do you want my charts for wallpaper? Do you want four seconds of light towards eternity, Monsieur? Do you believe that Noah should come back a second time instead of Jesus? If it rains forever, will you be uncomfortable spiritually?"

He looked at the sky, but the sky was just over the boat, descending like a liquid wall—vapor, then rain, rain, rain, geysers of rain. The captain was shouting, hauling me into the pilot house, holding the wheel with his right hand—"Rain! Rain! Like Paris in any springtime. And now we can turn this stupid little boat into a fine ark, for we have more than one specimen of every animal on board. We have Alsatian goats, German pigs, Czech sheep, Polish oxen—but no birds. We must have a little pigeon, Monsieur. I know, you will be the nice American pigeon and bring the good tidings back from Mount Ararat—yes? Also, I can make a ski lodge on the top of Ararat, so that the skiers in Turkey, in Russia, in Iran, can feel very spiritual while skiing down Noah's big mountain. See, I am better than André Breton—much better!" . . . and the captain hummed, "Da, da, da, da. Pa, pa, pa, pa. Yes, yes, yes, yes. No, no, no, no. Shit, shit, shit, shit. War, war, war, war. Kill, kill, kill, kill. . . ."

The cognac bottle, the dirty one, had been replaced with another dirty one—and after swigging, he filled a jigger for me, and barked, "*Votre santé! Votre santé* to another flood! *Votre santé* to you, *américain! Votre santé* to *votre santé! Alors,* everything spiritual is now mechanical—americanized! And the communists are now the Nationalists, and the Nationalists are now the communists—just like that! Mechanical—and who do they learn it from? From the capitalists, Monsieur."

Let the captain empty his heart and his Gallic insouciance—*absolument!*

"Are you not frightened at all, Monsieur *américain?*" he asked when he saw a row of lights blinking on the eastern shore. "If it is not Prey Veng in the distance, it's river pirates. How do they kill you? Like the Viet Minh. They cut off the head, find a pole, stick the head on the pole. You like that?"

My face was twitching, but it was from the ghastly heat and the torrents of rain. My body felt old, sodden, worn down. I wanted a bath, not his lousy cognac.

I tore off my damp clothes and stepped out into the torrents. Below, everybody was under tarpaulins, cursing in Polish, German and French, with the even-tempered Annamites sitting by themselves, silently contemptuous of the Europeans drunk under the makeshift canvas roofs strewn everywhere.

The rain was warm and sticky, but I felt cool. When it let up, the captain threw me a dirty towel.

"*Votre santé* to ice, snow, mountains—and to hell with mankind!" toasted the captain. I lay outside the pilot house to get the river breeze. It came hot and vaporish. I thought of the war nights ashore in New Guinea. Now it was another war. Who was out to make the world better now? Who was out to make the world unsafe? The heat was worse than the war. It killed with God's infinite grace. It was God's weather for everyman on the windless river and the oppressive paddies steaming up.

And the legionnaires, drunk, down to their shorts, were just ordinary heroes acting out international scenarios. They would fight anywhere and for anything with their philosophy of muscle, mystery and egocentricity. How did they differ from Captain Mallat, the Parisian? What were their basic oppositions? The captain could become like the Alsatian in time. The captain could become like the blond German, whom he had threatened to shoot. They were as united as they were divided. As for their basic loyalties, they were loyal to themselves—a complex universal enough to include an American trying to sleep through the inferno in back of a battered pilot house.

Captain Mallat pulled out a hammock for me. It was cooler than the hot deck. He said, "This is the last peace you will know, my friend. San Francisco—that is a peaceful city. I was there with the French Navy during the war. You like San Francisco?"

"The only city left in America! I was there under the American Navy," and again I was handed the communal cognac.

"My radio now is broken. But every night, I listen to San Francisco—jazz, news, Mozart. Mozart! He was an Austrian just like Hitler, but he did not murder. Do you know how many people are murdered every day in France and the United States?"

Now he was adding up his fatal nuances and it was like his figures at the gambling tables at Cholon. A million piasters would give him a ski lodge—but now he was killing off, statistically, Americans and French by the millions.

"They die every day, but not completely. Whole cities! Death, it starts in the lungs, in the nervous system. Then it reaches the real death—French and American boredom. But they do not have to bury these people, because they are alive-dead people."

The legionnaires had gone to sleep. The Annamites were sleeping too, sprawled in varied shapes, looking like coiled hawsers. Yet each one was less offensive to look at. They were shaped in prayers even in their sleep. Near the exposed engines, a child was awake, staring at the thrusting pistons, watching the steam curl up, trying to catch the steam with two cupped hands.

On the faraway eastern bank a light glowed for a few seconds and then blacked out. It went on again, blinking like Morse, spelling out some arranged signals. Captain Mallat pulled a switch and the ship blacked out completely.

"It is the Viet Minh," he said. Just then a flare-gun went off, with a sudden explosion. It was a Very light, shrieking from the faraway bank.

"Can you swim, *américain?*"

Shots slapped the water, way off. The legionnaires were aiming at the source of the flares, but nobody was hitting anybody anywhere.

"Asia is very noisy tonight," said Captain Mallat. "And Paris?"

"The Popular Front is very quiet in Paris. Europe is waiting," I said.

"Everybody is waiting—Stalin, Truman, Ramadier, de Gaulle. Waiting for nothing."

The rains started again, and the guns stopped. The Alsatian was bellowing out some song in German—the Horst Wessel song. We were the terrorized!

"What animals they are!" said the captain. "What Alsatian goats! What German pigs! What Czech sheep! What Polish oxen! The French Foreign Legion—*merde!*"

Pnom-Penh was different. It was calm outwardly and cool inwardly. The Cambodians were another sort of people, people of the Little Vehicle—Hinayana Buddhism—which was more primitive and purer, given to less pomp than the Big Vehicle— Mahayana Buddhism. It was like Martin Luther at Worms against Pope Leo X, or the primitive Christians of Ethiopia against the pomp and gold of contemporary Rome.

In the tree-laden, canal-cut city, many of the one hundred thousand descendants of the ancient Khmers lived like bonzes. They were dedicated to smaller enterprises of materialism and larger spiritual conceits. On every street, from Quai Lagrandiere and Quai Sisovat, to Boulevard Doudart de Lagree, were the tonsured, saffron-robbed young bonzes—heads shaved, lashes and eyebrows shaved, carrying wooden bowls, spoons and cups. They walked into homes, knocked on doors, begging—though they were not beggars, nor were they treated as beggars. They were bonzes, holy. They had taken vows—one meal a day, prayer all day, Buddha Forever, Man Never, God in Permanence, Man in Nothingness. Their quiet faces, so emotionless, gave you the feeling that they were in permanent suspension, out of dreaded thoughts, away from the universal fears, aloof—higher than the one-story buildings, vats and pagodas; for no man dared walk higher or above another man . . . and all men, including King Norodom Sihanouk, were equal. For Sihanouk, too, had walked about for six months as a bonze, to learn humility when he was not playing his saxophone.

Pnom-Penh was the route to Siem Reap, to Angor Vat, to all the ancient Khmer temples and pagodas. On Quai Norodom were a hundred steps leading down to the great lake, the Tonle Sap, which joined the Mekong in Pnom-Penh. On the quai, King Sihanouk's dancers, in tall headdresses of silver, would come every afternoon to dance for the fishermen, peasants, grocers, pedicab drivers, pot menders, street dentists, shoemakers—all from the liege line of Khmers, though some were now less regal looking in their Cambodian *langouti's* and *sampot's*.

I saw the varied French influences. The colonial French, who had taken on *congai's* (concubines), left their *sale meti's* (improperly called bastards) when they went back to France. And the Catholic Church, as the moral arbitrator, soon brought up these bastards for the inner and outer glories of Catholicism, Indochinese style. I saw them near the dancers, looking half-and-half, their Eurasian faces hardly happy, adrift between two intermingling cultures, standing near the dark nuns, watching the dancers.

The dancers moved like soft winds on water, fingers detached, faces powdered into white masks. Their silver towering heads were going from shoulder to shoulder, as they posed and gestured through Indian myths about dragons, Siva, Ananda, Buddha, in the eight-armed combats of good devouring all the evils of the earth. . . . And the old gamelan musicians, bored with it all, were hoping King Sihanouk would stop this bid for culture and go back to the serious business of being a modern king.

I went to the Palais Royal for lunch once, and to dinner twice. The palace was on a street called Rue du Palais. Up ahead was a French garden, followed by the Vat Prah Keo for the king's Khmer descendants. And the king told me, in soft French and halting English, the history of Pnom-Penh, founded by King Ponhea Yat in 1431 and named after a lady. For Pnom-Penh meant "Hill of the Lady Pnom."

He sat in a regal chair, his right arm in a splint. His jumping horse had balked at a barrier—and over went the galloping king. I asked about the war up north. My French interpreter, however, changed the subject as Sihanouk smiled. I would, obviously, not get his views about the war—then. To talk about his wives— then said to number one hundred—was less embarrassing. I wondered, if at age 29, he ever tired of so many women around him. I did not ask him that.

Every question was obliquely phrased. We talked about poetry. He liked Baudelaire. We talked about jazz and he liked Charley "Bird" Parker, Fats Waller and Duke Ellington—all the kings of jazz. We talked about the saffron-robed bonzes and Sihanouk showed me pictures of himself as a bonze. Obviously, he had been a protected one, hardly starving. He was quite chubby, handsome, always smiling—and his Hinayana Buddhism had a colonial French touch to it. I thought of him filling up his beggar's wooden bowl with France's cuisine and his wooden cup with champagne. Ever so humble King Sihanouk, who, much before 1966, was to become the neutralist—in favor of Ho Chi Minh and Red China. In 1964 he was to kick the United States, including the United States Information Service and American aid, out of Cambodia—for some American had written that one of Sihanouk's kinfolk owned bordellos.

One night, after dinner and cognac, King Sihanouk brought out six of his dancing girls. I thought of the friezes and statues at Angor Vat and the grand walk, the chiselled megalomania in stone, leading to the Bayon. The dancers, under sixteen, supposedly wived with the king, wore brocaded costumes. They moved like stylized statuary facing the four faces of Pnom-Penh and the four bodies of water that enveloped the ancient city.

It was a Khmer pageant. When Sihanouk's father, King Monivong, had ascended the Khmer throne during the Twenties, it had taken six days of pageantry to crown him. It was the Year of the Dragon. Each of the six days was devoted to some interior humility and external flowering in costumes and roaring cannons. And on the sixth day, King Monivong rode a white elephant to the four ends of the Pnom-Penh—and by nightfall, he was the king of Cambodia.

And now there was his son, King Sihanouk, who played the saxophone. He played with more than adequate professionalism. He had composed a Cambodian Symphony—and belted it out like a tooter at a jam session. After that, I made some sort of return cultural exchange. I had a choice of singing sea chanties,

learned during my seven years at sea while a boy, or doing
Russian dances. I did a Russian sailor's dance.

Later, culturally exhausted, we managed to get to political
thoughts. He was not a French puppet, he said. One day he
would resign and allow his father to become the king again—for
Sihanouk would rather become the premier, the man of action,
"so that we shall have a sovereign Cambodia, a free country, just
like the United States became free in 1776. . . ." He read one of
the miscellaneous precepts of the *Dhammapada*—the conceptions
of discipline stemming from Buddhist psychology:

"He who does not rouse himself when it is time to rise, who,
though young and strong, is full of sloth, whose will and thought
are weak, that lazy and idle man never finds the way to knowledge. . . ."

Some years later, the king abdicated in favor of his father. As
premier he took the Oriental road to socialism. At the United
Nations he denounced the West—meaning, the United States—
for alleged interference in Cambodian internal affairs. But in
1947, King Sihanouk was a mild jazzman playing at his kingship,
riding his jumping horses, running off to Paris, hoping for sudden peace, thinking of humility, and proud of his saffron-robed
bonzes with their begging bowls. He was, not strangely, later,
most daring and most adventurous in politics. With Red China
as a not-too-far neighbor, he made his peace through every political invention—the ex-saxophonist turned Marxist.

At the huge door, with the king's dancers and courtiers looking
on, we shook hands French style. I bowed out Japanese style,
saying in Yiddish, "Ziy gizint, chaver."

The Central Market had every kind of craftsman—jewelers,
weavers, tailors, barbers, dentists, peddlers and musicians.
Women rushed by carrying suckling pigs in straw baskets.
Lemonade hawkers sold their *tia krowch chuhmss* to a vast com-
mingling of the poor, the bonzes and the wealthy. Across I could
see the peninsula, Chroui Chang Var, that divided the Mekong,
the Tonle Sap and the Bassac. Ahead, too, was the Silver Pagoda
flaring in the night lights—and bonzes, endless bonzes, all pious
and faceless; the light within the light, with nothing of man's
darkness. Even the night had its sun in their seeing, knowing, all-
being, fearless world. Poverty was enough. Poverty was Buddha,

air, water and bread. They had nothing of violence, hurting not even a blade of grass. The world they knew was the world without the senses—exhalted by the poverty of their total abdication. Ho Chi Minh and Mao Tse-tung, by mail, could have taken over Cambodia. . . .

At the square near Avenue de Kampot, I saw three French soldiers hosing down the grass and the earth. They splashed the water in equal doses, trying to dissolve everything there. A French Union Expeditionary Force ambulance, with its back door flapping, was parked to the left. There was blood on the door, dripping to the street.

An empty pedicab leaned against the walk ahead of the ambulance. To the right of the ambulance was something covered over with a piece of canvas. And now, the hosing-down done, the three French soldiers lifted up the bulging canvas in a clumsy movement. The canvas fell back, exposing what they were hiding —a headless body and the kind of hat the French Foreign Legion wore in the tropics. The head was somewhere else—in a sack the soldiers had already tossed into the ambulance.

Who did the head belong to? They did not know. It was a head, bloody and unrecognizable. Was it a local head or a French head? It was just a head.

I left the next day for Saigon. No one would say, certainly not the Press Officer, who shrugged away my questions.

Who was the dead legionnaire? Somebody, any somebody had lost his head in courteous, quaint Pnom-Penh.

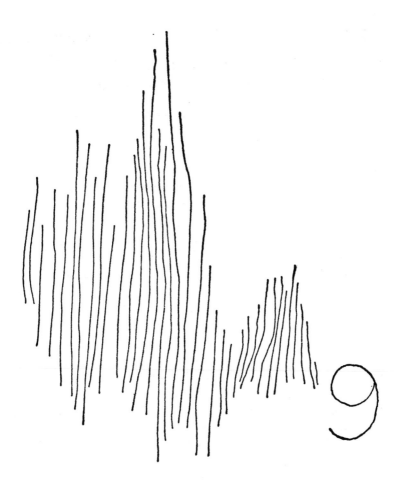

THE CITIES OF THE SENSES

THE K.L.M. PLANE was almost empty of passengers when it left Saigon for Europe.

It was to be Cairo for just one night, and hardly time enough to misadventure in any classical Arabian direction.

The exotic city between the hills of Mokattam and the Gizeh pyramids had enormous visions—when you were not suddenly marching through a stinking alley. Cairo's founder, Emir Ahmed Ibn Toulon, had built the base for Cairo's extraordinary history in A.D. 870, and the mosque to the visionary Emir was a copy of the Kaaba of Mecca, the holiest Moslem shrine. In Cairo, however, the four pillars of the Moslem faith did not blend with their

141

stringent, puritanical idealism. Cairo was like Havana had once been—where the girls were. Mohammed and his *suriah's* of behavior were in another country.

From Mokattam, where the gambling casinos sat on the trailing sands of the Sahara, you saw the Citadel that Saladin had built. And in 1811, the real rulers of Egypt—the military hessians and servitors, the Mamelukes—were finally killed off by Mohammed Ali. Later, Mohammed Ali memorialized his small contributions toward assassination and murder by building the Mosque of Ali, a replica of St. Sophia in Istanbul. . . . We soon saw enough of Mokhattam. We took a taxi to Cairo's suspected inner delights —downtown.

"It must have been a permanent hell—five years in a Japanese prisoner-of-war camp," I said to my friend the Dutchman, who was always trying to please me. I was his host, and he was broke. Everything seemed to hinge on these odd factors. I felt sorry.

"It was terrible!" was his stock phrase. "It was terrible . . ." and he said that, literally, every time I looked as if I might think up another non-terrible but somewhat sensitive question.

The big man, reduced in size, thin as a wind, broke as a beggar, had just enough money to get to Amsterdam—and into another hospital. He mentioned enough illnesses to fill a chart. None of them would kill him, just cripple him, until. . . .

I said, remembering what he was after, "Without women it must have been a nightmare!" I thought it would bring out something that would release the man in him, make him talk freely.

"It was terrible!" he answered.

We walked on, observing the Arabs in their striped *jalebia's.* No one seemed to sleep, although it was very late at night. They sat outside their muddy clay homes and looked as though they were snarling-smiling-greeting you. It could mean a knife—or a cup of sweet coffee.

I remembered the last time I had seen the Dutchman smile. It was in Thailand, when we had walked up to the Palace in Bangkok and the guards pointed their rifles at us, ready to shoot. I thought it was the end—that a trigger-happy guard would let us have it. And the Dutchman had smiled.

"They are very nervous ever since the King was assassinated," he explained.

"I'm a bit nervous, too," I replied. "And you?"

"I don't have nerves anymore," he had answered. Too much had been dulled or expelled from his body during his long imprisonment in Indonesia.

Suddenly, he said, "I would like a woman! I would like a woman!"

"Here—in this place?"

"Anyplace. Maybe in that dirty coffee house?"

"All we can get there is strong coffee. Would that be a good substitute until you reach Amsterdam in a few days?" I asked.

"Please!" He pointed to the coffee house. "There are no substitutes. It looks not so dirty now—please!"

"Sure! Sure! The dirty women are inside."

"I don't care what kind of women—if they only feel like women!"

He was overwhelmed. He wanted five years of love in the next ten minutes.

We entered, walking up a stair that reminded me of Allen Street in New York. The room, large, dirty, smoky, had a raised stage. A small orchestra sat below, whining out sinuous sounds. A large woman was on the stage and she was wiggling so furiously that he almost reached for her.

"I want one like that," he said, even before we sat down.

"I'll ask the waiter for her. Do you want her in a plate or a cup?"

I laughed, he didn't.

"Any way—but her!" He was breathing sex, and his mouth opened to swallow her.

"Maybe she has a friend for you?" he said with belated courtesy.

"I'll ask that, too. Do you want cider or coffee?" I looked at the menu, and added, "It's for American tourists. . . ."

"Just the woman!" he said hurriedly. He stared at the wiggling houri in his heaven.

"Better have a drink!" I urged. "Take vodka!"

"What for? I'll drink her!"

The waiter came. I ordered coffee.

"Can you get her—for my friend?" I asked the waiter.

"She is boss' wife!" said the Greek waiter. "But, perhaps—if you pay him. . . ."

I shuddered, and so did the Dutchman.

"No—I don't like that! That's filthy!" he exclaimed.

"I send two girls from the back," said the waiter staring at the Dutchman.

"Better send six for my friend. He has been in a Japanese prison for five years," I said. "Send six big ones!"

"One *good* one good enough!" said the waiter, leaning on the table.

"Just one good, fat woman," said the Dutchman, now smiling.

"I bring back two fat ones—good ones. . . ." and the waiter left on his erotic errand of mercy.

The music had stopped and with it the wiggling woman. The customers went back to their talk, rhapsodizing about the boss' wife and her amazing hips.

Finally, the women arrived. Two very large ones.

"Better to order cider," said the waiter. "They like cider. Okay —cider?"

They liked it very much, they said, spewing at us in broken English from mouths jammed with bulging, gold teeth. Their massive hips spread over the chairs, resting on some abstract center. They were stuffed, from any view and angle. My Dutch friend touched one, then the other, appraising and fingering their bulk.

"We are wasting time," he said to me. "It is not necessary to drink cider. Let me go to their bedroom now . . ." His skinny body looked shriveled beside the two women.

"My friend wants to play now," I said to the women.

"We drink first—then play," retorted the one nearest to me.

"Now!" said the Dutchman, trembling again.

I explained that he had been in a Japanese POW camp, then a hospital.

"Terrible!" said the same woman. "He is dangerous man now. He tear me to pieces like a lion. . . ." She was sucking at her lips.

"No!" I said. "Let us go now. . . ."

"We drink first—then play," she repeated. There was no point in bickering, for the waiter had come with the cider. I tasted it. It was like cream soda.

"Some cider this is," I said to him.

"Very special. You have no headaches from that."

When he gave me the bill, I gasped.

"Twenty dollars? Is this for the girls, too?"

"Just for cider. For girls, much less. . . ."

The music began again, and three other women were wiggling their way into heaven. There was a lot of hurrahs and shouts from the men.

"This is terrible for my friend," I pleaded with the girls.

"It is good for him—it make him stronger," said the huge girl nearest to me.

They had finished the cider. They looked fixedly at the empty bottle.

"You order another bottle?" one of them asked.

"Not until you empty him," I said, pointing to the Dutchman.

"Then we go, we leave you!" said the more talkative one.

My Dutch friend was gagging, appealing to me.

"Okay! One more bottle. Then we go. Do you promise?" I asked.

"We promise," they said, sounding like a vaudeville team.

Now there were six women wiggling on the stage, the whole stage filling up with huge hips and thighs. The tossing torsos were all seemingly aimed at the poor Dutchman's eyes and hands —and he was reaching again for the two girls with us.

It was the last "show." The regular customers were leaving. Lights were going out. . . .

We left with the two fat girls. Outside, in the rain, we waited for a taxi. It was coming soon, said one girl. It would never come, said the Dutchman.

"Then you must pay now—or take away hands," said the fattest. "I want money now—twenty dollars for two girls. Very cheap for two fat girls. . . ."

It was very cheap for two fat girls—at three in the morning. And I counted out the money. Everything was very cheap! The Dutchman was at them again—and then came the taxi.

Actually it was a private car—and the girls got in hurriedly. They said something in Arabic to the driver. As the Dutchman began following his hands, he was shoved by the fattest girl. It was a hell of a shove, for he sprawled, falling against two sleeping Arabs on the sidewalk. They laughed, and kicked at him. The girls were howling, the driver was howling—and the car was dashing off. I was picking up the Dutchman and listening to forty dollars worth of cider, sex and laughter roar away.

The coffee house was dark, closed, silent. All the good and bad women in Cairo were asleep, said one of the laughing Arabs on the sidewalk. "Go to sleep—and dream of girls," he added, as we started to walk away.

Europe was a tomb. Every man and every woman had their separate and endless hungers. It started with food and it never ended, neither in the political visions nor in the belly. There was less food and more profiteering. That's how wars ended, but the churches and the synagogues left over in the rubble of cities, villages and towns, still had God. . . .

I flew over the vast death and I landed in it. Where the cities were whole and unscathed, I saw the second sights of all the indecencies of the war. Beggared clothes, beggared faces, and dead human eyes. The alive had come out of it by making motions. Arms moved. Faces moved. Wheels moved. Voices made sounds. Amsterdam, so sturdy and beautiful when I was a sailor, took on a remembered vision. The city of dikes on the Amstell was whole.

It was money whole. It was water intact. It was gold—to finance man. The Beurs, to broker your money. Diamonds, to undress your women. Ryks Museum, to open your eyes. Kalver Straat, where everybody cycled past. The Dam, where business meant business . . . and I recalled bits of Amsterdam of another time. . . .

But I was malarial again. It was always coming back, hallucinating inside of me like the slaughtering century—still less than half over.

I was in the poverty of myself. I lay in bed, thinking of the broken cities I had seen. Of Hiroshima—gutted—and then of the rest of the brittle cities between the Asiatic mountains and the Asiatic plains. I rewound the indelicate films of my travel. For malaria is a director, a cutter, a sound man—and then you have a movie. How rich and how poor I was! What a terrible journey it was—in myself!

My black market francs, two thousand dollars worth gotten for two hundred dollars openly in Saigon, were to be my first freebooting pleasure money for Parisian pleasures. It was my second visit to Paris. In 1922, a quarter of a century earlier, I had come to Paris for five days, taking leave from my ship in Le Havre. I walked everywhere then, and I remembered Les Halles, the

Butte, Montparnasse, then a field for cows and pigeons, broad avenues, long alleys, the smell of gamey meat and fresh bread. I was the kid-sailor, sitting at Le Dôme, looking at the statue of Rodin's tough Balzac jutting off a tiny island on Boulevard Raspail. Over a beer, at age fifteen, I had met Foujita, Kiki—because they were sitting at the Dôme—and Tristam Tzara, the nonsense prince of *Dada*, precursor of an older surrealism and the current absurd. Tzara was then lampooning art, politics, people, institutions—and postwar World War I. Now it was postwar World War II.

Paris, in the spring of 1947, was an erratic political city in a confused France. It was time for another innocence and the collaboration of Radical Socialists, Socialists and Communists in the Popular Front government of Premier Ramadier. But whatever Paris was, or had, there were victorious American soldiers pouring in on leave from occupied Germany, and ex-Vice-President Henry Wallace, who had been invited by the Chamber of Deputies, assorted French left and radical intellectuals, to talk out his new thoughts. Wallace, making his mystical trek through Europe, was about to launch his third party. He was to find out years later that he was then a political captive of the American communists. Wallace was, or had always been, a farmer, a maker of fine corn, a publisher of a good farm journal, and a democrat-liberal-mystic who had taken a long time maturing in Washington and on the Iowa steppes—and he was in Paris. . . .

It was another visual Paris for me in many strident ways. A quarter of a century had only aged the paint in the alleys. Tourism had not yet returned, though the ladies who had occupied the grand houses of tolerance suddenly found themselves, by edict, touring the grand boulevards. New laws, new governments, a new if momentary puritanism—and the girls now went about like marathon walkers, picking up their GI clients, with whom they were allied in one big military brotherhood and sisterhood.

Near the Madeleine, where the touring whores accosted their fatter democratic khaki comrades, they spoke of the great American, Henri Wallace, considering that sufficient protocol before engaging the GIs in still another democratic proposition. In between they denounced the German whores, Hitler, the German occupation. It was Paris, almost two thousand years old. I remem-

148   THE TERRORIZED

bered what Tristam Tzara had once said to me at Le Dôme—
"Paris, as Lutetia, 1900 years ago, had whores, priests and comedians. Today we still have the same cultural complex. . . ." It
was an overstatement, even in 1922. Paris was always a willing
widow looking for a willing bourgeois gentleman.

Wallace had come to Paris a day before, surrendering himself
to spring, fellow-travelers, eccentrics, and non-eccentrics—the
French communists. He was heading for the third-party push on
a Moscow steamroller, with leftist champagne, a French cuisine,
zany lectures, political dinners and innocent lunches—outlining
where he stood on every human and political proposition.

Like other journalists, I was not allowed to attend the "secret
address" that Wallace gave at the National Assembly. At a later
press reception, with Pierre Cot as the immaculate public relations host, we were promised a leavening handout about the
"secret address." When I finally managed to reach Wallace, there
was a champagne waiter with a tray alongside of Wallace. When
Wallace heard my accent, he listened. Obviously, I was the only
other American present. When I asked him what was still so
secretive about his politics, he handed me a glass of champagne,
remarking, "The champagne will talk for me." It fizzed. A moment later, still fencing, he asked, "What agricultural paper do
you represent?"

"*The New Leader,* and it's hardly agricultural."

"I ain't talking to you, no sir," and Wallace laughed with his
boyish geniality. Boyishness was, by 1960, to become a national
political asset. I tried again as another glass was handed to me:

"I used to write reviews for *The New Republic,* which you now
edit," I protested. It was Wallace's magazine, front to back, pro-
moting the forthcoming Progressive Party. "I wrote for it when
Edmund Wilson edited the literary section way back in 1939,"
I continued.

"I never heard of Edmund Wilson," said Wallace, slurping his
champagne. "Who is Wilson? Is he related to Woodrow?" (I recalled that Edmund Wilson, in 1939, had never heard of Dylan
Thomas. . . .)

Wallace grunted over his champagne and spilled most of it.

The French communist leaders, as well as their literary intellectuals, were pursuing Wallace, an Iowa rabbit, ready to cook
him in leftist wine sauce. *Ce Soir,* the communist paper, called

him the dove of peace—Picasso's little white dove. The dove, as bird lovers soon learn, is the cruelest of birds. However, within a few days Wallace was basted with French oil and garlic—the American dove that had flown happily out of the Washington coop. Wallace, soon enough, was an ever-present augur in Paris, prognosticating, presaging, divining. He was the free American eagle-cum-dove who had one leg or claw in a farmer's dungarees, and the other in proletarian striped trousers.

Feted, fancied, Wallace was described by the communists and the leftists as the last political American champion of the masses. Louis Aragon, who had once been a champion of surrealism before he became a communist editor, wrote a long article on Wallace. It combined surrealism, intense social dynamics and some reverence for Wallace's hybrid corn. And Wallace, still slurping his champagne, was telling me that President Truman was preparing to start World War III.

"But I'm the peace within Truman's war!" he barked, still boyishly exultant.

We had more champagne for peace and Iowa pragmatism, and I went on to talk with lesser mystical leftist politicians.

One non-mystic was five feet tall and one yard square—the fastidious communist leader, Jaques Duclos. He gave me the comic angle of communist realism. He endorsed everything that Wallace had said at the secret session. Then Duclos, over Vichy water and canapés, suggested a Christian-Marxist analogy: Christianity had been on earth for two thousand years, whereas Russian communism only thirty years, "so one must really give Stalin a chance—for Stalin, one day, will be as sanctified as Christ. Communism is as inevitable as the sun rising over beautiful Paris. It is a natural phenomenon just like the dialectical process of life and death. But in politics, especially in the politics of the Popular Front, there must be compromises. Today, with the atom bomb, there must be even more compromises—or we shall all die!"

"Has Stalin compromised on anything? He's gotten all of Eastern Europe, Monsieur Duclos."

"Compromise? Stalin has shown how cooperative he can be. Your ex-Vice-President, Henri Wallace, is prepared to compromise. However, since Germany ruined Russia, Stalin should immediately insist on stripping Germany of all of its industrial

output," said Duclos. It sounded like a Gallic version of the
Morgenthau Plan to turn Germany into a nation of pastoralists.
I had visions of Wotan, Wagner and the Rhine maidens dancing
over the Ruhr Valley.

But Wallace, instead, was dancing about Paris. His five days
there provided him with all the messianic choreography. He
danced twice a day, centered and staged for his progressive
adagios. At the Centre d'Étude de Politique, Wallace exhibited
his intellectual and aesthetic adventures among the French. He
spoke on populations and he quoted detached extracts from the
historian, André Siegfried, regarding the future of the world.
From an unknown, pre-Spenglerian philosopher, Wallace pulled
out still another quote: "The Twentieth Century will see the
passing of the Teutonic race and the rise of the Slavs. European
populations, including the English and the American, will be old.
Only in Brazil, India and Russia will there be a resurgence and a
burgeoning youth."

The Parisian spring wallowed. Postwar confusions and dreams
were natural now. Wallace had his new dedications. He had
been a *guru* once, and Nicholas Roerich had instructed Wallace
in Indian mysticism. *Guru* meant being "a teacher and a venerable one." He was a latter-day venerable one—and he could say,
on April 23, 1947, at a dinner given by the American Veteran's
Committee, "I believe that toughness breeds toughness and that
both the United States and Russia, by their actions, have already
undermined the solemn cause for which their young men
died. . . ." Wallace also said, "To the only two American communists whom I absolutely knew were communists, I said, 'You
believe in materialism as the sole explanation of history. I believe
in idealism.' "

Paris was green. Golden fountains rioted. But Paris was hungry
and sick. Parisian bread, always a meal in itself, was bad. When
the bread was bad, the rest followed in Paris. There was not even
sufficient newsprint about to wrap around the once-crisp, extraordinary *baguettes*. The wine too was sour. It was a time without
vintages, for all the vintage wines had been drunk up by the
recent conquerors. The restaurants had, long ago, lost their
superior touch—for what had been there to cook during the occupied years? Only gall. But whatever else Paris was in 1947—
gray, guilt-ridden, war-sodden, poor in everything—it had the

look of a brilliant, refugee-haunted city, with all sorts of social workers, native and foreign, establishing their sociological imprint. They were arranging a future for those with a past that needed no retelling before exiling them, by default, to some other countries.

I soon found five old American friends in Paris. They were dedicated to international trade unions, the Third Force in politics, revolutionary propaganda, black marketing—and assorted human nightmares. They worked at their crafts for all sorts of agencies, committees and distribution centers, engulfing the refugees with the promises of a future elsewhere. One of them, a sociologist from New York, a very pleasant and handsome opportunist, hated Paris. It was too good for the Parisians, he said. Paris should belong to New York—physically. He had no use for Paris spiritually. He knew everybody and he told you so a moment after meeting him. The names of great men were always on his lips. He had, in his quaint past, once loved the Soviet Union, believing that all sorts of national minorities had a future there, especially the Jews. But all sorts of national minorities, especially the Jews, had no future in the Soviet Union. So he changed. But no matter what he changed to, he was always coming back to socialism.

Larry, the socialist sociologist, burgeoned brightly over art, collecting Indian statues of Siva, the many-handed deity of the Hindu trinity. Siva, the transformer of forces, had an adequate answer to the problems confronting man in 1947—and onwards. More hands! Larry insisted that a many-handed worker would baffle the capitalists and was an extension of the Marxist theory of value. All we would have to do was to learn how to create contemporary proletarian Sivas.

We differed over dinner at Chez Rosalie, the Left Bank restaurant where I used to meet Foujita. I said, over pâté, to my friend lost between many ideologies and many hands, "What we need are more heads per man."

"Are you being physical or metaphysical?" he asked, eating his cold herring.

"Spiritual, Larry," I said. Paris made me feel strange. "The physical is always here and with us."

"But more heads per man will mean more problems, not fewer," he said. "Look how badly man does with one head."

COLLEGE OF THE SEQUOIAS
LIBRARY

"It depends on the heads and who is wearing them," and I looked analytically at Larry's big, handsome, somewhat Germanic head. He was, however, getting fat between his neck and his head. At least three chins.

"More hands!" He reached for more herring. Having discovered that his plate was empty, he called the waiter, "More herring, please."

The waiter brought another plate and Larry swallowed the contents like a school of herring. A third plate came. Then a fourth.

He sneered, saying "What kind of a Jew are you? I am not even a Jew and look what I do with herring. I swallow them! Herring is the salt of the sea. It makes man continuous with nature, you understand? Siva was a fisherman in his spare time—and he must have eaten herring, I'm sure."

"He was a vegetarian, I'm surer!"

"Madman! I read somewhere that he ate pork as well as herring. A vegetarian—impossible! If Siva was that kind of a god, I'd throw my fifty statues of him into the dirty Seine, you hear?"

"I hear, comrade. Siva ate women, not herring," I said, over my beef. "Women and vegetables. . . ."

"Vegetarians are troublemakers!" stormed Larry, eating his herring like Siva. He was all arms over his plate. "They distort the true image of man—all cannibal! How godly can you get with a carrot? A worker needs meat! Vegetarians are brooders who disturb the peace of the stomach, then the world. To hell with vegetarians! Give me herring!" yelled Larry, finishing his fourth plate.

"Was Karl Marx a vegetarian?" I asked. "Is Stalin one? He lives off meat—Siberian meat, in jail. I think, Larry, that you've turned yourself into an ex-Marxist German herring. . . ."

The second friend was dedicated. Rose R. had batted around Europe for a year as a social worker. Prior to that she had worked for the New York Welfare Department. She knew, professionally, the welfare of Europe's greater poverty. I had known her father, Hersch R., a Yiddish poet, whom I had admired for his lyrical Yiddishkeit. Rose, all heart, endlessly pained, running every human heartbreaking errand for The American Jewish Joint Distribution Committee, worked around the clock to get the Jewish refugees out of Europe.

They left from France, Holland, Belgium, Italy for new homes

on other continents, worlds away. One ship that Rose arranged
for took 750 Jewish refugees to Australia. A plane carried 25
Jewish children to the United States. Others were sneaked into
Palestine. Some refugees, waiting out the dread days and years,
sickening and dying, went to Brazil, to the Argentine, to Ven-
ezuela. It was a time to leave the Europe of the dead. The past
had been a burning oven, and the future was a ship moving the
saddest, the most wretched and wrecked people on earth—to
other countries.

The third person, a revolutionary from one of the never-able-
to-learn-anything Trotskyist groups, was a forlorn, hapless salesman blackmarketing through Paris' alleys and boulevards. In ten
minutes you were exhausted by his plots, plans, and markets. He
detailed everything, for he had once in New York been a maker
of blueprints. He had the permanent jitters along with the permanent revolution well engraved on his fat body despite his
twenty years of "comrading" about for the causes of mankind,
leftist variation. As pragmatic as he was phlegmatic in his marketing rounds, he hated New York and loved Paris for its revolutionary atmosphere, the cafés, the old world—the city that had
bred revolutions within its stones and bones. He was either broke
or suddenly rich. Both states depended on what had just been
marketed and where. He was constantly between reality and
fantasy, as the Marxist middleman. He had cars sent to Paris—
and soon he was speeding towards another country, where the
price was two hundred percent higher. Yet, as one of his old
Trotskyist leaders said, "John is the only idiot in Paris who can't
make a living on the black market!"

The next two friends of the past were also assorted idiots out of
the revolutionary zoo. With Paris' political stability very much
in doubt, they were involved with daily plots. The government,
approaching May Day, was about to lose its communist sector,
and my two sentimentally seized ex-friends were imagining another Paris Commune. Daily, over baths and lunches, they com-
muned in my room. The nationalized auto industry was on strike.
They insisted that it was the French Trotskyists leading the
strike. Soon the sailors would strike—and it would be like Russia,
1917, in St. Petersburg.

Harold, the more imaginative of the two conspirators, would
phone first, "Look, Harry—I've got the word. It will be a general

strike, at least. Auto workers, metro workers, bus conductors, waiters—all of Paris is about to go out. With Paris taking the lead, the rest of France will follow. And who do you think will run the strike—the Trotskyists! I'll be over in an hour for a bath and to tell you more."

He came. I ordered lunch sent up. He looked like Marat as he ate, in the nude, running between the bathtub and the telephone, for he was ever phoning. He talked French, German, English, Russian—all the essential revolutionary tongues for twentieth century conspirators. And every conversation, which started out with a sense of terror, ended up, "Can you lend me ten bucks? Can you take me to dinner? We'll meet at your place. Yes—without doubt—this is it!"

By the time I left Paris, Harold owed me a hundred dollars. He'd had ten baths, ten meals, and God knows how many bottles of wine and cognac. The general strike never got further than Harold's head.

The fifth friend came from Boston—a mid-Victorian lost amid modern artifacts. Actually, she was a specialist in early Americana, a poet who loved Brahmin meanderings. She lived on Rue Furstenberg, above the Delacroix Museum. She was sweet, delicate, warm, concerned, sympathetic to root liberalism, dignified as becomes some Bostonians, alert to art, worried about love, knowledgeable about food and wines—and she had faith. There was a future for all of us, she assured me. I took her to the Folies Bergère to view Paris' present and spend some of my dark money. It was money from a war in Indochina, not quite black-marketed, but stained. For years after it was to be a quick method of making a thousand percent, indulged in by soldiers, correspondents, government employees, tourists passing through a war. And whether we knew it or not, our dollars were going to the then Viet Minh and to the now Viet Cong.

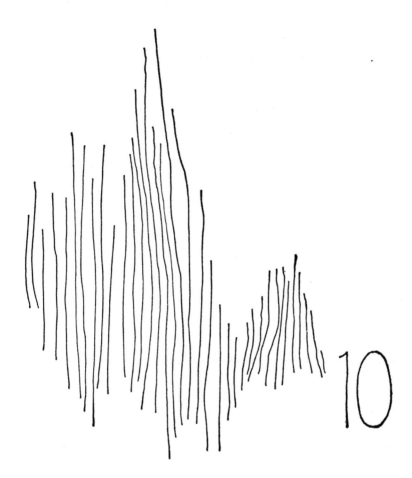

10

ENGLAND IN LABOR

IT WAS A miserable ten-and-six, bed and breakfast room near Hyde Park. It had a nineteenth century stove for making hot water and furniture that had been hand-me-downs after the Crimean War. Everything was run-down, indecent, worn away with the Empire's leavings—and the British Empire was no more.

It was no more on every street in London. England, with its middle-class thrusts, the "nation of shopkeepers," according to the fury-vented Marx, was in the second spring of the postwar. The Labor Government, between theory and practice, was lost in the economics of socialistic poverty, exporting everything for the sake of dollar credits. The English pound had lost more than half of its value. Only American gold and dollars would keep England from going down.

I spent a weekend at Hove with Jack Winocour, an English writer I had known in New York, and his family. Jack now edited, with dutiful proletarian grace, *The London Illustrated.* It was pro-Labor Party, pro-mass circulation, and full of messy photographic misadventures, like picture stories about the soliciting whores in Soho. They stood there in the thousands. The masses wanted that. Or it satisfied the extreme social conscience of Labor. But Jack wanted the guts of photographic journalism much more. The *Illustrated,* interested in the first round of the forthcoming Arab-Israeli War, had sent a photographer to cover a refugee ship running illegal immigrants to the then-called Palestine. I saw the photographs—British marines boarding the refugee ship, clubbing the terrified refugees. And all was again right for Foreign Secretary, Ernest Bevin, the Labor Party's unofficial anti-Semite. It was a pitiful comment all around. And the accompanying story, after the pictures, was even more terrifying. It cured me of any possible love that I might still have for Labor *in extremis* or Bevin as a leader—God wot! But the English loved dogs—and Hyde Park was full of dog lovers, spielers for every crackpot philosophy and batting, chirping cricketers. The sounds of English purring and fury died in the *Illustrated,* with Shakespearean accents over tea and toast. I was in England once again.

Decay had few charms, even when the process was speedy and unarrested. The English, hungry at home after a winning war, had inherited less than the toast after the victory. The nation and its people had nowhere to go—but hundreds of thousands were deserting England for Canada, South Africa, East Africa, Australia. None were going to India. They were about to be kicked out of India. It was all over in India. In a few years it would be all over in East Africa, for colonials. It was an empire merely being badly empirical. It was furtive, rat-eyed, isolated by Labor's incompetence. It was unable to satisfy the masses, the middle class, and certainly not the upper classes. It was to nationalize medicine and make doctors equally harried in their professional practices. Eyeglasses were to be worn by the masses, gotten free—to see socialism sooner. The teeth, too, were nationalized—to bite better into medicated socialism. If France were dying, and it had been for so many years in the Chamber of Deputies, England was a corpse not yet to be buried despite the hymns and the funeral sermons. I went on to visit Henry Treece and his family, at a town called Barton-on-the-Humber.

In 1938, I had written to the then poet, Henry Treece, to assist me in gathering together an anthology of English and American social-minded poetry. Treece had responded immediately, sending me the names and addresses of Dylan Thomas, Oswell Blakeston, J. F. Hendry, Nicholas Moore, Keidrich Rhys, Lynette Roberts, Julian Symons, and George Woodcock. Most of them were published in my *Exiles Anthology*. We were against war and against poverty. We favored social idealism. It was a simple statement, taking in the world's many woes, and Treece had done yeoman work for poetry's headier wines, to be drunk just before the oncoming war killed us all. I also published an excellent translation of Rimbaud by Lionel Abel. I managed, with two other editors, to put out both books for under five hundred dollars. Of course, we printed the books ourselves, in a country town in Illinois called Prairie City. Nearby was Spoon River—Edgar Lee Masters' river of the turn-of-the-century realism. We also arranged for Henry Treece's book on Dylan Thomas —the first critical commentary on Dylan Thomas' sources, development and lyrical Welsh furies. So I was indebted to Treece for all his literary labors and favors. And though we had corresponded since 1938, we had never met. There was the war, worlds apart, he in Europe and I in the South Pacific. We wrote during the war about death, about coming out of it alive. And much alive in May 1947, I was on a train going to Barton-on-the-Humber, in Lincolnshire.

The English are the most kind, the most moral people in the world despite their overdone accents, their historical understatements, their colonial brigandage and their abnormally bloody history. As the mandators over Palestine, no other country could have managed so well with the Balfour Declaration regarding the future state of Israel. I thought, as the train chugged towards Barton, of the many ragged edges of contemporary history regarding England in Decline in our time.

At the station, I was to meet Mrs. Mary Treece. Henry, a schoolmaster, was still at school with his cap, gown and overly bright pupils. Mary, engaging with English affability, was at the station to fetch an unfamiliar American lost in the Midlands. As we drove on, there were wonderful farms, stone barns, fat horses pulling plows, few cows, many sheep, some goats. We passed pub after pub, each with a princely name. I was to know many of them, through my many visits with the Treeces through the years. The pubs were to create every nostalgia about England, down at the heels but still up in the head. Once, to do a story, Henry and I crawled to twenty pubs, through many counties, drinking ale and stout when it was not Scotch. We started on Rent Day, going to the Nelthorpe Arms, in Ferriby, when the owner played host to the farmers and the locals. For rent, paid yearly, they had a day of free ritual drinking and a gala night with dinner and cigars. When I asked the owner how old his pub was, he said, "Oh, I don't rightly know. It was here before the flood-out."

"You mean, before the famous flood of 1900?" I asked. Henry had given me the local history and its liquid artifacts. I was a smaller historian of the moment, that second.

"No, Noah's flood-out, sir."

Later, we crossed to Nottingham to drink at the oldest pub in all of England or the world, Ye Olde Trip to Jerusalem Inn— where drinks, bed, and food had been on tap since the tenth century. It had been hewn straight out of a mountain. Above the pub were the remains of Nottingham Castle, where Roger Mortimer, the Earl of March, used to keep a rendezvous with an English queen. A narrow tunnel climbed up hundreds of feet to the castle, and eventually to the queen's bedroom. One day, Roger Mortimer, in haste to get at Queen Isabella, lost his head and was done in by some moral-minded knights. The pub, once called *Tryppe,* which in Old English meant "halt," had been a Crusaders' hospice after the First Crusade. And it was a crusading hospice for Henry and me before we started for other pubs around England, like The Bacchanals, which had as its real name, Bag O' Nails, and Goats and Compasses, which had as its real name God Encompass Us. A few days later, our pub crawl, so Joycean, ended at the Star Inn at Alfriston in Sussex. The Star Inn, built during Tudor times, had been a rendezvous for odd-job mayhem, robbery, anti-king plotting, ribald wenching and murder with a marlin spike. Now it had us. . . .

But now Mary had the car home with the American visitor from afar. The Treece home, in 1947, was on Ferriby Road.

Across the road and a field away, was the Humber River and Hull, the fourteenth-century city, where the poet and political satirist, Andrew Marvell, had a statue of himself in the middle of an Elizabethan square. The poet, Henry Treece, was in front of me, with his extraordinary laugh, smile and warmth. He was pumping my hand like an ex-boxer and remarking, "At last, we meet. Come in, Harry. Meet my old dog, Rags. Meet my young daughter, Jennifer. Here, let me take your valise. And do sit down, Harry. Scotch or Guinness, which do you prefer? Was it a bad ride on the poor old train? Man, all those countries you've just been through! Are you all right, Harry? Not tired a bit—no? Here, take this stuffed chair. By the way, we're having some friends over for dinner—Vera and Granville Canty. I thought that you'd like to meet the real Barton people, the good local folk; not intellectuals, but real people, of course. . . ." And Henry, speaking a cadenced, soft English, was getting up the Guinness and the Scotch, patting Rags, smiling at young Jennifer, who was trying, hopefully, to ride Rags. But Rags, already on in years, was jumping all over me, acting like a very old puppy—fourteen years old, shaggy around the eyes—and, like England, going towards the end. . . .

The England of the Treeces was falling apart in their own home town. You saw it in a sudden look, in the understated comment about the local cycle works, "All out at the spokes and the gears are not meshing anymore. If there's a choice, a workingman would prefer a lot of beer to buying a needed bicycle to get him around. . . ." After that, we walked to the local pub, The Volunteers Arms, to meet some of Henry's friends before dinner.

It was a walk to introduce me to people, shops and streets. Barton-on-the-Humber, with less than five thousand relaxed Lincolnshire citizens, was a village of Saxon times. The church, around the bend of the one-story and two-story brick houses, was a flowering, time-laden, sculptured, soaring edifice. People nodded, said, *Hello, how are you, Good day, Good afternoon, Good evening,* and spoke as locals do about birth and death. Yet, some years later, I was to learn how much like Spoon River, but on-the-Humber, was Barton, with British sin—much evident despite the understated sexual ways of the people of the little island.

At the pub, feet laced at the bar, or sitting over heavy wooden tables, were businessmen, farmers, salesmen, and Henry and I.

I was always introduced as a "Visitor from America." This always got me another Guinness as I drifted between English goodness in sequence and style. One Scotsman, an engineer, was asking me, "Are you in favor of Mr. Robert Burns or do you prefer that terribly vague American classicist, Mr. Thomas Stearns Eliot— Mr. Treece's friend?"

Henry, in RAF Intelligence during the war, was attached to the famous Dambuster Squadron at Scampton. All that he and his colleagues did was breach all the German dams they could find between the North Sea and the Weser River. They made mud villages and liquid cities from the air. After the war, the poet became the prosewriter. He wrote a hundred books, many of them for T. S. Eliot's publishing firm of Faber and Faber. He was enthused about what money could do, and he set himself an enormous task, as a writer, craftsman and historian of the times of King Alfred, the Druids, and the Greek myths. He was the scholarly Englishman who sat down to do a book and got up when it was finished. One draft, in depth, as a rule, meant one good book. The story and the language came with a natural force for Treece. He had the grace of the raconteur, the phrasing of an Irishman, the mystique of the Welshman, and the conceit of the Englishman of another time, and none of them were around anymore. The maker of books and the filled glass was the host of the language. Six of his books were to make Henry most famous, most wealthy—and to the critics, most bloody. He was, in his warming fashion, to become the memorable literary squire of Barton-on-the-Humber.

He was bloody, said the critics! War, gore and death—tales of ancient England and ancient Greece were his basic reality. He had abdicated from 1947. His forceful poetry went into his prose, set there like a flowering *abattoir*. He delighted children, frightened some critics, earned more than most successful writers, bought the big old house, East Acridge—right behind the Saxon church. And year after year, on the visits that I made during the next twenty years, Henry accumulated historical artifacts to fill up East Acridge. When he bought, he was also part Scotsman, loving the tumble and the jousting with the antique dealers. He was as expert as they were about Henry VIII furniture. He was, certainly, Henry I, in Barton's little kingdom off the Humber.

Bloody? Not bloody likely. We saw antique England at ease. If there was blood, it was not oozing where we went—to old churches, older inns, ancient eateries, old friends, all seen with the pride of place.

Treece had his loyalties, but he was an objective friend. Though Treece was a good friend of T. S. Eliot's, he had a one-act play that I'd written about Eliot's various religious, moral and private affirmations read at a special evening given over mostly to lauding Mr. Eliot.

It took place at a famous university. Obviously, this was not the time to take up the converted American poet's transgressions—the anti-Semitic phrasing in the poem, "Burbank With A Baedeker: Bleistein With A Cigar." Mr. Eliot, I was told, was present, too. My play took up five stages of Eliot's growth and decay. I had, after all, grown up with Eliot's poetry—and once, too, my poetry was praised in his magazine. I was the Marxist, then, with my own trespasses. I had, too, on occasion, lampooned Mr. Eliot. In the Twenties we had chased him down his private alleys. For he was then, to us, the poet of decadence. In my one-act play, which had five characters, all of them variations of Eliot's different postures, there is a desert scene. All the characters are dying—and Eliot, now a Lay Preacher, makes his last speech.

There is no salvage, no salvation, but memory.
We beget dust and dust soon blows away.
Add up the Songs, the Marches, the Statesmen,
Who have briefed the world—then gone quickly;
The Summary is a machine, the natural carbon of essences.
The Gentile is unkind to the Jew,
The Jew to the Jew,
The Gentile to the Gentile.
Every century has piety and more poverty.
When is man complete?
When he has said everything he has said.
There is only death, alas . . . when he is dead.
There is only Fire, Water, Air, Earth—then rebirth.
The hothouse will soon consume itself; the rose
Will dry, and the end END . . .
And the end is just endlessness.
What did I say my name was?
I was the poem of the Trinity. I was three men, once . . .
But now every epitaph is my final laugh.
Ashes, ashes, ashes . . . the masses have ashes.

Let us leave here. Sand! Sand! Sand!
Homeless and dead we are.
Dante said: "For I treat of what good I found there,"
And that is all, all, all.
This goddamned yellow sand is our world forever.
There is no key to this mystery—it oozes
Only our everlasting death . . .

As an offbeat traveler through the years, every trip that I began started at the Treeces. I took a Vespa scooter around the world in 1956–1957, leaving from Henry's house. In 1959, Henry, on an old airfield, taught me how to drive a Hillman Husky station wagon. Some weeks later I was driving through East Africa, following the Nile from its source in Uganda to its mouth in the Mediterranean. The Treece home was always a symbol for going and coming, a safety medal for my dangerous journeys away. Henry had his roots and I had the wilderness still left to unbreathe man's contemporary poetry.

I write about Henry Treece with some finality. On Christmas, 1965, I was his guest. The Saxon church dutifully rang its ancient songs, bell on bell. It was a time for a two-week holiday, for I had just come out of Paris and a brutal month of rain. I had written a book about bohemian Paris during that rained-in month. And I looked forward to this most unbohemian, most conservative English holiday.

It meant pub-crawling, of course. It meant journeys through adjacent counties in search of English history. Henry, though overworked and overly sick for seven years, knew of a pub that had old harnessings, brass, copper, iron, wood. We admired another time, the time that had harnessed horses running over the roads and fields. Later, in the same mood, we climbed to the top tower of a castle, the first all-brick castle in England. I was puffing on the clammy, stone stairs. I was happy to reach the top, to pretend that I was admiring something. But all that I wanted was a breather. Henry, discoursing, was not puffing at all. He talked of the craftsman's woodwork, the fieldstone fireplaces, and the paintings that told you who had dwelled in the castle since the fifteenth century. One family, English. Handsome men, beautiful women, lovely children—a history of five hundred years of a family. It was an art gallery, regal and bardic, rude, rough—yet gracious, as became the English.

As we descended, watching other tourists dropping cigarettes on the great stone floors, we were no longer in the times of myths. It was as real as the clammy stone stairs, the broken stained-glass windows, and the caretaker chewing gum. The moat, too, was without water. It was as real as the outdoor toilet, with the engraved names of tourists. It was like the winds, when we left the first example of a brick castle, blowing cold over the moors. It was as real as the next beer at the next pub as we drove back to Barton-on-the-Humber. And I was leaving the next day for New York. It was the end of Christmas, 1965.

On June 12, 1966, *The New York Times* announced the death of Henry Treece, to end still another era. On June 20, a long letter from Granville Canty, Henry's old friend, told me everything. They'd had a leisurely evening, on June 11, at The Volunteers Arms, and only three pints for Henry. He was seized at two in the morning—another heart attack. In the morning, at nearby Scunthorpe Hospital, Henry, given only a ten-percent chance to pull through, took the ninety-percent end out of the world. . . .

I am writing this a month later, on a hot July 7, New York morning. I am still stunned as I think back. Hundreds of letters had crossed between us since 1938. Treece's letters to me on all sorts of timely, literary, public and warring things are with Syracuse University. My answers, most of them bitching about everything, are with the University of Texas. We had deposited in repositories all the ills of the Thirties and Forties. We had, during those years, climbed all the proletarian and princely castles. We had been poets, once, and we gave it back to nature and not to man. Death was the last poem.

Before leaving London I made a small party to say hello and to say good-bye.

Stephen Schimanski came, a friend of Henry Treece. He had edited a series of books with Treece just before the war broke out. Under the title of *Transformation,* a personalist view of the times, they developed a philosophy of *personalism,* "a name and an idea neither of which was our invention. In fact, the idea which interprets the world from the point of view of personality is as old as the history of human thought, and Ralph T. Flewelling, in an essay on Personalism in a survey of twentieth-century philosophy, traces its origin back to the sixth century B.C. In brief this philosophy (which, it ought to be repeated, we are not so much concerned with stating as with letting it evolve from our discussions) sees in the *person* the key to the meaning of the universe and believes in the creative and not mechanical evolution of man; it acknowledges God as the creator of our being, but it also stresses man's independence of God, for the realisation of the individual is an end in itself, whereas the spirit of God is the link between the individual and the outside world. In this respect, 'personalism' owes a great deal to the catholic human philosophy of all-unity."

How I got into this literary, theological, philosophical, personalist nightmare was beyond me. Treece had asked me to write something during the latter days of my Marxist contemplations. And like all anti-war writers of the late Thirties, I wrote about the political eccentric wheel—about the Russian-German Pact, about Vision and Beauty, about The Writer, The Cause, The Politicians, The Division of Labor, The Poets and The Critics—and what the coming war meant to me. I saw no victors and few values until I learned about the German concentration camps. The *Transformation* contributors, which included anarchistic Sir Herbert Read; liberal-straddling Stephen Spender; the culture-of-the-cities iconoclast, Lewis Mumford; the sexual virgin, Henry Miller; the metaphysical-muddled Kenneth Burke, and others, were not always in favor of World War II. Hitler, however, soon made raging patriots of all of us.

Transformation offered up vague expositions of twentieth-century rebellion with fifteenth-century methods. It favored the donkey over the car. It preferred the candle to the electric bulb. It suggested that we eat unpackaged food and the raw things of the earth rather than Wheaties. But nobody had mentioned, in their mummery of meanderings, bottles. And over a bottle that I bludged for five pounds, I challenged Schimanski's defenses of his prewar philosophy. While we were semi-saturating ourselves with the bottled goods, with the days of the endlessly exorcised Thirties, with the future suddenly upon us, in came George Woodcock. He was a gentle anarchist who edited the magazine *Now*, which was dedicated to man's kinder reminiscences regarding his human possibilities.

Everybody is always kind to the man they are saying good-bye to, almost as a sober-hearted reflex for one's own sadness. Soon enough, however, everybody, even an atheist, will go back to

God through the bottle. The bottle often turns out to be God. For with anarchists, God is always in the back room, somewhat trapped by old books, untidy desks and cluttered files.

George Woodcock and his German-born wife, Inger, wanted to leave England. But before leaving, Inger wanted to see her sick mother in Germany. There were travel restrictions. If you left, you were given something like five English pounds for your overseas expenses. The flight of currency was an endless battle for the Exchequer. You could, however, breathe the clear German air, said the authorities, without adding to England's financial woes. I managed, however, with my refugee expert, Rose R. in Paris, to get Inger into Germany a few months later. But right then, over the emptying bottle of Scotch, the Woodcocks were questing about for a home, an anarchist's home, where a literary historian like George could sit back, most anarchistically, away from trade union struggles and political battles, and write a good book about one of his earlier social ancestors, William Godwin.

"I must migrate," said George, "but where shall we go? You've recently been to Australia—shall we go there? It's at the other end of the earth and so far from England. You've also been to New Zealand, shall we go there? I want to migrate for good, Labor government or no Labor government. Where to, Harry?"

We talked about the various embattled countries of the Commonwealth. New Zealand went quickly as a settling place for an anarchist. "Do you hunt and fish?" I asked George.

"I wouldn't kill!" said George emphatically.

"Then New Zealand is out. Australia's too far—yes?"

"Too bloody far!"

"That's out! There's only Canada left—British Columbia. Go west, George! It's virgin country. It's excellent for anarchists. Besides, you've got colonies of Doukeboors and Tolstoyians, all living handsomely on nature's bounties, with the state only occasionally intruding. When the Dooks make one of their naked parades, then the state insists that they put on their shorts."

I sounded like a migration expert. Years later, I was to visit with the Woodcocks in Vancouver, and see what I had, so persuasively, brought about for the migrating Woodcock family.

We argued about the political *state*. The bottle was empty.

"The terror is everywhere!" sighed Woodcock. "Eastern Europe will soon fall to the Russians."

"It's already fallen," said Schimanski.

"We have the glorious United Nations."

"It's for moral eunuchs."

"Eunuchs of the world unite!"

Now's quarterly message, to less than one thousand anarchist readers around the world, sang out the final gasps of polite anarchism. It was the last literary dream before man, most cultured, ate his own entrails. *Now,* to which I had contributed poetry, was a minor Gregorian chant to purity, with Bakunin as the Godhead of anti-statism. It said *no,* metaphorically, to everything probable, possible and impossible. It was against *our* kind of a world. It was also kid stuff, made up of enchanted playthings of the mind. It was righteous but hardly real. It used wonderful images, passions and metaphors for its superior dreams, a magazine without the vision of the century we were still in—the twentieth.

Schimanski had other political views. He was much more worldly; the sober, philosophical editor who was hardly anarchistic about anything. He had just done a book about Germany for Gollancz—to even out Germany's past, if not its future—an angry book, as only a good Russian Jew would write even after English citizenship was supposed to have mellowed the man. Germany would never reduce itself to humanism. It had the wrong instincts. Modern Germany, he argued, was like ancient Germany and just as tribal. In twenty years, said Schimanski, Germany would out-produce Europe. Whether divided or united —and division was what Russia, England, and France wanted forever—Germany would rise to be a menace again. By nature, by philosophy—from Hegel to Marx—Germany had its tribal *ubermensch* still within its psyche. It would always be *Wotan uber alles.*

In his travels through Europe, Schimanski had met and written about many contemporary philosophers—some German, some Swiss, some French, some Expatriate. Many of his articles had appeared in *World Review* in a series on philosophical thoughts and systems. He wrote about Martin Heidegger's metaphysics and Karl Jasper's continuum of history as founded in the Christian faith. He wrote about Paul Tillich's existentialist personal attitude and Martin Buber's *I And Thou* and *What Is Man?* And Schimanski could say, like Descartes, "Thus the whole of philosophy is like a tree: the roots are metaphysics, the trunk is physics, and the branches that issue from the trunk are all the other sciences. . . ."

Schimanski took me to the plane, but he refused to see it leave. He spoke of Icarus, the son of Daedalus, who had flown too close to the sun. He headed for the bar and I went on to board the plane. I had a world view below the sun. The plane would sever clouds and skies and reach God. In the plane I would be lost between time, space and being—airborne towards New York and my American infinity. I was coming back with a private doctrine of truth. Had not Neitzsche written, "Truth is the kind of *error*" (I would say *terror*) "without which a definite kind of living species would not be able to live. . ."?

In June 1950, when I was in Paris, I ran into Schimanski. He was on his way to Korea as a war correspondent. The philosopher was gone. He looked haggard and was due to fly to Tokyo the next day. We had lunch at a Right Bank café—for the impolite people. The café was filled with standing and sitting-around whores. Schimanski, off to the wars, wanted other playthings for his existentialistic mind—to test out all of Descartes' branches of the human tree. He would reach Tokyo and die in a plane crash without getting to Korea. It was an existentialist's death.

At La Guardia Airport I could see my crippled mother beyond the barrier. She was still leaning over heavily to the left. Her amputated right arm had not crippled her peasant smile nor her engaging eyes. She would hug me passionately, wondering—in Yiddish—what I had done going around the world.

Once, somewhere, Robert Louis Stevenson had written: "It is a better thing to travel hopefully than to arrive," that "process becomes its own goal." I had arrived.

I was in America again, if hardly the way my parents had come in 1895, with their packs, their tattered baggage, their copper candlesticks showing through a bundle, their religious books—the Jews who had, after centuries, finally wandered out of Russia to America the *gonev*. A more modern wanderer, I had come back with some gifts smuggled through customs. I had wandered about, with or without a total religion as my guide. My parents had had God and the synagogue. They had been unworried about money. There was no money. They had grace.

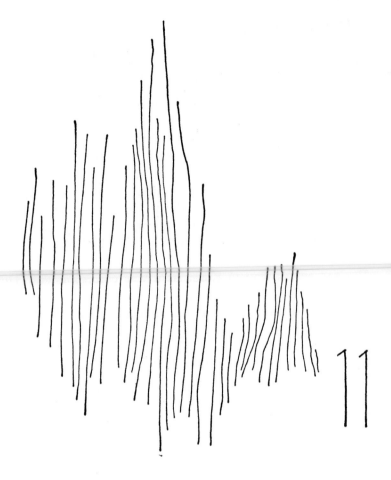

11

DIANA

IT WAS MY fortieth birthday. I was alone, writing a poem to myself.

I tried laughing away my sudden aloneness. I stared at the phone as if I expected some "Hello, Harry, best wishes" to spring from the electronic black box—not even ringing for a wrong number. And I saw various faces on the receiver, on the dialing arc. Then the phone rang once—and died before the second ring was completed. Obviously it was only half of a friend.

Feeling subjective, I took a slug of whiskey. After that, a poem began to form . . .

> Pour yourself the sun and say,
> You are forty years of age today.

An hour later I had a hundred lines and a half-empty bottle. Was it worth the hangover? I had a poem for a birthday to myself. I mailed it along with three others. And a month later they were published in a literary magazine.

In the end, it was a poetry birthday. . . .

When the magazine arrived, I found some poems about China alongside my poems. I had, also, by some mystical process, included several of my own poems about China. The memory of my harrowing visit was still acute—death in the cities, starvation everywhere, the civil war between the communists and the Nationalists. The magazine had two views of China—mine, with some realism, and a girl's, Diana Chang, who wrote lyrically about her memory of another China.

Who was Diana Chang, the author? She also wrote about her father:

> If you remember the geese flying south
> The year you were alone in Chefoo and walked
>   by the sea-edge
> And carried upon you the imprint of the
>   unbearable autumn light and wind . . .

My poems seemed related. I had written about Chinese gamblers in Cholon and the girl who ran the dice table:

> It is her singing—the shock of rituals
> Weighed in traceries of the gambling eyes;
> Echoing in the cold duality of vice
> The shining, chiselled mountains of dice.

Entranced by our juxtaposition, I wrote my first fan letter and then I forgot Diana Chang, the winds of Chefoo, Cathay, and the South China Seas.

My apartment, then, was a museum of Foujita paintings—fifty of them on walls, behind doors, in closets, under the bed. Worth fifty thousand dollars, said one art-minded expert. They were worth twice that much, said another, better expert. They were worth anything I could get, said a third voice of reason. In my now-saddened eyes they were worth nothing. For nobody was dashing up to my flat and buying them. Nobody but a man named Ben, who was no expert at all, whom I had met at a Parke-Bernet auction. I was bidding on a Pascin lithograph of a girl named Nina, whom I had known. Mr. Ben was also bidding.

Mr. Ben, inexperienced in bidding on art, had his right hand up whenever the auctioneer called for a rise. He had his left hand up as well. His right hand was bidding against his left hand. Several hundred dollars later, I called to him, most genteely, "Fellow-collector, you'd better put your left hand in your pocket or you'll go broke. You're bidding against yourself."

After that, with my assistance, he saved a few dollars and collected a great collection of late-hour junk. Mr. Ben liked large, flamboyant canvasses with gilt frames.

"Do you collect or are you a dealer in art?" he asked later over a drink at a bar.

"I collect myself," I said, drinking to his collection.

"That's enough for any man," said Mr. Ben, who was in real estate, collecting rents, and a real feather merchant as well. "So what do you have outside of yourself?"

I mentioned the fifty Foujita paintings lost in my apartment.

"I knew Foujita in Paris, years ago, when I was a millinery buyer," Mr. Ben said, ordering another round. He was small. He was whimsical. He was still laughing about his *yontif* as an auction buyer. A minute later he wanted to see my Pascin lithograph. A green Tyrolean hat perched over his head like a yodeling basso.

"She's real sovtic. So why did you pick on this Pascin? More Scotch?"

"I knew the model. A friend of mine, Phil Kling, committed suicide over her. That makes me a collector of sentimental memories. Kling was a poet. The girl was a beautiful slut."

"So what do you need her for? Here, sell her to me. I want to tell my Mexican wife how romantic some men are. They kill themselves—imagine! Will you take a hundred in profit?"

Mr. Ben began to count as I answered, "No, Mr. Ben. I don't want any profit. I merely want this deadly lithograph."

A week later Mr. Ben phoned: "May I come up with my beautiful wife to look over the Foujita paintings?"

"Come. . . ."

The Foujita paintings had been on exhibition for six weeks. All the critics had said nice things about old Foujita, the great cat painter. I had spent over a thousand dollars to help out the gallery. We advertised, we sent out circulars, and we went after the great collectors. The American-Japanese artist, Kuniyoshi, whom Foujita had befriended years before, attacked Foujita. He called the old man a fascist. He also called Foujita a Japanese imperialist and an expansionist, who had marched, as a professor of art, with the Emperor's troops into Indochina in 1941.

Poor old Foujita was a samurai, armed with a Chinese brush, at least. "Obviously," I said, "Foujita and Baron Tanaka, in collaboration, had worked out the military aesthetics for the East Asia Co-Prosperity slogan—'Asia for the Asiatics.' Better still, 'The Madison Avenue Market only for Kuniyoshi.'"

The exhibition died on the white walls despite excellent reviews in *Time*, *Newsweek*, the *Herald-Tribune* and the art weeklies. Foujita was an imperialist artist, said Kuniyoshi. Not one sale—and the last of my money was gone. I had, however, paid my debt to Foujita.

One morning, lost between non-poetry and minor dreams of non-money, the gallery owner called me. A very rich man, an oil king, who had fled from communist Roumania with his money, and left his oil holdings, wanted to buy one of the Foujita oil paintings. It was a large nude, red of hair, including the pubic. She was breathlessly Renoirish. She was a fleshy, abundant female.

"We've sent it over to the oil man's apartment. He wants his girl to see it," said the ecstatic gallery owner. "How much do you want?"

"The thousand that I spent to bring Foujita back to this most phony art world," I said gamely. "And you can charge the oil millionaire what you like up to a million."

Two days later the painting was back at the gallery. The nude was too beautiful, said the gallery man. The millionaire's girl friend, who was present when the picture arrived at the Pierre Hotel, was spitting angry.

"I don't want anything in his bedroom that looks better than I do!" she had screamed. "Get that Goddamn bitch out of here! Do you think that I can measure up to that dame's ass? Scram!"

Now I was awaiting Mr. Ben. . . .

Ten minutes after Mr. Ben arrived at my furnished, well-contained walk-up, which had the kitchen in the toilet, he was convincing his pretty Mexican wife that Foujita was the greatest cat painter in the world.

Mr. Ben looked over the fifty paintings of cats, nudes, Indochinese scenery, Peruvian peasants, llamas, dogs, tigers, mermaids. He selected six on the spot. He did it half by size and half by subject matter. Then he asked, "How much for the lot of sexy crap? Look, this is not an auction, you understand?"

I understood most concernedly, and so did his wife, who had gone from aesthetic embarrassment to financial harassment in a second.

"But, Ben, we can't afford another painting. We have to see the children through college. You promised, Ben. You're showing off again, Ben."

"So I promised—so what? Harry, here, a poet, is very poor. Since he almost died for his country in New Guinea, I can afford the pleasure of a bad conscience. Did I go to war—no! Do I write poetry—no! Nu, so how much do you want, poet?"

I added up the value ridiculously. Instead of pausing, offering him another drink, pushing a pack of cigarettes at him, trying psychological nuances of indifference to his last "nu," I said, hurriedly, "Three thousand dollars—on terms. . . ."

"Terms? You sound like a businessman suddenly. And I thought you were a poverty-stricken poet? So, nu?"

"By terms I mean in twelve installments, with five hundred dollars down." How did one talk to a feather merchant? To a real estate owner?

"Okay, so let's haul the crap down. That is, you haul it down for I've got a bad heart. Here, take the first five hundred. . . ." and Mr. Ben shoved five green hundred dollar bills into my fumbling hands.

I hauled hurriedly, all nerves and sudden money. I gave Mrs. Ben a drink. Then I gave her a Chinese fan, for she was perspiring. Another "nu" from Mr. Ben might end everything.

I gave Mr. Ben my best wishes as an art collector and I managed to fit all the paintings into his car. I bowed to them with a Buddhist gesture, cupping my hands before them, to bless their household. At that, Mr. Ben pulled his auction-prone left hand out of his pocket—the costly hand—and said, "Look, I hate to owe a poet money, even though you're the first poet I've ever met. I never read the crap now but once I wanted to be a poet, an artist, a doctor, a diplomat—and I became a feather merchant instead. I don't mind owing the banks, they're stuffed. So, here, take the rest of the gelt—twenty-five hundred dollars— and sign some kind of a piece of paper."

I signed. . . .

Christmas 1947 was bleak. I had become a father, wrote Emily from Melbourne, earlier. I added Deborah to my daughter's other names. I was a father from afar, with letters telling me about Deborah's progressions. She looked like my mother— blonde, high-cheeked, blue eyes, fair. I phoned—to hear Deborah's little sounds. I made moral statements again—to marry Emily. "Harry," said Emily over the static-lined telephone, "you must not live alone . . . get married. Even if you came back to Melbourne, we'd be separated. This wowser country! This Catholic-ridden, taboo-laden, empty land! My divorce will take more than two more years. . . ."

Christmas 1947 was bleak. As the occasional poet, I was more the reviewer of books, the writer of articles, disenchanted with poetry's void in America. I was leaving two-thirds of my private world, making another hole in my interior sky—and drifting back to politics.

We had gone beyond the vague beginnings of the Cold War. The times were public nightmares. Poetry was suddenly an effete adornment, hardly a magical emblem for our earth. It died in the privacies of words, lines, images, lyrics, completed poems, finished books—in the nowhere of America. Out of conscience, I recalled Shelley's essay, "In Defense of Poetry," which I had used on many occasions in doing battle. The playthings of my twenties and thirties were leaving me in my beginning forties. I was either maturing, losing sensibility, or learning to be a normal American.

One night, early in January 1948, the phone rang.

A small voice asked, "Is this Harry Roskolenko, the poet?"

"It's Harry Roskolenko. . . ."

"This is Diana Chang."

"And who is Diana Chang?" I had been asleep, dreaming of a political speech I had to give on colonialism at the Rand School.

"You wrote me a letter some weeks ago about my poems," said the tiny voice.

"I did? How nice of me. Did I say something objectionable?" I asked, not then recalling the winds of Chefoo, Cathay, and the South China Seas.

"No, you said very flattering things. Don't you remember? Do you write many letters to lady poets?"

"Not even to men poets. Are you sure I'm the Roskolenko you want?" I said, kidding back. Poets were odd fish, said Marx.

"How many are there? Are you a split personality?"

"If you spell my name like Raskolnikov, I am. . . ." Then I remembered those Chinese poems alongside mine in the magazine. I was soon apologizing.

"It was the first fan letter I ever sent. Are you calling from China?"

"I'm calling from Barnard College where I go to school. I'm graduating very shortly, Mr. Roskolenko."

"That's wonderful. Are you joining Chiang Kai-shek and the Nationalists as a poet-diplomat?"

"Please be serious. I am a New York-born Chinese. Can't you hear from the way I speak?"

It was Cathay—New York. . . .

Somehow we arranged to meet for dinner.

I was to meet her at Barnard. It was like being a scholarly freshman coming over from learned Columbia University, just across from Barnard, I was looking for a Chinese girl and I was excited by various associations. I thought of the China that I had seen briefly, of Kweilin, and of the vast interior that I had flown over that week with the U.N.R.R.A. Mission team. I thought of the sick and dying sleepers in the rain on their beds of sacking.

There was Diana Chang coming out of the elevator. Five girls, four of them fat and one of them slender, small, with large eyes that were blacker than black. Black bangs cut across her forehead.

A small right hand was nervously shaking mine. Her face was animated and serious, her voice even smaller and its delicacy wounded my ears.

"I thought you would be a taller man," she finally said. "You sounded taller on the telephone."

We laughed like tall people.

"I grow taller—talking," I managed. "It's a Jewish way to become an athlete. And now, do you prefer American, Japanese, Jewish, German or Chinese food?"

"Jewish . . ." and we laughed even more tautly.

"Why?"

Then her mystique temporarily disappeared. She sounded tremendously practical, aware, and New Yorker to the bone, saying, "Most of my friends in Shanghai, where I lived during the war, were Jewish refugees from various countries. I even speak some Yiddish. Shall I try?"

She tried. She spoke. She made puns. The Oriental girl with the bangs was giving me her version of ethnical and linguistic burlesque. "You can't help that at Barnard. It goes with the courses you don't take. But I can talk very seriously about T. S. Eliot, William B. Yeats, and James Joyce. Do you know anything at all about Barnard?"

"It's a school with four fat girls and one pretty one."

"Then you don't really know Barnard, Mr. Roskolenko. I'd rather talk about China, which I miss because my parents are still there. Do you know more about China than about Barnard?"

"It's divided, like Gaul. The peasants of Chefoo can't talk to the peasants of the provinces of Lapchung or Tsang. Isn't your name really Tibetan? Didn't your people migrate—like the Jews, from T—s—a—n—g?" and I drawled that out.

"Like the Jews?"

"I mean, like the Chinese. Anyway, now we're about to have a Jewish state. It means. . . ."

"More tzimmes," said Miss Chang. "And in China, what?"

"More Hell! Today every Jew who is not ashamed of himself is a Zionist. Today I'm for the Irgun! Ten years ago I was for Trotsky! By tomorrow I'll finally be for myself—all Jew!"

"I'm a Zionist," she said, as if to accommodate my political reflexes.

"You're a what?"

"Seriously, I sat on the dais at the last Zionist Congress. Of course, I was with a red-haired Jewish delegate, who took me there as a national minority. I am, after a Chinese fashion, a national minority in New York. In New York the Jews are a city-wide majority just like the Irish. But I am one-fourth Irish, or can't you see? My very black hair has a tinge of red in it."

I saw. And now Diana Chang, who had written poems about

China, turned out to be a Eurasian born in New York 24 years ago. She was as cosmopolitan as the sky.

"Aren't there some Chinese Jews in China?" I asked, feeling universal. "Don't they have red hair just like the ancient Jews? Have you ever met my Chinese brethren?"

"They live in the northern part of China and I've never been there."

"Are they single-lidded?"

"Some are, some not. I'm not single-lidded. They are Chinese in all ways except—that they're not. Please, I'm not a cultural anthropologist. Imagine a Chinese Jew!"

I imagined Miss Chang as one by the time we reached the Jewish restaurant.

After I took her back to Barnard, I was walking down Broadway, past the scholars of Columbia. I saw Chinese students, Jewish students—then a Eurasian. Miss Chang was Eurasian, split within the complex, part of two worlds, part of no world, rootless. I had seen them in Asia—lost, beautiful, apart in themselves, apart outside, separated by their eyes, their skin, their psyches. It was all fear. I was about to enter the Eurasian complex. But as a Jew, that was much too easy after our racial Gehenna.

I phoned her a week later. She was very busy with English Lit. examinations.

I phoned two weeks later.

I phoned a third time. She was no longer busy. Yes, I could take her to a party.

We were at Charley's large apartment, lost with fifty people. He never invited less. He invited the heavily laden. There was Dr. Edmund Bergler, the psychiatrist, who had discovered the *writers' block*. It was not a street—but your blocked mind, somebody gagged. Charley, when drunk, used to say that he'd handed over, in heavy installments, the ten thousand dollars he'd gotten from Governor Thomas Dewey for the socialistically-slanted speeches that Charley had written for the governor.

Charley's parties talked—Charley's ecstatic ivories. Etched in bulk on a sagging black settee, his Buddha-like shape, eager eyes and flaying hands told the world off by the hour. They were parties that always left scars, wounds and regrets, as well as strange tokens of warmth and affection. It was Charley and the world—his guests, equally adjusting their riot of rhetoric. It involved declamations, lectures, ego-training and frantic furies regarding trade union ethics. And Charley knew enough trade union leaders to let us know where honesty began—it began nowhere in America. After that, when the new novel came up, Charley announced, "After James Joyce—there is nobody!" Apparently, in his heat, he included everybody. . . .

He had his raging editorials—for everything. Once, for a year, he had written a political column for a weekly, cutting off a head a week from Washington's large bureaucratic supply. The sting, the cut, the blow, the rapier was Charley's gentlest way. His happy guests were, at times, Max Eastman, e. e. cummings, Eugene Lyons, Charles Abrahms, James T. Farrell, famous French ladies—as well as actresses, editors, comedians, labor leaders, politicians. If you talked and drank, it made a party. If you listened and did not overly argue with Charley, it made a party. If you parried back, it was hell! In his right hand was a glass of gin, which he drank straight because the doctor had told him "It's good for my kidneys and it opens up the ventricles. It also opens up my mouth, my visions, my typewriter and my checkbook. . . ."

To Diana, trying to bridge the fantasias that Charley created, it was frightening, impressive, serpentine. She said, in the taxi back to Barnard after the party, "I feel as if I've been swallowed by a human cobra. How does his good wife take it all? You mean, this is after four years of intense psychiatry?"

"He's unblocked! He's Jesus, Napoleon, Hemingway—and wonderful Charley!"

The following week Charley gave another party. When he was not writing, he gave parties. Someone came up with a recorder —and tooted out "Danny Boy." A saxophonist tried playing "Finlandia," by Sibelius. Diana and I danced to South African folk music, inventing what we were dancing. Dr. Bergler, again a guest, was taking notes; for everybody present, obviously, would one day call on him. He was a busy psychiatrist, I'd heard. He wrote early in the morning, blocking out his many books—and his blocked writers came after 9 A.M. Suddenly, as we danced past him, he said to me, "Are you marrying that girl? If so, you're an exhibitionist. . . ."

We danced on, my Jewish Id and Diana's Eurasian Unconscious fusing with the South African folk songs. Freud was playing the saxophone, Charley was lambasting Stalin, and Max, one of Charley's wittier friends, was later to say to me, "Charley was not analyzed. Charley was Berglerized!"

Id! Yid! Jew! Poet! It went with the folk songs. But I was a Jew without a religion. I had unlearned every ritual. Ritual was the death of Faith. I could no longer read Yiddish or Hebrew. When asked, I would mumble something about Spinoza and Pantheism—"God is all, and all is God." "There is no choice, no chance." "Love God intellectually." It hardly sounded like Liberalism—in Faith. And what did I really believe in—after God? I had given up every dream about socialism—for neither man nor God was ready for it. But I was anti-colonial—for I had seen that world and had just come back from it. I was still joining noble causes, with Max, my oldest friend. . . . We formed an anti-Dutch organization for the liberation of Indonesia. We set it up, ran the meetings, denounced the communists who tried to take it over, wrote letters to the press, argued, sat up late— and eventually, Indonesia, with or without our small assistance, became independent. Prior to that, when the Dutch wanted to show the world what progress they had made in Indonesia as colonizers, they organized a planeload of journalists to come over and see what their three hundred years of colonial stewardship had brought in progress. I was invited, then scratched because of an article I had written against Dutch colonialism. The plane took off after a gala party. A few days later, when the plane crashed in Indonesia and killed more than forty journalists, I decided that I was slated for other physical misadventures in the octane-laden air and on God's gray, post-colonial earth.

When Al Jolson died, Charley had held a wake, with nostalgia, gin, and—"Mammy, Mammy—the sun shines east. . . ." But we'd had many wakes at Charles's literary boozery and ecstatic dinery. We held one for President Truman when he removed General MacArthur from Korea—for you did not have to drop dead for Charley to celebrate your life. It was part of his *Walpurgisnacht* dictum—then the celebration, the gin, the great meals, with Charley often up all night over the hot stove. When Charley's dentist took away his upper and lower bridge, for a month Charley thought of serving soft foods at his parties—cereals, mush, baby food—and he said, "If I can't eat filet mignon, neither can anybody else in this Chambord, after-hours club." By the time Charley got his upper and lower plates back from the dentist, he'd written a cookbook for old gourmets without teeth.

Charley was never unblocked, except in his wonderful phrase-making speeches. As a writer, he was battling *himself*. For the next seven years he was in an inferno of his own sad creation. When he died in 1954, it was from everything in the pharmacy, the kitchen, the liquor store, the psychiatric parlor. Max and I mourned like a hundred better brothers. You loved him—despite his vitriol-with-gin-and-bitters human concoction. It was the way a man wanted to live—when the critics in the quarterlies did not write essays about you. He was not Hemingway, Faulkner, Steinbeck, Dos Passos. He loved his own contemporaries as meaningful stylists. He loathed most of the new novelists, especially Norman Mailer—calling him drek.

In the taxi back to Barnard, I kissed Diana prudently. I talked about myself, the boy from Cherry Street who had wandered about the world.

She asked me questions that were not intended to fend me off as much as to get to my legal antecedents.

My rich brothers made antecedents to impress Diana. The Chinese, like Jews, like success. My brothers had come up the tough American way, in the style of East Side Jewish boys who knew only the finite curve of ambition and the work that ambition creates.

I talked about my religious one-armed mother who had suddenly gone blind at 85. I had been with her, when I was six years old, as she crawled under the ice truck down on South Street. I had seen her run over. I had tried to stop the driver. I had dropped the ice she had shoved out to me. Even the little red wagon that I had made, for just such excursions during the hot summers when we were too poor to buy ice and had to filch it, was run over. My mother lay under the ice truck. She was mangled, bloody, unconscious—and I fainted. Then came the cop on the horse, then the ambulance, then Gouverneur's Hospital, then my father—and her right arm was amputated, shoulder and all. And now, 36 years later, my mother was blind.

Diana was crying and I was sorry that I had told her all the terrible things of the Cherry Street past. I kissed her to quiet her and she leaned into me. She stopped crying. She smiled, and I said, having felt like it since our second meeting, "I want to marry you, Diana. I love you. Will you marry me, Diana?"

The taxi's radio was on. The taxi was at 72nd Street and Broadway. Diana said, "Yes, Harry. . . ." The taxi at that moment was dashing past an awesome red light.

The driver had heard my proposal. He heard Diana's acceptance. He passed the red light and said, "Congratulations!"

She preferred a Jewish man, said Diana. Jews, because she knew a few from Shanghai—as refugees—were racially outgoing. They were warm and emotional. Love was sacred to them. It was like the Torah, she said. Jewish families were like Chinese families—given to each other. Jews were Orientals, she said. We were getting some racial facts mixed up at the non-racial doors of Barnard—which now resembled the Wall of China and the Wailing Wall. . . .

I preferred a Chinese wife, I said. Years ago, in my sailoring days, I had made that decision—only it was a Japanese girl, I meant to say. But we were saying nonsensical things in our joy, our hands tightly wound into each other, our eyes sharing our mixed Oriental delights.

Could the wedding take place in Washington, D.C. in April? Her aunt, Lomay Chang Buck, lived there with her husband, John—a former husband of Pearl Buck. Lomay was her only close relative. And Washington was very official for marriage, acts of law, great decisions, said Diana.

My brothers were told and so was my sister. My mother, too orthodox to conceive of me marrying an Oriental, was not told. Orientals to her were goyem with different eyes. My mother would know, however—in the non-seeing-feeling, when and if I brought Diana to her. I felt sickened and we agreed I could not introduce Diana. She would think that I married to spite her, for, through the years, my mother always said, "If you marry late, you make a bad husband. Find a nice Jewish girl—and marry her! It's time! It's time!"

One afternoon, Diana brought along two of her Barnard colleagues to inspect and test her future husband. One girl, tall, Jewish, with a spectral body, came from North Carolina. The other, shorter, came from the northern part of Texas. Most southern, most sociological, most literary, they helped make the afternoon tea and researched my world with all sorts of questions about what a poet did for a living.

It was a practical session—how would Diana be provided for? I was confronted, almost, with how I paid my rent, what I ate, what my habits were, whether I had a temper. Who was I? And Diana, embarrassed, came to the fore, saying, "Harry publishes in the serious literary journals. Here is an article on art and poetry in Japan," and she shoved over a copy of the *Sewanee Review.*

The girl from North Carolina wanted to know if it was a folk song magazine.

Diana picked up a copy of *The New York Times* Book Review containing another piece of mine on Japan.

"But what do poets do for a living?" went the girl from North Carolina. "Mr. Eliot is an editor, Mr. Frost is a teacher, Mr. Sandburg is a hog packer—and you are. . . ."

"A pickle salesman!" And we had tea after that.

I found another magazine in which I had just published an article on, "What Poets Do for a Living." I had written to 22 major and minor American poets asking that question to get at their interior reactions. I got savage answers, retorts from ambushed and anguished men strangled by the spent American earth. I gave it to Diana's two feminine investigators.

In 1948, poets were not classed with bankers, con men, brokers, politicians, psychiatrists, atomic scientists, morticians, fashion designers, diplomats, or union leaders. They were, as poets, occasionally everything but poets. Some were truck drivers. One played the numbers—as a collector. Several taught English courses and wrote textbooks—after they wrote their poems. Others were editors, readers, handymen for publishers, errand boys for aged females, and salami salesmen. A few lived off genteel ladies who had an income or a paying profession. When they sold a poem, they got upwards from fifty cents for a lyrical line to two dollars for vintage humorous verse. And living off the sweat of poetry then was as real as living off the sweat of your brow—Biblically, if you preferred "God's Language" in your head.

All these poets published in the literary quarterlies, in the fashion magazines—to fill in a spot below an enlarged picture of a Maidenform bra. And when the poet had a book ready, a publisher—who was a minor patron—gave him a five-dollar lunch, a cigar and a hundred dollars in advance of royalties . . . and from the answers to my queries to these poets, I summarized the following poetic condition in 1948:

Paul Goodman, then 37, had published 25 books of poetry and prose. His total earnings came to $4,000—or a $160 per book of faith, grace and anarchism in our city primeval. Professor Mark Van Doren, most esteemed, most learned, most read, earned two percent of his yearly income from poetry. Dr. William Carlos Williams, a baby doctor *extraordinaire* and the paterfamilias of contemporary poetry, made one hundred dollars a year from magazines and about three hundred dollars from all of his books, as royalties. Over a span of twenty years, said Dr. Williams, he had averaged two hundred dollars yearly from writing—but more than enough from delivering God's children to bring up his own family. Raymond Holden, on the staff of The Book-of-the-Month Club, was able to buy a friend a drink from the impractical art of being a poet. Kenneth Rexroth, translator, poet, raconteur, lecturer, columnist, wrote, "I support the Postmaster General, not myself, from poetry. . . ."

One poet, to live, played with a jazz band. Another, who lived badly, wrote documentary films. A third, who was worse off, worked for his father in a bindery. Each of these poets, dedicated craftsmen, made under fifty dollars during 1947 as a serious yeoman of his poetic fancies. Kenneth Fearing wrote: "My own earnings, from poetry alone, have fluctuated from virtually zero to around three thousand dollars a year. The latter figure includes magazine sales, book royalties, reprint fees; and what is startling about the economics of writing poetry are the fluctuations themselves. A poet is a gambler . . ." and Fearing knew what the green-shaded gamblers looked like. . . .

The teachers—ah and alas! Peter Viereck wrote: "They little know of poetry who only poetry know. Exclusive preoccupation with verse breeds the exquisite, obscure coteries who are the enemies of poetry today. A poet is also a citizen, and this can help, rather than hinder, his poetry. . . ." And Professor Viereck concluded that poetry brought back only his poetry.

Another teacher and editor, John Frederick Nims, made five hundred dollars yearly from poetry, reviews and miscellaneous writings—and he had been an editor of America's most continuous magazine of poetry, *Poetry Magazine.* Hugh Chisholm, editor and poet, could not even mention the infinitesimal sum. Howard Moss, poetry editor of *The New Yorker,* made $250 yearly from poems published in magazines, including his own *New Yorker.* . . .

There were others among the elite and the celebrated; names not to be used, though the economics could. Among those to be mentioned was Langston Hughes, then 46. Poet, author, lecturer, script writer, playwright, popular speaker on the political platforms of protest, member of ASCAP, an earlier fighter for Negro rights, he wrote that he made about two thousand dollars from these varied, yearly, frontal activities as a poet.

It was a composite qualification. There were others, who preferred to keep their secrets about money earned from poetry— Carl Sandburg, T. S. Eliot, Robert Frost, Horace Gregory, Karl Shapiro, Allen Tate, Wallace Stevens, Robert Penn Warren, Randall Jarrell, Delmore Schwartz. The list ran on, ran over, and gave me back Literary America—or what Melville, Poe and Whitman had known at another time. It had never been anything else, or better. It was America's answer to its poets. It was the United States in 1948. What is it like in 1967? Ask a poet! Better, ask the foundations that keep a few of them. . . .

The three Barnard scholars finished with my disenchanting essay on what poets do to live, and I awaited the reaction. It had been mostly an economic session, hardly taking in prosody, styles, the conditions of man, the condition of women—and love. It was, basically, my condition—or how I would provide for Diana, when married. Now, in a huddle, to continue their evaluation, their appraisal—and what I was or might turn out to be— the two girls insisted that I leave the room. There was only the bathroom-kitchen, out of range of voices, especially if I ran the water. I ran the water after I closed the bathroom door, and the girls went into a ten minute examination. What was asked, Diana never told me, but the door was rapped, out I came, the two girls kissed me, and Diana announced, "Mr. Roskolenko, I can now become Mrs. Roskolenko. . . ."

One weekend we went into the country for the snow. We spent a Saturday night as the guests of a lecturing psychiatrist, a German postwar émigré who loved poetry in a postwar German fashion, and who, as a psychiatrist, suspected the meanings behind every word of Dylan Thomas. When the words sounded more than magically right, then "the bardic qualities" of Thomas were objected to, that Saturday night until early Sunday morning.

After dinner, he went after Dylan Thomas with all of his profound German energy and exactness. He picked a poem at random and was hardly selective. He merely flipped towards the center of a book of Thomas' poems and he announced, with Wagnerian tremolos, "Let us see what there is to this poem— 'My World is Pyramid.'" With that he drank a full glass of whiskey, spit on the floor, grunted a few times to get himself into voice, and becoming all things in a moment, bellowed:

> Half of the fellow father as he doubles
> His sea-sucked Adam in the hollow hulk,
> Half of the fellow mother as she babbles
> Tomorrow's diver in her horny milk,
> Bisected shadows on the thunder's bone
> Bolt for the salt unborn.

I defended Thomas' poem. The psychiatrist was vehemently answering, "They are only ecstatic sounds. The poem is full of unborn furies, distortions and mythic convolutions. If this is energy and lyricism, then I am Freud and Jung joined up together in Israel. But what am I? I am merely trying to keep incompetent American women from committing suicide."

I had never seen a drunken psychiatrist, nor a really happy one, nor one as vehement. But I was, a few years later, to encounter one of our great myth-makers, Robert Graves, who was also vehemently anti-Dylan Thomas. It was at Graves' own birthday party, in Deya, Mallorca.

Graves was somewhat deep in his own red wine. A play about Graves had just been concluded. His many American, English and Universal protégés never disagreed with him. He was the supreme intellectual squire of Deyá—and so various forms of worship came easily to many. Now they were sitting and standing about the Master. . . .

One of them was thinking aloud about great, contemporary English poetry. Out of habit, I mentioned Dylan Thomas, who had recently died. I had been to the last party that Thomas was seen at and heard alive—at Ruthven Todd's Greenwich Village apartment. In 1938, I had arranged to have the first critical estimation of Thomas published—Henry Treece's evaluation. And now, Graves, who was only half a poet, and the other half a myth-writer, was calling Thomas a bard and a bad poet.

As his guest—also somewhat drunk—I should have been more constrained. Instead, reaching for more bad wine, I said, "Mr. Graves, I hear a little echo of envy drooling from your mythic lips. If you're not somewhat ashamed, then you're totally insensitive and envious."

I expected to have my face slapped and to get the heave-ho by his massed coterie. Instead, Graves looked on with astonishment—and we argued, bandied, sallied, told poetic tales, and drank more wine. There was no winner regarding Dylan Thomas, Welsh bard, Welsh poet and international lyrical drunk.

We were married in Washington, by a Justice of the Peace, to whom one also paid fines for speeding, for being drunk, for cursing out our legislators, and for spitting on the sidewalk. Ten dollars made us man and wife, civil style, though I think God was mentioned once. An hour later we began our honeymoon at the Smithsonian Institution's relics of American history. Then, to celebrate with more aesthetically-seized emotions, we spent an hour at the Mellon Museum, to see America's official collection of great art. It was a most esoteric and sanitary honeymoon, though Diana thought we could have included the Lincoln Memorial, the White House, President Truman, General Marshall, Dean Acheson—to argue out our "give away China" policy. We settled for everything at the Smithsonian Institution and the Mellon Museum, where our past was buried.

We were like students trying to manage between the sudden physical mingling of our unknown bodies and our questing minds —two sets of reflexes that were to act in harmonious accord, two

poets exaggerating their poetry. Black eyes and blue eyes, fair
skin and delicate Chinese skin, and then the token-minded bal-
anced words of two races meeting in the touching of the hands.

It was in the touching of the hands that we met and dissolved
our early awkwardness. I, now forty, was about to have a home.
Diana, 24, her education interrupted by the war in China, be-
latedly graduating *cum laude* from Barnard, was about to have a
home. We would be rooted in a vast city, in a small furnished flat
filled with Oriental art. All my instincts were that of the man
who walked alone late at night, for the city's grim poetry and the
silent, fast walk; who needed isolation, then the gregariousness
that made my isolation fruitful. . . .

There had been an East-West reception by thoughtful, warming John and Lomay Buck, with some Chinese friends who
worked for Chiang Kai-shek's embattled government coming in.
They left little Chinese gifts, felt awkward, though some had in-
termarried. It was East-West in the going protocol day, in the
flagging, faltering, nervous conversations, with everybody trying
to please everybody and nobody really knowing what they really
wanted to say.

We were stared upon in the New York busses and subways. At
parties, some women looked acidly and inquisitively. Unformed
questions made their eyes bulge or narrow, depending on their
racial tolerance. It was easier to marry a Chinese girl. It was not
like marrying a Negress, I kept hearing. It was miscegenation in
any event. It was the "twain meeting" as poets in their own vine-
yard. There was no wrath, no exhibitionism, no scholarly questioning about racial differences, and those close friends who
wanted to ask more intimate questions never did. Diana was a
lovely woman and I was, I was certain, her most loving husband.

The year 1948 was the Year of the Pig for the Voice of Amer-
ica, where we were soon employed. It was many sorts of political
dragons and animals in our midst, regarding Nationalist China.
America was giving up Chiang Kai-shek and withholding aid.
The White Paper was soon to be issued, and the death of the
Nationalist Government was in the planning stage.

For Diana and me it was to be a part-time job, written at home
—three fifteen-minute scripts a week, done like a soap opera,
regarding Chinese-American relations from the nineteenth to the

twentieth century. We wrote about the Christian Missions—to show our charity and beneficence—about the history of the soya bean and what it had done for American agriculture and the plastic industry, about medicine, Chinese herb healing, old wive's tales, Western magical pills, and Eastern folk medicine. And we wrote about the whaling ships bringing back Chinese art, to make up America's great hoard. We took up every facet of our past and current interrelationship. We wrote about all things except intermarriage.

One of our scripts would read like this:

CHANG FAMILY SCRIPT NO. 15
HARRY ROSKOLENKO AND DIANA CHANG

(*music: signature phrase, establish and fade under.*)

The story of a friendship between nations is best seen in the friendship of its peoples. The Voice of America presents another chapter in the story of the Chang Family of China . . .

(*music: up to climax and out.*)

ANNOUNCER: The Chang Family—three generations of men and women whose experiences cover a hundred years of Chinese history! (*pause*) Professor Chang Wenlao's family is living in New York City, where Professor Chang is doing plant research at Columbia University. His daughter, Jennie, is a problem. She is a clever but not a serious girl. She graduated from high school in June, but is not making any college plans for herself. Fortunately, her cousin, Yu-ming, arrived from China recently with her grandfather, Chang Ching. Yu-ming is very worried about Jennie, and has just called a family meeting to discuss Jennie's future. . . .

YU-MING: (*in her best collegiate-meeting style—which she imitates through most of the script*) Will the meeting of the Chang Family please come to order. Thank you. Yes, Jennie—why is your hand raised?

JENNIE: (*very formally*) Miss Chairwoman, I wish to make a suggestion, Yu-ming.

YU-MING: Certainly, Jennie.

JENNIE: Ladies and gentlemen—whom I usually address as Grampa, Ma, Pa, and big brother—since this meeting concerns my humble future, may I propose that careful consideration be given to every suggestion *before* it is aired on the floor. For instance, I *do* think it is wise to suggest only the name of a college which is coeducational. I do not think an all-girl college is good for my development as a member of society—a society which is mixed. I think it would be difficult to enter me into an all-boys college. In fact, coeducation is the only thing—these days. It is the latest thing—as new as—as bebop.

YU-MING: As chairwoman of the family meeting—I think all suggestions like Jennie's should be kept as brief as possible. Two or three sentences a time, please, Yes, Grampa—let us hear your opinion.

CHANG CHING: Education—oh, yes! (*in his lofty, narrative style*) Education is related to tradition, to beauty, to a painting—a Chinese painting, of course. I am reminded of the stone boat that stands in the Garden of Modest Gaiety! Ah, such memories! I am reminded of Ho Shen—the confidante of the Emperor Ch'iem Lung.

YU-MING: (*using her gavel*) Grampa, Grampa . . . it is my duty to interrupt you. Such memories do not seem related to the subject under discussion, which is "what college Jennie should attend next fall."

CHANG CHING: Yu-ming, a good chairwoman can see subtle relationships. As I was saying, Ho Shen's estate in the Garden of Modest Gaiety had numerous buildings with 1360 objects of art. Nearby was the Jade Fountain Palace, and a little further the rooms of Kenadu. The Great Wall loomed not far away.

JENNIE: Yu-ming, Miss Chairwoman, Grampa's lectures are always educational, but I still have to go to college in order to get a degree. It is your duty to bring Grampa back to the subject under discussion.

CHANG CHING: My grandchildren, what do you suppose I have been discussing! The Garden of Modest Gaiety was to become the grounds on which Yenching University was built.

WEN-LAO: Miss Chairwoman, I am only Jennie's father. But I would like to have the floor for a moment. Ho Shen's Garden was purported to hold great treasures which Ho Shen gathered during his service to Chien Lung. For centuries, the Garden has been dug up, by people who hoped to find Ho Shen's stolen hoard. But the real treasure of Ho Shen's old garden is the Yenching University that we know!

YU-MING: At last we have come back to the subject under discussion! Uncle Wen-lao, will you please continue . . .

WEN-LAO: With pleasure, Miss Chairwoman. I suggest that Yenching is the college for Jennie, for Yenching is coeducational, the brother college of Princeton and the sister college of Wellesley! There are two hundred girl students and six hundred men. That means, Jennie, that there are three boys to one girl. That should suit your plans!

Of course, since the Voice of America's sociological forage was government-sponsored, we did not write about a few disturbing subjects like the Opium Wars and England and America's past commercial enclaves running from Shanghai to Manchuria. The scripts were mostly timid affairs, while the Nationalists were being kidded out of existence with their own help and by America's gallant misconceptions about communist methodology. And like our scripts, our State Department, then operating sartorially under Dean Acheson's co-leadership—in 1948 and 1949—became a White House opéra bouffe regarding Chinese-American affairs. The year 1948 had been the Year of the Pig, and 1949, on the Chinese calendar, was the Year of the Dog. We had, by some, once been called the running dogs. And we were living up to that image, in China.

Our bosses at the Voice of America, which was then in New York, were a mixed grill of old men, a few young homosexuals, and some professional civil-service-minded gentry who had been gelded in the service long ago. With them, as specialists, came an admixture of missionaries who had been chased out of China by events and who now practiced a more informal liberal religion for the Voice of America. It was a holiday of ancient Old China Hands. As Diana used to say, "Old China Hands dragging their flat feet, their senile minds, and their square asses for the Verse of America." We were, all of us, great comrades for the vague script and unholy political scriptures at the Voice's muffled and rattled mike and typewriter.

We lectured too. I, having been to Indochina, then a totally unknown Annamite and Cambodian world, was now a sudden expert on the burgeoning war there. I also knew the Pacific islands, the Orient—the places of wars and revolutions—and the Rand School of Social Sciences booked both of us. We lectured on Trade Unionism in Asia, Women's Rights in China, Poetry in Japan, the colonies about to enflame, emerging New Guinea and Samoa—any place that was coming of age, with or without the help of the United Nations.

At one lecture that Diana gave to a woman's club, and which I attended, she was asked by a lady who wore a tall hat with a large rose stuck on top, "Is virginity in China a feminine asset as much as it is among Jewish and Moslem women?"

Diana, flustered by the question, spoke up quickly, saying, "My husband, who has lived in the Orient and is an experienced journalist, is sitting in the back. Will Mr. Roskolenko please answer this question. . . ."

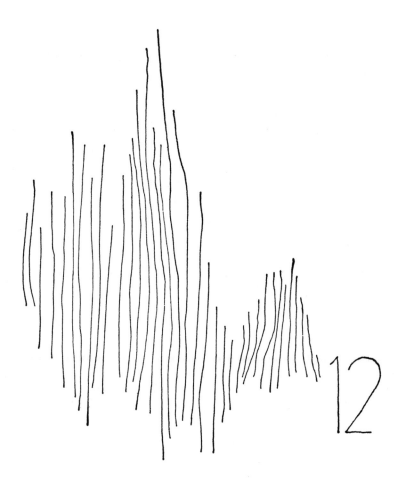

THE HOLIEST YEAR

IN OCTOBER, DIANA suddenly became a government-sponsored Fulbright scholar. Based on owed-to-America war loans, it was Senator Fulbright's way of getting young Americans, once abroad, to study foreign culture, foreign languages, foreign fantasies—to enhance our TV-, American-made current infancies.

Diana went off and I remained behind for a lonely month to work up various journalistic assignments in Europe. One of my non-assignments was a literary party for Ray R., the night Diana's ship took off. I went from the ship to the party, unhappy at the thought of going to the party. I wanted to go to a movie and see how much I missed Diana in two hours. Instead, by ten P.M., I was celebrating Ray R.'s departure. Ray, a good old friend, was going to Italy to rediscover the Italian source of his recent hero-ism. He had been badly wounded at Salerno and he had a purple heart for his heroism.

Diana's ship was student-laden, carrying all the classical brains for the future of America. They added something unique to the forty thousand total tonnage of the wines, the menus, the chefs, the waiters—and the bored crew. It was a ship floating away with young exacting scholars. I soon staggered off to Ray's party. I left the garlic and champagne smells of the ship for the whiskey and marijuana smells of the party at a top-floor apart-ment on East Tenth Street off University Place.

It was a Greenwich Village radical affair, long down at the heels and high up in its smoky head. Ray was going to Italy to find the bandit, Salvatore Giuliano, and do a book about the latest Robin Hood in Sicily. The tight apartment was one room tall, wide and full. A big bed had ten of its recent sober intel-lectuals. Spread across was *Partisan Review*'s best writer, Isaac Rosenfeld. Isaac had gone through Dr. Wilhelm Reich's orgone box for a few semesters of boxed-in psychic-zinc penetration. Now he was boxed-out—and out. Above, as the master of the dialectical ceremonials, was Bernard Wolfe, then doing most of Billy Rose's newspaper column—and writing serious novels. The whiskey I had brought was on a table. When I tried to reach for a drink, another *Partisan Review*er reached for my bottle. I waited, hoping to get one slug, then go on to my movie.

The party was unevenly divided. More than half of the drinkers, talkers and non-dancers were from *Commentary* magazine, the better paying soul mate. Often this complex literary labor was confusing. Nevertheless, the Jewish and Gentile friends of Ray were all talking at the same time. If you talked, you did not have to listen. If you listened, it meant that you did not have a new universal idea going, or any ideas, for that matter. If you argued meekly, but continuously, it meant that you had the same idea—last year's—and you were still proving its possibilities in October.

All the smells and all the talk came together into one huge smell-echo about the emergent New Left, Marxism Revisited, the Third Force, lost within its quaint virginity, and China, lost within the State Department. Then someone vaguely said some-thing about a problem dealing with Negroes.

If you did not write for either *Partisan Review* or *Commen-*

tary or, usually, for both of them at the same time, you were beyond the Marxist-Liberal, Judeo-Christian-Liberal inner frontier. Some of the literary celebrants were related as fourth cousins to the Labor Movement. Others, recently total Marxists, were about to become accredited sociologists at great universities, performing for the "new science" with the same kind of rhetoric they had contributed to an older "science"—Marxismus. A third grouping at the farewell party, and much better dressed, had their own interior profession. They were the elite schnorrers who had discovered a variety of Jewish causes they could live off. Not one of them had been to Israel or in the Second World War. (Ray had, of course—and he was different—a man.) Nor had any one of them spilled his blood for Zionism except, perhaps, with some red ink—and paid for. They lived off various agencies, organizations and charities as the schnorrers of a specialized dialectic. They had, too, no real religion except "making out." They were a breed of handy-job professionals with their self-contained, payable-on-demand margins of value. As conscious Jews, they were moral cretins. As Christians—the same. Godless, emotionless, nervous, gutless, they were mostly ridiculous. Once in their overall presence, you ran for a quick drink and made for the crowded, hard-to-get-out exit.

I tried, once again, to get my one drink from my bottle. I finally got my pint—hoping to salvage that one drink—when I was pushed by a drunken writer. My drink dropped to the floor.

I refilled my little glass. I had already said good-bye to Ray and to Bernie Wolfe, who had once been Trotsky's secretary. I tried to sip my drink and run. This time it was slugged out of my hands by the same writer who had just pushed me.

Sadly, I gave up the thought of my one farewell drink. Instead, I reached for my battered raincoat. By this time Isaac Rosenfeld was sleeping on it. I tugged, managing to get it without waking Isaac up. Why disturb his many kinds of sleep? Isaac was a genius, to me. He did the best takeoffs in Yiddish of T. S. Eliot's "Prufrock." He was brighter than all the other writers in his various ways. He had, by now, a small cult sleeping on the bed with him.

Coat in hand, I headed for the crowded door. I passed other famous "in" and "out" writers. In the room, final opinions were made—theirs. As I was exiting, I was pushed again.

This time I sprawled across the dirty floor. Standing above me was Stanley Grimm. He looked heavier, taller, much younger, and most *avant-garde*. He was complaining about something. The party was lousy, I said, getting up. It stank physically, morally and intellectually. The four or five people that I liked there, I could always see. Ray was going to Italy, Bernie to Hollywood. And I was going to a movie, I thought. . . .

"Okay, fella, you've had your fun," I said to the drunken big pusher, Stanley Grimm, as I moved towards the door. Good-bye, intellectual party!

I was, however, pushed again in more rear-*garde* ways by Mr. Grimm. If he was drunk, that was his luck. I was totally sober. I was going to a movie. I was, by now, feeling impatiently angry. My jacket had been torn too. All the hazards of the mind were being confronted. I thought of a discreet Ernest Hemingway in such a situation but my mental reflexes were too objectionable to mention. Without doubt, he would have shot the beast, no? He would, like Humphrey Bogart, have committed some likable mayhem. I kept seeing myself at the movie. I was thinking of Diana, a hundred miles at sea, and I wanted to unbreathe all this intellectual garbage—when I was shoved again.

Not a boxer, not Hemingway, I slugged Mr. Grimm. Mr. Grimm fell against the table and all the whiskey came tumbling down. It was a moral disaster for many, as the whiskey rolled into rivulets. Bernie Wolfe was irritated. Ten others called for a fight and they made a boxing ring. Bernie Wolfe, soon to be in Hollywood, for better realism, called out, "Goddamn it, take the fight downstairs!"

We took it downstairs, four flights, with mobs of intellectuals surging ahead and following up behind. I led, since I had punched Grimm. It was protocol. I kidded, to keep the protocol in hand. Mr. Grimm looked huge and grim—professionally. He was a good writer, I knew. He kept ahead of the *avant-garde* circuit. He had more zany ways. He also boxed with one of the Gentiles, who was always getting a beating in the Village bars. It was the Hemingway thing to do. . . . Ah, poor Ernest Hemingway—what a comedy he had brought to these infants! The importance of being-like-Hemingway was their major motivation, drunk or sober. . . .

Not a boxer, I waited and feinted. I found myself more awkward than I thought I would be. My last fight had been in New

Guinea, when I was called a Jew bastard by a sailor. A minute later the sailor was converted to pacifism, to reconciliation, to great fellowship, and "Let's win the war first. . . ." Now I slugged away at big, equally awkward Mr. Grimm. If you can't box, slug!

It was over. Grimm was in the gutter. He was lying there breathless. The mob of writers acted like a mob—we were not professional enough for them. We should have taken it to Madison Square Garden and sold ten tickets to Hadassah.

I bent down. Mr. Grimm was elsewhere. Had I killed him? Had his head hit hard on the pavement? I massaged his heart. I talked gently. He stood up finally, sheepishly, then said something about publishing—that I published more poetry than he did. I laughed! He laughed! He was weak. He was hurt. He was breathing badly. Soon, I was carrying Mr. Grimm up the four flights.

"You put up a lousy fight!" said somebody to whom I was subletting my apartment.

"Was that important?" I asked.

I said, still hoping to make the movie, "Look, Hemingway, shall we both make the trip down the four flights again? Let's go!"

It ended there. He did not walk to the stairway. He was still the greatest boxer of the cafés—another make-believe Hemingway. I went off, found a movie on 42nd Street, and I dreamt of Paris while seeing a film about Paris.

I was in Paris late in November. It was unlike 1947—when hunger knew every other Paris street.

Diana and I were living in a non-scholarly, unheated, cold-water duplex studio at 28 Rue de la Sablière, in the Fourteenth Arrondissement. It was large, freezing and Parisian. Diana usually went to sleep looking like a stuffed China doll, wearing five Chinese jackets and American sweaters. The walls sweated in the studio. The bathroom was an adventure in climatic change. Mushrooms grew on the windows. A small cat that we had picked up outside of the Luxembourg Gardens, in the rain, suddenly found that it had a family—in one of the closets. I was just as surprised, as I helped the poor little cat become a mother, the cat not knowing what to do when six kittens, in three hours, made up her first family.

It was Paris and we had money. We made a party. Our guests brought bottles and delicatessen. Our guests were mostly Americans, though some of them were normal Parisians, like our Chinese neighbor, Zao Wou-ki, or the Swiss artist, Giacometti, or Tristam Tzara, the Roumanian mother and father of *Dada,* or C. F. MacIntyre, a permanent expatriate from everything American. But our Americans, loyal to the dollar, if not to normal Democratic-Republican-Socialist politics, evened out the professional expatriates. They came with their bottles of wine and champagne. Robert Carter, then a Fulbright and an excellent poet, and now one of Doubleday's major advertising artisans, popped the bottles when MacIntyre would let him. James Baldwin drank from the bottles and borrowed needed money. Baldwin was, like the Fulbrights, always broke. It was sad to be broke in Paris, or so said many Henry Millers and thousands of other expatriates. In any event, it made you a writer of letters asking for money. It had also made thousands of naturalized Frenchmen through the centuries, before the American Express had an office on Rue Scribe, be what they were—Parisians. Now Jimmy Baldwin was the Parisian in self-exile. The Negritude culture in him was slowly developing. He talked, between gulps of champagne, about a book, *Go Tell It on the Mountain,* in fast, nervous clips—a monologue.

Saul Bellow, who always looked shy in Paris and hardly spoke Yiddish, claimed that he could not understand Diana's Yiddish-Chinese jokes; he was then working on *The Adventures of Augie March.* In his entourage was Herb Gold, about to launch himself into letters via Bellow's ambience. Both were studying book binding—to bind their future books in leather. Gold had sold a few stories—and soon his world of gold, leather, salt and onions, and existentialist yeast was to make up his literary bread. Gold talked away, with nimble excursions into everything regarding the market place. He also rode a battered bicycle—to be very French, culturally. Gold, who was thin, always wanted to help somebody with his diagrams for literary success. To me he always looked like the small owner of a small bank locking the bank's door, and saying, as he extracted the key, "Good night, money. I'll see you tomorrow morning, money." But Saul, hardly then a Herzog despite his interior, handsome quiescence, used to baffle me. He sat taking everything in, like a burgeoning book, writing itself into the memory. But Bellow could, after you wrote him a sad letter about your life by likening your past to, say, Herzog's meanderings in love, offer to sponsor you with a selling blurb for your book jacket. . . . But in Paris, when he talked, it was talk of no interior intensity—which made him nobler. All of us talked with interior intensity. It was Paris, after all. But some writers did not talk about their books. Nor was Yiddish, in Paris, an essential linguistic adjunct to humor. Diana used it for shock purposes; I, for *hamesha* expressions. Amid Sorbonne French, Roman Italian, and London English, it sounded all the more like a bizarre language—to disenchant the moment of grace.

On Christmas, 1949, we went to London, and to Barton-on-the-Humber, to see the Treeces. Bellow was in London, too, at our garish hotel. One afternoon Saul and I went walking through Soho where Saul was to pick up a Dolmetsch recorder. We tried three stores—no Dolmetsch. Literature, obviously, was the continuation of art by windy instruments.

Ten writers I knew had learned to play "Danny Boy" that year on recorders. We sampled, after that, all the secondhand books at Foyles. We had a few drinks. We walked about London, talking about what we had talked about before—the interior lives of our friends. Careers came with tokens of gossip, as evaluations. I had met Saul before *Dangling Man,* his first novel, came out. It was either in the Village or at a party that Harvey Breit had given. Yet Saul was a kind, sensitive, withdrawn writer who gave off other appearances. You liked Saul and you waited. But what you waited for came through in his work. It came through in the writer if not in the talk.

Suddenly I was another dangling man. As Saul and I were walking about Soho, I saw Laura striding towards me. We embraced. We were in another country. Our words were lost. Explanations became impossible sounds. I had gone all the way to Australia to marry her—and now she was explaining that she was divorced. Knowing words, token words, blonde hair words streaming from her mouth in childish fashion. She was still Laura, beautiful from her speech to her hair. We exchanged addresses. I was invited to tea—tea tomorrow. Love tomorrow. Memory today . . . and there was Saul, embarrassed, gaping at lovely Laura, and later asking me too many private questions. . . .

Should I tell Diana? I did. I was, not yet, Herzog. . . .

It was to be tea tomorrow, then thousands of tomorrows for the next eighteen years, when Laura came to New York. . . .

Since liberalism, in France, was the first refuge of political indifference—and usually led to its own authoritarianism of the liberal variety—I saw its political handmaidens whenever I visited the Chamber of Deputies. The Left, the Center, the Right all practiced a form of political importuning for votes. It was a classical Parisian performance for the professionals. They made a government one month and overturned it three months later. Their names occurred and reoccurred, like calendar dates— Halloween, Thanksgiving, Christmas, Easter, *et al.* Whenever you looked it was Georges Bidault, Robert Schuman, Jean Letourneau, Pierre Schneiter, André Colin for the Popular Republicans. Or when it changed, it was René Mayer, Henri Queuille, Yvon Delbos, Edgar Faure for the Radical Socialists. Or to make for still more quixotic balances, there would be Eugène Thomas, Jules Moch, Guy Mollet, and Lucien Coffin— Socialists. Questions of confidence followed, and a vote of confidence was taken on schedule. It solved nothing, not the colonial war in Indochina, where Emperor Bao Dai was the put-up, anti-colonial face-saver for the French. And it solved nothing in Algeria, soon to unloosen its own civil war.

The year 1950 was to be a year of indecision, but some natural decisions were made. Stalin and Mao Tse-tung recognized Ho Chi Minh. President Truman ordered the construction of the hydrogen bomb. Leon Blum died. An American military mission went to Saigon—to advise the French. Another government was dissolved in Viet Nam. Dean Acheson talked about the Soviet world menace. General Lucius Clay favored German rearmament. General George Marshall became Secretary of Defense. Red China said it would not tolerate the invasion of Red China— as they invaded Korea. General MacArthur met President Truman on Wake Island. The French communist leader, Thorez, went to Moscow. René Pleven got a vote of confidence; and General Eisenhower, still on leave from Columbia University, was suddenly head of S.H.A.P.E. in Paris.

In Paris, the Fulbrights met daily in little restaurants on Rue de Tournon or in their little rooms. One night was like another night—the talk and trouble of French culture, poetry, prose and politics. It was wine and dinner, with too much wine. The writers wrote and most of the Fulbrights did not study. Diana read, deciding after a few months at the exasperating, quixotic Sorbonne that reading at home was better for her classical education in Paris. Some girls got pregnant from Bohemian French Gentlemen, and were sent home—no longer pregnant. The Fulbright Act took care of everything in a proper American way. My friends were scholars with dollars—owed by France, and paid out in francs to make young Americans glory in Gloire, Fraternité, Rimbaud and Racine.

Among the writers, I preferred the poet at Le Dôme, C. F. MacIntyre. Mac, wearing a blue beret and a turtleneck sweater, used to race about in his red MG before parking it at Le Dôme or Le Sélect—to work on his endless, wrap-around-in-a-brown-bag translations. At Le Sélect he would engage Ramon the waiter, from whom all borrowed money, in the matter of making poets by the name of Baudelaire, Mallarmé and Verlaine come through—in English. Mac's spoken French was unique. But his translations were exacting and compelling. He sat at the cafés through the years carrying his fragrant lunch and his brown bag of books. Daily he had dozens of glasses of beer as he munched at sardines, cheese, bread and Mallarmé. Tall, whimsical, gaunt, he made that area of Montparnasse his private domain for poetry, statuary, and slow dirty stories. He was as permanent as Rodin's great statue of Balzac, just across at the intersection of Boulevard Raspail and Boulevard Montparnasse, where the working whores used to congregate.

Mac was outgoing, strident, infectious, and salacious. He made my year in Paris warmer with his zestful companionship—the old poet, full of Rilke in his softening bones, if often fuller with beer—"for translation purposes." He was, later, to leave a teaching post at U.C.L.A. because "there was a man from Wisconsin called Senator Joseph McCarthy and there was a law that wanted you to tell stool-pigeon stories about friends who may or may not have been radical. The Senator is not Rilke. The Senator is not Mallarmé. The Senator is not Dante. The Senator is a yente. And, for that matter, Marcel Proust is a yente."

A stroke, in 1959, suddenly put the poet Mac to bed. His pithy conversations gave in to age and another form of poetry—the impossible words, hard to mouth, harder to understand, yet tearing with joy as Mac's eyes sparkled after a small cognac, with his young lovely wife, Marian, adding in the missing words. Despite his stroke, he was still lord of the language. When I saw him last in December 1965, he had just published another book of poems—*Tiger of Time*. He was a tired Clemenceau. His portrait on the cover of the book, painted by Jim Callahan, made Mac look like a flying Scotsman reflecting about another time—1890, before the calmer nineteenth century ended and the twentieth thundered in to tear up the world. On July 3, 1967, *The New York Times* announced that Dr. Carlyle F. MacIntyre had died in Germany. I cried. . . .

Rue de la Sablière, where we lived, was two blocks off *bis* Moulin Vert, once an area for painters and sculptors. At 51 *bis* Moulin Vert, our Chinese friend, Zao Wou-ki, shared a Parisian garden with the sculptor of lean, tall figures, Giocometti. When we came for a Chinese dinner, Zao Wou-ki and his pretty wife, Lan-Lan, who studied composing, took us into the strange garden. There were old walls, and things that grew as only Paris, in the cold and dampness, can grow things—much as if sculpture and painting were natural to the garden's many old graces, faces and fancies.

As Chinese as he was by now Parisian, Zao Wou-ki painted the imagined images of the gaunt garden. His big, high studio was canvas-filled. His work, Eastern-Western, took on a French reality and a Chinese metaphysics. Reality came from his recognizable tiny horses, tiny animals and tiny human beings—in a forest of great green, white and red light. . . . And one day, at our once-empty studio, which was gradually filling up with paintings, Zao Wou-ki said to me as he drank another glass of red wine, "Why don't you write a book of poems about Paris? I will illustrate it for you."

I did it, during that winter. I sat over a large table, an oil stove under my feet—and in two months I had eighteen poems about Paris; a sad, savage, imagistic book written out of compulsion; Paris as a city of whores, cyclists, bakeries, pissoirs, shuttered windows, café gamboling, mermaids in the Metro, stranglers of love, citizens of the holy franc, endless strikes, the water shut off, the gas shut off, the Metro shut off, the Chamber of Deputies in a panic again, governments changing, scandals again, and Sunday in the Bois de Boulogne. Picasso was an opportunist in politics and in the arts. Those great Parisians of the past were no longer around except as some memory engraved under gas lamps, on doors, on old buildings—recreated for their relationships. They had been the architects who had framed the high blue sky and the manners of a sighing, blue, brutal city. It was the withering Seine flowing its garbage of Spring and disordering a lonely artist at Notre Dame. It was the pity of Parisian love; the pity of lewdness and stripping nightclubs. It was the time of Winter going into Spring. It was priests without prayers; a Parisian crucifixion softly breaking as art into the Seine's subtle vapors, rising over the bookstalls on the Left Bank. It was the children in the Luxembourg Gardens, with their balloons trapezing like flotations—they were the murderous infant armies in the gardens, kicking at their Scandinavian nurses.

These are the heroes, standing as iron and bronze,
Ghosts of the nation on abrupt carrefours:
Danton weeping over the Metro at *Odéon*.
The old man at *du Maine*, a sans-culotte of history.

All over the city they tower as literature,
Dancers of rhetoric, swordsmen of the people;
They lean in winds above the Friday markets,
Polished by cries of bread, wine, cheese—and the rain.

Each square is a carnival, with actors and fringed walls,
The blood of verbal wounds sighing in the stones;
The satin mornings, a guillotine of fog,
Cry in the winds of ancient revolutions.

The derelicts depart to their night apartments—
A room of shadow—where sadness rehouses them
In mansions of grief. Apostles of winter,

They pray in sleep around some bivouac
For warmer days, around hunger
For more food, around life for sweetness

Of flowers, the scent of summer giving them
The affection of no residence,
A heaven of their special innocence.

My cat is a striped critic of Paris,
Gray in fur, full to nose and purr,
He tears the daily journals, a scavenger
Etching toilet tissues from immense issues.

Often the cat is a theatre of goats,
A menagerie of arts, the zebra of all
That walks handsomely, his tail at Picasso,
And his balls pointing toward the Academy.

A magician of moods, the cat is Rimbaud
Eating all languages and alphabets,
Or Céline down below the last silk sewer,
Waiting for plush meat to adorn his whiskers.

But when sleep entangles his claws,
He dreams of females, alleys of bitches
Singing in *Provençal*, many pregnancies
And progenies, all bound for the Academy.

Zao Wou-ki did six lithographs for the book. Daily we went
to the *atelier* of Desjobert to watch how the finished lithographs
came off from the old lithograph press, hand-handled, wetted
down, screwed down, with each page taking ten minutes to
finish. Near Zao Wou-ki was Max Ernst, working on another
book. On the walls were the past and the present—an encyclo-
pedia of names. We printed 99 copies and sold them for ten
dollars each to friends. A few years later the books sold for seven
hundred dollars each—to flatter both of us for a cold winter's,
wine-warming last book of poetry.

There was some literary comedy as I wrote the poems. I sub-
mitted six of them to Karl Shapiro, with whom I had feuded
during the war, when both of us were in Australia. Karl now
was editing *Poetry Magazine* in Chicago. Would he publish me
under my own name? Doubting it, I sent the poems to Karl
under the adopted name of Robert Ballard, giving the American
Express as my return address. Two months later Karl wrote back:

"Dear Mr. Ballard: We should like to publish four of these poems. Please send us some brief autobiographical notes about yourself."

I sent Karl some *proper* autobiographical notes. I was Roskolenko, not Ballard, explaining the half-forgotten reasons for my pseudonym. A Yiddish poet friend of Karl's, in Chicago, Selwyn Schwartz, meanwhile, had been advised of my little con game. Selwyn Schwartz was an older friend of mine. I used to read his Yiddish poetry, which he had translated into English— and I would advise him. Now he advised Karl, who by now had received my brief autobiographical note and my real name. Some weeks later, Karl wrote back—"I am of course keeping these poems, which by any other name, are just as good. Cheers. . . ."

In advance, the poems were published in various university quarterlies. One much respected quarterly, in publishing the poem about my cat, where I said, "And his balls pointing toward the Academy," changed "balls" to "rounds." When I told my male cat about it, he meowed, wanted more kidneys, nipped at some champagne in a plate, remained at the champagne, nipping away—and then suddenly started to do handstands, backflops, jump-ups. He was the perfect critic of poetry and Paris.

Our *femme de ménage* came every Friday to spend her day of chores by improving, she said, Diana's spoken French. She swept, scoured and talked. She talked more than she swept. She drank the cognac, then went after the red wine. She was a small battle-axe of a *femme de ménage*, capable of cutting off your head. When she saw our collection of accidental kittens and the mother cat, she said, with conspiratorial awe, pointing across the courtyard, one flight up, "Watch all your cats! Register them at the Préfecture! Photograph every one, because, where I am pointing, there lives a cat-eater. During the war he made cat stew, cat soup and cat steaks. It smelled like a . . ." and Diana added, in French, *"Chat ménage!"*

"No, please—like a sewer of dead cats. That man ate hundreds of them—and now, I have been told by the horse butcher, that he sometimes comes by asking for cat meat instead of horse meat. So, Madame, watch your tender little kittens—and that bitch of a mother!"

My assignments took me through Paris' many physical Jewish catacombs. Out of a similar past, in 1895, my father had come to New York—from the Ukraine. Paris now was a refugee city. My father had migrated after soldiering for twelve years in the Czarist Army. He had migrated by running away—Siberia, Japan, United States. And in Paris, the runners were people left over from the death camps—the fortunate ones who had managed to be one step ahead of Hitler. . . .

In a huge gray building near Montmartre lived forty Jewish refugee writers and their families. Having come from Poland and Roumania after the iron curtain descended, these forty writers were the last literary remnants of European Jewish culture on French soil. Temporarily housed (more than three years then!) in a house given to them by Baron de Rothschild, but awaiting visas to all countries, from Palestine to the Argentine, they dwelled amidst the grayness of a past through a present that was hardly less gray in the dismal color of a Parisian winter.

Their refugee past was constant, surrounded by its immediate terror, their clothes, their children born en route, their interim arrangements that now made up a thousand harrowing days. It issued out of everything they did and thought. Since their language was Yiddish and not Hebrew, they were learning English, French and Hebrew—and the languages of the lands they expected to leave for when they finally emerged from 9 Rue Guy Patin. That all of them were not going to Israel, despite the emotional appeal of the new homeland, seemed to Sz. Kaczerginski, the writer, not at all odd. "We are Yiddish writers. Yiddish is our language. In Israel we could not publish, except occasionally. To learn a new literary tongue in our time is difficult. A tailor can work anywhere, but a writer must write and publish in the language of his greatest intimacy and fluency."

Sz. Kaczerginski, age forty, my historian of another hell, knew too well the brutal past. He had written a book called *The Nazi Liquidation of Vilna*—a people and a city liquidated. Another history, *Between the Hammer and the Sickle,* was a study of what has happened to Jewish culture in the Soviet Union, where Kaczerginski spent time during the war. And a book published the previous year in New York, edited by Leivick, the *Songs of the Ghettos and the Concentration Camps,* was based on material gathered by Kaczerginski while lecturing in the concentration camps and the remnant ghettos of Europe.

In his little room, more bare than furnished, lived his wife and his three-year-old daughter, Lieba, who sang little ditties in a mélange of languages. French, Russian and Yiddish came out, helter-skelter, with infinite charm. The little girl was an heir to the past, though she was born in France. She was precocious with her multilingual echoes of pain. The studio bed had several of her dolls draping one end. Along the wall was her crib. Further away was the sink, K.'s desk and a shelf of books, written by various members of 9 Rue Guy Patin. These books had a history as grim as the day and the surroundings. Once a rich culture had blossomed from the countries which the authors of these books had come from. Now the authors preserved the leftovers; men still en route, temporarily the inhabitants of this self-imposed ghetto.

Number 9 Rue Guy Patin was not known to the world of Yiddish letters. Initiated by the Federation of Jewish Societies in 1946, it had become the home of writers. Within this building, too, was Club Tlomacke 13, formerly a writers' club in Poland, a center of literary thought and practice. There were many other organizations—from the French section of the Jewish P.E.N. Club to the Verband, the Writers' Canteen, the Marionette Theatre and sundry other organizations working for a refugee, on-the-run culture.

The inhabitants of 9 Rue Guy Patin that one met in the dining room, around the hard benches, were men like Abraham Zak, age sixty, author of fifteen books of prose and poetry, translated into Russian and Polish. At the benches, over the soup and the pot roast, the faces raised up still seemed to wander. Intense, yet speaking softly, they laughed at something a puppeteer, Schwartz, had just said while trying to eat, to finish the puppets and to erect a stage, his hands full of food and theatrical implements. The atmosphere was as natural as pain. But in their faces one saw acute Jewish laughter, merriment away from hell. There was Moisse Grossman, a novelist, who had written novels on Marx and Rosa Luxembourg and had recently published a book of his seven years in Russia, called *The Wonders and Legends in the Land of Stalin*. He was called the Jewish Kravchenko. At another bench sat the lyric poet, essayist and journalist, Yitzhak

Yonasowitz from Poland, the author of three books, including *Poems from Pre-War Poland.* The poet Raizill Zichlinsky sat across from me. All of them had been housed within the Nazi terror and the aftermath. Raizill Zichlinsky had a special and original Yiddish tone. There, near the coat rack, sipping some seltzer water, more water than seltzer, was Rochman, who told me that he knew a relative of mine, another Roskolenko, from Bialystok. "Your name I could remember. He was a dramatist. He was killed by the Nazis." I did not, until later, really learn of my relative, the killed dramatist. But we were all relatives now.

I met Joseph Wolf, the author of *Critical Essays,* a book on Jewish and world literature, and Leo Lenneman, who was well known and had contributed to American and foreign Yiddish newspapers and periodicals. One talked of migration only. Letters just received from other writers, who had gone abroad, were passed around. A few had decided to alter a previous decision. They would go to Canada, to America, to South America—to Israel, where many wanted to go, but as Kaczerginski constantly reiterated, "We are between two fronts wherever we go, that of the communists, whom we here oppose, and that of a crisis culture—a people still in transition, having left their past but still awaiting some future."

Kaczerginski had also written a book of short stories while in White Russia, a book about Jewish partisans. Formerly a pressman in a lithography plant, a member of the "Young Vilna" group of intellectuals, Kaczerginski had managed to leave Moscow with the Polish refugees. He went to Lodz where he worked for a year in the Central Historical Commission, compiling a history of the Nazi occupation of Poland. Arriving in Paris in 1946, he worked for the Joint Distribution Committee, lecturing in DP camps in a gaunt Germany. He was a delegate to the Jewish Cultural Congress in New York, in 1948. Later he went on a six-month lecture tour throughout the United States. And Hadassah ladies, the people of the Bible, the Bronx, the Borscht Belt, were to learn anew how Jews died. . . .

A vote had been taken by the tenants of our cold-water building regarding hot water—for some minor payment—and all had voted against it. As a result, taking a bath was a Cherry Street affair, something I had done around 1912, when my mother heated a large copper vat and poured it into our huge two-part sink in the kitchen. Then, one after the other, the whole family took turns at getting clean. In Paris, however, it meant going to the public bath off Avenue du Maine.

On Friday mornings, carrying towels, soap, clean underwear, Diana and I raced the four blocks. We passed the Friday open markets where ski books, fruit, herring, winter clothing and pants were sold. In the public bath, in *cabinettes,* were all sorts of couples, married, unmarried, pickups from the cafés—some there to bathe and some there to fornicate in a public bath that was cheaper than an old hotel.

We bathed properly and then we dashed back, cold yet sweating, racing for our neighborhood café. We swallowed two hurried cognacs, to keep the heat in us before we went back to work at our freezing studio. There, earlier, we had tried various technical aides for heating. With little electricity available, we could not use electrical equipment, though we made several attempts to use an on-the-spot, easy-to-use, American hot water maker. You attached one end to the faucet, and the other end plugged into a wall socket. You waited for hot water. It steamed and exploded, blowing up part of the sink.

Paris was and is art; Paris made art a sexual, physical, visual joining-up. It fell into the streets like in no other city. It sat at cafés in the same orderly disorder of the senses, like Rimbaud's poetry. It was art when Tristam Tzara played a pinball machine with me. We bet for drinks, of course. When I introduced him and Albert Cossery, the Egyptian novelist, to Chicago's greatest twentieth century creation, at an off-beat St. Germain des Prés café, Tzara said, "This is better than anything we did with *Dada!"* The machine glowed. The ball shot away, hitting lights, cushioning off, smashing against electrical registrations, piling up numbers. Cossery, awaiting his bid, believed that it was like Creation; that Chicago had, at last, found God in a pinball machine. Tzara, who was still putting out his rare, expensive *Dada* books, using every great artist he knew to illustrate them, answered, "Albert, this is beyond God! It is the Age of Electrical Annihilation. After this, who needs art?"

But Jean-Louis Barrault wanted art at Theater Marigny, when I interviewed him as one would a mime-turned-talker. I talked Yiddish to Barrault, to keep a joke going. Not being Jewish, he was puzzled at my accent. He kept nodding and so did his wife,

Madeleine Renaud. Barrault was another Scapin within his postured antics. His acting, miming, and movements came, literally, off his nose. He had just done Gide's translation of Kafka's *The Trial*. He had, in the past, done Knut Hamsun's *Hunger*. I had, during the hungry Thirties, heard that Barrault was interested in Trotskyism. We admired him then for his politics as well as his art. Trotsky was his faraway political mentor and Charles Dullin was his teacher of mime. Trotsky had been assassinated. Charles Dullin had died a day before. Puzzled by my accent, he finally said in English, "Does Monsieur Roskolenko come from the *Midi?* You have a *Midi* accent—yes?"

It was Yiddish-*Midi*, I said. Diana explained that I thought everybody should be Jewish. It would end anti-Semitism. If Christ could be a Jew, why not great Parisian mimes? Christ, too, had been an actor in his time.

Barrault was still puzzled. Madeleine Renaud thought it was a droll philosophy, and for two hours I argued with the son of a pharmacist from Vestinet. Barrault had studied mathematics at Chaptal College and art at the Louvre. At 22 he had accepted the world of art to study with Dullin. "It was like trying to chain Leonid Massiné down to a haberdashery shop. I sprung for the Parisian heavens instead," said Barrault, as he grinned from his nose to his toes. It was that kind of a body in "Drôle de drame" as we went through his elastic autobiography, which took him from his first major film, *Children of Paradise*, onwards to the nationalized Théâtre de France. Prior to that he had been against the subsidized theater, remarking, "It makes the actor lazy to live always on a subsidy. At Marigny we must earn our salaries by keeping the theater full." He was to change that view by the time he took over the Théâtre de France under André Malraux's de Gaullist tutorship.

In 1966, Malraux had to appeal for money to subsidize Barrault, then doing Genet's *Les Paravents*—a scandal-stirring play. Opportuning for more money, Malraux said during a debate on the culture budget, "The hands of liberty may not always be clean, but this is no reason to defenestrate her. I am not saying that Genet is Baudelaire, and he may be anti-humans; but so was Goya—and Goya was subsidized by the kings of Spain."

Malraux had once, during the Twenties, when he had lived in Indochina and China, been akin spiritually to Mao Tse-tung. He

had been, in turn, the revolutionary novelist, a borrowing archae-
ologist in Indochina, and the philosophical novelist of an uprising
in Canton, during 1926. As I write this in 1966, he is the Minister
of Culture under de Gaulle—an exceptional irony for our times
and our age. Barrault had aged. Men of older rebellions, now less
idealistic, had only a few cynical insults left. We subsidized, now,
like socialists and Nationalists. . . . And I came away, having
heard Barrault say that he detested the plays of Tennessee
Williams, of another age-in-being. "A play is like soap for washing. The public purges itself through drama," said Barrault, digging into his curly hair. "Williams purges nothing as the dramatist
of excesses and psychopathic mechanisms," Barrault mimicked,
adding, "It is 'If-my-father-was-that, then-I-must-be-that' sort of
theater." Barrault insisted that plays with inherent psychopathic
nuances were mechanical and uninteresting. And to illustrate his
meaning, Barrault took a sheet of white paper, studied its un-
relieved whiteness with comic relief, turned the paper in all
directions, posed the sheet as a character in a Williams play, then
broke into Gallic laughter. "Are you impressed, Monsieur?"

He was Hamlet, Kafka, Shakespeare, Racine and Faulkner, his
hooked nose and body doing what his voice could not always do.
Barrault with his Theater Marigny was the theater in Paris after
Louis Jouvet's death. It lay dying behind great facades and
greater hamming, posing like some Left Bank characters we saw
about—believing they were still in the Napoleonic era. They
wore cockade hats and the silks and satins to match the Emperor's clothes.

I free-lanced through Paris' ancient comedies, its current politics, its private heroes and its public disorders. On one such misadventure, I was soon quarreling with Maurice Nadeau, the
literary editor of *Combat,* over Louis-Ferdinand Céline, about to
come up on trial in absentia. I had loved Céline once.

In 1950, it was more than seventeen years since Louis-
Ferdinand Céline had burst into "great" literature, with his
echoes and refrains of damnation, misery and hate. Though
misery was only a literary part of Céline, he raided the whole
moral frame of our society. Hit and miss, he spewed up, with
hate for the bourgeoisie, his exercise in frenetics and fancies of
what he conceived all of society to be. From his special hells

Céline dug a bigger grave for "bourgeois man." Céline had participated in many strange amalgams. His sense of pity, vast as it was, got into the way of his man-in-the-gutter language. Irony, sarcasm and splendor ran riot in Céline the creative writer. Not that he was a novelist. He was the universal intimate reporter before his self-exile to Denmark for collaborating with the Nazis during the war. But Céline had a cosmic ego. He could collaborate with no one, especially not with those whom he himself had helped to convince of his racial notions, his anti-Semitic psyche, his parlance and posing. I saw the amazing contradiction that Céline himself created, as a creative act almost—which would no doubt save his neck: *the Germans, with whom he had collaborated, were no better than the bourgeois he hated.*

Céline saw Paris as a gutter, and his work was a functional exorcism, a Black Mass for the bourgeoisie. But like other writers during the war, including Ezra Pound and Knut Hamsun, he created his largest contradiction in the humanist image he had of himself. He was, despite his past art, as humanitarian as Hitler! Hitler murdered with gas—he with words. Céline, at the end, was a gutter doctor. His mind, his hatred (for his strange intellectual comfort) was part fraud, part iconoclast—and partly the writer assembling his choice of characters and characterizations. Hatred alone has no love. Love alone has no hatred. Between both, there must be a fusion. Objectivity is rare—and Céline wrote in one key. He raked man from his desk, the doctor turned author, angry, petulant, resentful, digressive, inventive—like a clown waiting for God to praise him. But it was the Nazis and other fascists who praised him.

Some imagined hurt, when younger, gave him his future prescriptions. There is always the Jew! The doctor was not the doctor as a writer—but the pus-creator, the healer of nothing; a primitive medicine-man spewing out magical words—of venom. But then, this old soldier of the First World War, who had been wounded in his head, was living with his head, his wound, his childhood among Parisian and Jewish storekeepers, the people of Rue Lepic—and his "Jew bastard!" was like giving France a prescription for aspirin tablets.

Céline's trial was on. I was fighting with an editor who was defending Céline . . . and I was meeting Céline's old friends as I researched the man, his work, and his earlier history. . . .

I went back to his first book, *Journey to the End of the Night,* feeling sick. I was now aware, autobiographically, of all the special echoes of dread that Céline later let loose. His work as a ship's doctor, his eight years of investigating sleeping sickness in Africa, and his job in a Ford factory in Detroit later made up Céline's unforgettable writing. Céline's war wound gave him a permanent headache. Under his hair was a metal plate. Since he could not sleep, he wrote. And, as he said, "My own trouble's lack of sleep. I should not have written a line if I'd been able to sleep."

This relationship to his work was not peculiar. He had become a writer under a midnight sword of Damocles. I was under pressure then to pity him for his sleeplessness, his lack of balance, his cockeyed view of the daytime when his perpetual night was a constant nightmare. We were not dealing with normal reactions, but with a man whose mind underwent all sorts of terrors, drafted into literary journals. Dr. Destouches, later known as Céline, condemned his own spirit. Later, speaking of his past work, he said, "In the course of my life, I have spent so many years as a bard, a hero, an official and a doormat in the service of so many thousands of madmen that my memories alone would fill a whole insane asylum." They had, and he had populated it with lunatics.

The wretches he had known were not all phantasms . . . they existed only too well. His great book was his first. In that he was the anarchist attacking all the rituals of bourgeois society, giving up the sham and slum of life, with endless marvels of observation and writing. But it is Céline writing an indictment when he himself is the prosecutor, judge, jury and, later, his own victim. Céline is always the victim as the endlessly wounded hero. Though Leon Trotsky said of Céline: "Céline walked into great literature as other men walk into their homes . . . ," Céline also walked out. He began another journey into darkness.

Most critics, except some few, like André Gide and Milton Hindus, gave Céline up when his second book, *Death on the Installment Plan*, appeared. It was a comedown from the Olympian plains to the mud flats. It lacked discrimination and sensitivity. It was full of bombast and brittle conceits. But when Céline's book of horrors, *Bagatelles for a Massacre*, made its appearance in 1937, even Gide's patient criticism was of no avail. Céline had doomed himself with all but the anti-Semites and the racist mobs. Gide was forced to consider this book a total farce, intentional, to make fools out of the professional anti-Semites. So over-drawn had Céline made his caricatures that even Hindus, in 1947, in his introduction to the new edition of *Death on the In-stallment Plan,* was forced to walk gently on the tightrope of Céline's ridiculous circus. But since Hindus had such a hand in the renewal of interest in Céline, as a study in literary demonol-ogy, Hindus' journal, *The Crippled Giant,* written while visiting with Céline in political asylum in Denmark during the summer of 1948, was of acute concern. Hindus, a Jew, was trying to con-vince Céline of his racial transgressions.

I read *The Crippled Giant.* I walked for a week around Céline's former home, 98 Rue Lepic. I was in the environment of Céline's *Journey to the End of the Night.* I sensed all the grayness of a Sunday in Paris in the winter, the horror of Parisian weather, another postwar reality, another day—in the climate of Céline's older despair. Hindus wrote: "Céline is a splinter in my mind that I've got either to absorb completely or eject completely." The journal was a painful investigation and ejection, sincerely thought out and written, full of fine criticism for isolated ele-ments of Céline's attitude, psyche and work.

I quote: "Céline said that during the war he used to say to collaborators like Brassillach: 'What are the Germans doing here? They're just ordinary bourgeois and Pan-Germanism is their ideal. If only they had brought with them socialism or some other idea, but nothing of the kind. If only they had behaved like brutal conquerors of the French, that still would have been better than nothing. But they are bourgeois out for a good time, a weekend in Paris, and the only ideas they have are bourgeois ideas—to eat our bread, to drink our cognac, and to assault our women. What do we need them for?' "

Céline's conversations with Hindus were aflame with irrelevant notions and irreverent ideas, with digs and *pastiche* decorations of his state of mind. He admired children and had contempt for the Danes who had given him asylum. Céline said that Hitler was a fake, "insincere," because he had no anti-Semitic program.

Hindus says of Céline, "He limps with rheumatism. He seems completely sick physically and mentally. His trousers are so old they have large blotches on them as if, like a Bowery bum, he had peed on them while rolling around the sidewalk drunk." Céline was repetitious and egotistical, said Hindus. He knocked everybody, including his wife, comparing her to the Danes, whom he despised as "the least Hamletian of all peoples," never troubled by anything. "He's a mess, no doubt of it," wrote Hindus. "He's got more excuses than most."

Céline was not interested in books, not in the new editions of his work and the reviews of them, but in the money they would bring. That was, indeed, the reflection of the bourgeois with goods for sale, the sale of anything. Hindus quoted Sartre, who accused Céline of selling even anti-Semitism, if it could make him money. Céline drooled on. He was afraid of the police. It made him nervous to stand before a Danish police station, which they passed on their walks. He took an hourly dose of veronal to sleep. His language was forty percent *merde,* wrote Hindus. He likened the Vikings to the Nazis, "the original Nazis—unbelievably barbarous and cruel." Hindus said further, "Céline rants against the Germans, his new scapegoat. He says he prefers a Jew to a German any day, and he'll be glad to say so anywhere. I object to his making a lump sum of the Germans for the same reason as I object to his doing likewise with the Jews, and that enrages him against me." Further: "As to the abuse he heaped upon the Jews ten years ago, he repeats a hundred times: 'I was stupid, stupid, wrong and stupid. I was a pacifist and a patriot.'"

It is a journal and a journey through all the folklore of the semi-deranged, with enough resemblances to normal behavior to make one shrink with horror for a man with a self-pitying mind like Céline. As Hindus says, "He pities himself incessantly and sees no real hope for the future. He can't sleep. My own explanation of that—a mixture of migraine, worry for the future and conscience about the past."

To sleep was the endless problem. Céline's explanation of German anti-Semitism sums up his confused mind. Hindus says: "The Germans interpreted anti-Semitism as killing the Jews, but Céline didn't mean anything like that at all . . . Céline wanted to try to bring up the Aryans to the level of the Jews, to make them 'as smart as the Jews' and thus be able to compete with them better. He didn't want the Jews killed—that was just another instance of German treachery, stupidity and brutality."

At Céline's trial, in absentia, on February 21, which I attended, Céline had many defenders, including Henry Miller, Pierre Mac-Orlan, Marcel Aymé, Thierry Maulnier and Mme. Arletty, the actress. Most of them offered up sentiment, Parisian and Gallic, like the spicing for a ham sandwich. It came as easy as pouring a glass of wine or stirring a gravy. Three doctors gave evidence that Céline was suffering also from gout, and that if the Danes evicted him and he was forced to stand trial, he would die. His various defenders said that he had not really collaborated—merely accepted Nazi hospitality. His publisher, Robert Denoël, assassinated by a Resistance fighter, had urged Céline to write *Les Beaux Draps,* one of his worst anti-Semitic books, when the Germans were in Paris.

Céline had two letters read in the court. In one of them, Céline wrote, with his usual tongue-in-rhetoric manner: "The Jews should raise a statue of me for the harm which I could have done them, and which I did not do. . . ."

Combat, once liberal-left, took sides. That is, the literary critic Nadeau took sides. Céline was only a fool.

His sentence, one year. His property, real and literary, was confiscated. His future—a French abstraction. When I talked it over with Gen-Paul, the crippled artist—and Céline's boyhood friend from Rue Lepic—Gen-Paul, busily painting a horse for me, said, "Céline is a criminal. Here, I made the drawings for his first book—take the book! Here, you think he is a great writer—have a photograph of Céline before he became great! I piss on him!" Gen-Paul hobbled about. We drank a cognac and coffee. Across the street was a famous windmill café. Up the hill, the street ran to the Butte's Sacré-Coeur. I had loved Céline as a writer, once. Down below was every element of *Journey to the End of the Night.* It was Rue Lepic, pushcarts, whores, pimps, strip joints, and Pigalle's alleys of disenchantment—1950. During the 1910's it had been the same, if more petty bourgeois.

As for Céline, after the trial in absentia, he returned to France in 1951. He died at the age of 67 in 1961—forgiven by La Belle France. In 1966, he was morally vindicated by the questing and more confused younger generation. He had died the same week that Hemingway died—but Céline's death "was dwarfed," said a French critic, by Hemingway's suicide. It became fashionable in 1966 to admire Céline, to admire Hamsun, to admire Ezra Pound. I had admired them all in my time.

Great literature had something to do with love, love of country—apparently. To some minds, if you betrayed your country, you became even greater.

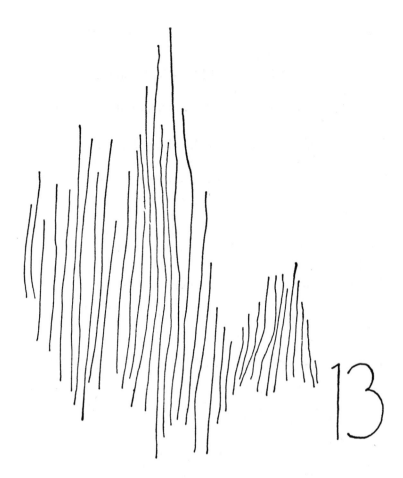

13

NOT HOLIER THAN THOU

IN SUPER COUCHEVEL, I was skiing. It was spring of 1950. Diana
was in Paris feeding cats and studying for her final examinations
at the Sorbonne.

"I'm the color of old copper," I said, phoning Diana. "Come!
Give the cats to a cat house—or pay the concierge to feed them
horsemeat. Come!"

"I've been that color since I was born. The Sorbonne, remember? Racine! Molière! Culture! Cats! Do you want me to fail
Racine?"

"To hell with Racine! I've met two great atomic scientists—
come!"

215

"Who are your scientists?"

"Frédéric Joliot-Curie, and his wife, Irène Curie. Are you coming or are you dedicated?"

"Racine! Examinations! Sorbonne! The Fulbright Act. . . ."

I'd met Frédéric Joliot-Curie hurtling down the main slope of Super Couchevel. He was, though a communist, the head of the French Atomic Commission, a thought that frightened Washington but not the anarchistic, adaptable French. We became friends despite my objections to his communism. Apparently my name gave me a Russian-posed, sympathetic character. He kept pronouncing its syllables—*Ros-ko-len-ko*. He introduced me to his wife, Irène Curie, over a drink at the chalet, remarking, "Monsieur Ros-ko-len-ko does not like my politics. He likes my science. We are *engagés*—to science and to communism. . . ."

It was a word the French Left intellectuals loved—their pledge and enlistment to Stalin, in Paris. It gave them more than a belch after a large dinner. It gave them an emotion for politics they had not had since Jaurés' assassination in 1914. It made them as revolutionary as Marat and Robespierre. It gave them a red flag, mass meetings, denunciations. They thought of the day they would take political power. And we toasted to power, science, peace, poetry, French cooking—and kindred anarchistic arts.

As we skied down the blazing, deep snow, I plotted to get Mr. Frédéric Joliot-Curie to talk about his *engagement* to French communism. As an ex-Marxist, I had, by 1950, an old hate-love sentiment about my own revolutionary past. Frédéric Joliot-Curie, within his political and scientific world, had added the last name of his wife, Curie, to his marriage symbolism. I thought that strange for a revolutionary, for a man. I could only put that down to opportunism—a very old French disease. Astute, suave, always courteous, he risked, by his outspoken politics, his post with the French Atomic Commission. He was under political fire all the time. The Russians were working on the Bomb, and any communist sympathizer in the field was a natural prey—a scientific informer—said the opposing French press every week as they attacked Mr. Frédéric Joliot-Curie.

"You can interview me in Paris at the office of the Atomic Commission," said Mr. Frédéric Joliot-Curie, arranging to meet me there in ten days. "For whom will you do it?"

"For *The American Mercury*." I mentioned its former editor, H. L. Mencken, to the scientist. He had never heard of Mencken. We talked again about political and social power. France had none, we agreed. It was no longer La Belle France. It would have power when the communists took over, he insisted: "We have a heritage. We will expand socially, internally, politically, and not geographically. We must give up Algiers, our colonies in Africa and Indochina. But there is not one politician outside of the communists who is ready to do that!"

"Your classical heritage is totally opposed to giving up anything in any country! Even as communists you would not!" I said indiscreetly. "Do you love Stalin's methods? And how much Asian land has he given up today?"

"It's always Stalin! Do you think that he alone represents Russian communism? Come on—enough about politics! Let us wait for the Paris interview. We will ski now."

We skied. He was a much better skier—the scientist who had made major discoveries in the transmutation of matter, especially regarding neutrons. His skiing was as scientific as his blueprints for the future. We raced down the major slope. He won like an exploding Stalinist proton. He slid over the liquid corn-snow like solid, dialectical matter. I paid for the cognacs.

In Paris, instead of an interview, there was a scandal ten days later. It was in all the papers. Frédéric Joliot-Curie was no longer in the French Atomic Commission. He was lost between political protons and neutral neutrons—fired for his communism. The interview had been preempted by Paris' heated political science—and Frédéric Joliot-Curie disappeared, temporarily incommunicado amid Paris' atomic and leftist political scenery. The published political attacks in the communist press, however, made him twice a martyr to peace and three times a hero of his scientific, compulsive communism.

All sorts of American adventures in the arts and in the theater were being tried out that spring in Paris. Art in the U.S., it was said, depended on the Internal Revenue's concept of "tax loss." The tourists were coming over to blossom on the broad, green boulevards—Americans with their careless pocketbooks, their spangled shirts, their endless complaints, and an older innocence. It was art, nevertheless, that spring. Even Orson Welles, an old

Hollywood and Martian hand, tried to create an American theater in our midst. After all, a hundred thousand nimbly lost Americans now made up Paris' permanent expatriate colony. Abroad, America was saving Greece, France, Italy, and all of Western Europe, with our huge international civil service and our American-posted, khaki divisions. Paris was the ideal location for the Marshall Plan, for NATO, and for flair in matters non-military, non-commercial, non-scientific—in the seven American wandering arts abroad.

Orson Welles, actor, director, adaptor, opened up his erratic American Theater on the Right Bank. Nearby, sneering at our culture, lived surrealist André Breton—who never came to see what Welles had created. A friend of mine, a girl who used acid to oil her atavistic tongue, was Welles' assistant. When Welles barked, she screamed back louder, "Eat less ice cream! Direct! You're getting fatter than William Randolph Hearst—and he's dead, Orson! Direct, genius!"

And all sorts of dedicated people came to Paris that spring— Canada Lee, the actor, who was a New York neighbor of mine, arrived in an actor's hurry, en route for a part in *Cry the Beloved Country*. Before taking off for South Africa, he spent a day frying dozens of Southern fried chickens in a large flat overlooking the crowded cemetery on Rue Schoelcher. As if he were questing the future of fatalism, he fried his chickens and stared out at the gravestones. "They are certainly dead out there!" he said, cutting another chicken into halves. "They're basted forever!"

The guests had brought their skinny French chickens—from their own beloved *bouchères*. Ten hours later Canada Lee was still with the French chickens, and moaning, as he drank, to keep up his flagging expertise—"That goddamn cemetery! What a hell of a place to have an apartment! You go straight from your open door to a closed pit. I'll bet some of them died in bed, but with a girl or two. Some of them died in the cafés of this beautiful city—and how come I never came to Paris before? It's been hidden away from me. What a city! What a creation! What a civilization!" and he fried on—the actor between chickens, the cemetery, and *Cry the Beloved Country*.

When the film was made, it was badly directed. A few years later, in his 57th Street Sherwood Arms Studio, as he was recuperating from a heart attack, he said, "The wrong Korda

brother directed it, unfortunately." The cemetery was still in his
eyes; the boxer turned actor, a Caliban no longer. The tempests
were gone. He would die and his world of 57th Street and Sixth
Avenue would die with him—when the high-risers were blue-
printed and our little walk-ups went with the bulldozers. We
were, after his death, all Calibans—deformed from our toes to
our heavens. New York was a concrete God with a Hollywood
contract.

In June, as the Korean War broke out, I made other, tentative
plans. I was in the Naval Reserve, and if the Korean War spread,
I might, once again, be floating away on water. In the non-
spreading peace-war interim, Diana and I planned to see Terra
Europa before it burned up again. It was the end of many things,
we knew, summing up. The Fulbright fellowship had not quite
made Diana a French scholar, nor I the found-myself poet. I had
done the book of poems about Paris to stretch out the little
magic left in the poetry-seized impulse. And Paris had what
Paris is to all frozen-out Americans—unlike anything we had
in our tightening, clutter-built, indifferent land. It had been nine
months of Paris, pregnant like a chattering, drunken, poetic
fishwife. With two motorbikes, a map of Europa not yet at war,
Diana and I purred into the scenery.

We were camping out, though Diana soon tired of it. I did all
the camping chores at streams, in woods, on beaches, wherever
the paved and the unpaved roads took us—Tours, Poitiers,
Angoulème—on to Arcachon. There we stayed with a French
actress, Christianne, to drink her father's vintage wines and eat
four days of his superior cooking. In return, Diana made a
Chinese dinner by inventing her soya sauce, her Chinese shiny
noodles, her Chinese cabbage, snow peas and *fan-teo*—bean
curds. And I cooked one meal, a chicken that I had learned to
do up as a Boy Scout. I wrapped the chicken up in a cake of
mud. I thrust it into the heart of a fire that I made on the beach
and I went swimming in the Bay of Biscay. An hour later, I
returned to the heart of the fire. The table was set. Christianne
was dressed for dinner, like her father and Diana. We had two
aperitifs. Diana looked worriedly at the heart of the fire—and
she had a third aperitif. They watched. . . .

I got the now-hardened mud ball out of the fire. The ball had
a smell of its own—Imported Boy Scout Chicken. As I broke

the mud away, Diana smiled happily. Christianne had a third drink. Monsieur Cauet was taking down notes, querying me about every stage of the chicken—the mud, the ingredients, the heart of the fire—to make certain that he had not missed any of the extraordinary pains I had taken before I went in for the swim.

The mud was finally chipped away from the chicken, and Monsieur Cauet was gallantly exclaiming, as he toasted—"To Monsieur Roskolenko's primitive American chicken—*à votre santé!*"

We drank the toast. Out came the finished chicken—a ball of black-charred, boneless, meatless, Imported Boy Scout Chicken.

By the time we were on the way to Narbonne and Montpelier, we became somewhat possessed to see an old abbey—the Abbaye de Font-froide. Picasso had painted murals there for the abbey's windows in 1910. It was way off the beaten track, in a wasteland of no place.

An odd moon shone over the craggy hills as we cycled on. It made us feel like cosmic pilgrims arriving to worship—Picasso. We went through desolate places, past scrubby fields filled with boulders. It was a biblical, vacant land.

"It's so ghostly," said Diana, as we turned on a sandy road running through pines and boulders. "All for Picasso?"

"All for God and Picasso! I've never slept in a church. . . ."

"Must we sleep in a church?"

"There's only the ancient abbey there—the cold front of God," I said.

"Ah, God! The Jew in you is coming back—no?"

"The Chinese in you has gone away—yes?"

"The camper has gone away . . . everything is frightening!" Diana pointed towards the dark, scraggy desolation. "It's for nuns, monks and God. . . ."

The road ended. A huge, walled-in building with towers and parapets gleamed—the Abbaye de Font-froide. It was tenth century in twentieth century time—stone, moss and agony. To the left we heard farm animals—then a farmer, coming towards us with a swinging lantern.

The Abbaye was closed, said the monk-like farmer. It would open in the morning. We could eat with him and sleep in the barn, said the farmer. We ate soup and black bread. We went to sleep on the straw.

We heard the roosters too soon. We washed in buckets. We ate lumps of bread and sipped black coffee for breakfast. I tried to pay.

"Pay God," said the farmer. He had been dour, yet kind. He had smiled a long time ago—in the tenth century of his face.

Everything was very Christian, before and after that. A young man, in polished boots, told us about every stone, the tenth century religious architecture, as he marched us up and down the courtyards, the chapels, the private chambers, until we reached what we had come to see—Picasso's paper murals. They were tattered, sandwiched between glass panels. We heard a small lecture on Picasso, mostly exclamations—"Ah, Picasso! Oh, Picasso! *Formidable! Extraordinaire! Fantastique!* A great, great French artist!" the young lecturer in boots kept repeating.

"He is Spanish, not French," said Diana, annoyed.

"He is French, Madame!"

"He is Spanish, Monsieur—and a lousy communist, too."

The lecturer in boots stammered, *"Jamais! Jamais!"*

"The French are worse than the Chinese, whom they resemble, as Nationalists and egotists," mumbled Diana, becoming firmly American before the lecturer. She tipped him a few francs—to hurt his pride. I tipped him more, for we were the only Americans, or pilgrims, to have ridden through the mad desolation. His pride became French again. He stared at her, listening to her speech, uncertain of her country and her origin. . . .

Angered, she felt her Eurasian complexes all the more. It came with the Abbaye, with French flamboyance—and with his exclamations. We mounted our motorbikes and went back through the desolation, heading for Montpelier. In Montpelier, I planned to put Diana on a train and meet her in Nice. From Nice, we would take the train to Rome—for the *Anno Santo,* the holy year.

Saint Peter's was holier with pilgrims massing in the square, on the steps, inside the massive cathedral. They arrived on busses from all countries. They came on foot from hotels. They drove up on motorcycles from Wales—miners in their work clothes, their lamps lit as if they were on the way to Golgotha. They carried huge wooden crosses which they had rented a square away. Though it was a rented fraud, their faces had a candle-lit passion as they passed the local Romans. Some older Romans had put Christ on the Cross—Christ the Jew. Now Welsh cyclists, laden with hundreds of pounds of wooden crosses, crossed into the Christian crucifixions as they stumbled towards the huge, bird-swamped entrance. They were passing their own stations of the cross, God-swept, enwrapt, fixed to heavens, sundered from their motorcycles, weeping like the women all about us. I bowed to the Welshmen and took their piety to myself.

In its time, pre-Christian, this ground had been the circus of Caligula—the place of martyrs when Nero reigned. In 1450 it became truly holy ground as Saint Peter's rose, slowly, for the next 176 years. We stood before it, then we walked through its flowing, regal, over-rich gilt-laden marble vaults. Later, as if part of the holier essence, our guide said, "Do you know that there is more gold stored away in the Vatican than in Fort Knox, Kentucky. . . ."

I wrote a sarcastic poem about the gold stored away. It was published in a very Catholic city, Dublin, in *Envoy*, a Nationalist magazine. I was in a circus, the Circus Maximus of the spirit . . . and I gave myself questions and answers. I was to remember older conversations with Henry Treece, who wrote a book about the Crusades. Over stout and Scotch, it was easier to answer Christianity's total defects—conquests, crusades and permanent wars. When in the name of God and Jesus, it was conquest first, gold first. God came in as a pious afterthought. Killing, we had agreed, was basically what heathens, Moslems and Christians did to settle nothing. The Jew, always condemned for his alleged love for gold, seldom drew blood, except in defense. It was time that Christianity gave up its frauds and confessed its reality. We left Saint Peter's. Rome was too rich to be too holy. I wept as I left Saint Peter's Square, watching the Welsh miners leave with their huge wooden crosses, bringing the crosses back to the hiring place.

Three hours later, Diana and I entrained for Salzburg to hear Mozart at the Mozartium.

I left Diana to rest in Salzburg. I cycled off for Germany on a totally compulsive mission.

Germany was a moral and physical graveyard in August 1950. I saw it as a sleepwalker, barely observing the tidy reconstruction of the destruction. I was the observer who could not observe enough or listen enough to the chatter in the beer halls, stubes, wine cellars, bars, cafés, hotels and guest houses. My route became a mélange of routes. In Passau, just before the Bavarian Forest, I had dreams of Heine's walks in the Black Forest. But Passau had been another Dachau—an earlier pyre, I soon discovered. Passau had burned its first Jews in 1477. Dachau, near enough, was Germania of the modern Huns. In the cafés and restaurants, they looked like people of delicate sensibilities—blond men, with saddened, embarrassed eyes when non-Germans looked at them.

I overheard an earnest, breast-beating discussion that was intended for me, near Kassel, at breakfast. A large leather-panted man was addressing two of his fellow citizens with his bitter complaints. "Yes, I heard about those atrocities, but who could have believed those rumors! We were always such a civilized people. Who can forgive us for what we have done as a nation, as a people? True, Hitler did some good things—but to destroy people like that! It was the Alfred Rosenbergs, and those other people who were responsible for it. . . ."

In Passau, when I asked a hotel clerk to change my traveler's checks, he said, "If you want more than the official exchange, there are Jews on the corner. But I can get you a better rate!"

Outside of Nuremberg was Furth—where the novelist Jacob Wassermann had been born in 1873. Wassermann had made my youth younger, more romantic, more ironical, most vexing, and terribly lost—the Jew within the Jew. And Furth, too, had been the scene of one of Wassermann's most searching books, *The Dark Pilgrimage*, a novel about the False Messiah, Sabbatai Zevi—the Smyrian Jew who had declared himself the Messiah in 1666. From Furth, too, had come some of the wanderers and followers of Sabbatai Zevi. "On to Zion! The Messiah has come! Join! Follow! Sabbatai Zevi is the Messiah!" These words turned thousands of Jews from all of Europe into wandering gypsies, Palestine-bound, to meet Sabbatai Zevi. And Wassermann had chronicled the Jews wandering out of Furth, for Palestine.

I saw Furth now, 289 years after the hosts of Jews had marched towards Palestine. It was half a town, bombed in part, bourgeois in the middle, lost to its past, a suburb of Nuremberg—where the Nuremberg Laws had indicted the Jews of 1933, when Hitler was the Messiah for the German folk. I walked through its darkness looking for resemblances to another time, another exodus, another emblem of faith. I remembered something that Wassermann had written, something without balance, something of the self-hater, oddments that went for analysis in Wassermann's meandering sadness: "The Jewish race is strong and tenacious; but Jews are great only when a little success is granted them, and they are not great for long, for they easily become surprised at their own greatness. Sabbatai Zevi was a Jew, perhaps the most typical of Jews, a scrap of Jewish destiny."

Wassermann's last published book in New York, in 1933, was *My Life as German and Jew*. In Furth, walking about early in the morning, Furth was *Judenrein*. I was the only Jew in Furth—walking back to Nuremberg.

I thought of another German Jew, Theodor Herzl, the spiritual founder of the Jewish State, and his wrath during the 1890's regarding the men of money, the men without Judaism—who were later to become more German than the Germans.

Herzl had known every pilgrimage in his wanderings—dark, darker, bitter, after and before he published his small book, *The Jewish State*. He had known dukes, popes, czars, kings, emperors, sultans—the regal gentry of the world who, in many instances, would happily have sent their Jews to Palestine for their own political reasons. Herzl, a determinist with tremendous literary skills and the practical idealism that eventually killed him in 1904, would say, at various times during his journeys between the Jews he knew and the Gentiles, as he planned the future state of Israel—"I do not need the rich Jews—what I need are men. *Donnerwetter*, they are hard to find!" "Every day I observe with painful attention the sufferings of our people in every land. I believe that this pressure is bound to make men out of even the most abject wretches."

When Herzl was even more irked, he would write in his diary: "There are Jews who live on Judaism, and those who live for it. . . ." In Turkey, when the Russian *chargé d'affaires* said accusingly: "You have among your people perhaps twenty percent who are not any too ethical—the same as among other peoples," Herzl could reply, as a riposte, "Yes, but in our case they are counted double, so that people come to believe it is forty percent. . . ."

He could also say, with intense anger, "I am an opponent of the House of Rothschild because I consider it to be a national misfortune for the Jews. The only member of the family who by his past behavior has awakened general sympathy is Edmond de Rothschild—a man whom I held, and still hold, to be a good staunch Jew; and shall such a man refuse to contribute to our national salvation?" And, later, when other prosperous Jews turned Herzl down, he wrote, "The prosperous Jews are all against me. So I am beginning to have the right to become the world's worst anti-Semite."

As I wandered about Germany, on a side road, not too far from the Rhine, I saw a sign—*Valhalla*. I was lost amid green mountains. I thought of Germanic myths and of Nietzsche. On a hill there were marble myths to blood—the flushed green and red of birth and dying. There was a garden for warriors of the sword and of the death camps; a column of white to a blacker history. The sandy road now became an *autobahn*. There were cars and horses, blond children on bicycles, all rushing past the serried haystacks—and *Valhalla,* on a hill of dung.

Nietzsche had been turned, by editing and lies, into a supposed racist by his sister, Frau Forster-Nietzsche—to Hitler's acclaim. It was the lie within the lie. Had not Nietzsche written in *Human, All-too-Human:* "The whole problem of the *Jews* exists only in nation states, for here their energy and higher intelligence, their accumulated capital of spirit and will, gathered from generation to generation through a long schooling in suffering, must become so preponderant as to arouse mass envy and hatred. In almost all contemporary nations, therefore—in direct proportion to the degree to which they act up nationalistically—the literary obscenity is spreading of leading the Jews to slaughter as scapegoats of every conceivable public and internal misfortune. As soon as it is no longer a matter of preserving nations, but of producing the strongest possible European mixed race, the Jew is just as useful and desirable an ingredient as any other national remnant. . . ."

Later, in the 1960's, when they blamed Nietzsche for the death of God, I went back to Nietzsche himself. I quote what he actually wrote—before he was distorted by latter-day priests without religion, by ministers without hope and by dunces of despair in their churches, mosques and synagogues:

The Madman. Have you not heard of that madman who lit a lantern in the bright morning hours, ran to the market place, and

cried incessantly, "I seek God! I seek God!" As many of those who
do not believe in God were standing around just then, he provoked
much laughter. Why, did he get lost? said one. Did he lose his
way like a child? said another. Or is he hiding? Is he afraid of us?
Has he gone on a voyage? or emigrated? Thus they yelled and
laughed. The madman jumped into their midst and pierced them
with his glances. "Whither is God" he cried. "I shall tell you. We
have killed him—you and I. All of us are his murderers. But how
have we done this? How were we able to drink up the sea? Who
gave us the sponge to wipe away the entire horizon? What did we
do when we unchained this earth from its sun? Whither is it moving now? Whither are we moving now? Away from all suns? Are
we not plunging continually? Backward, sideward, forward, in all
directions? Is there any up or down left? Are we not straying as
through an infinite nothing? Do we not feel the breath of empty
space? Has it not become colder? Is not night and more night coming on all the while? . . . God is dead. God remains dead. And we
have killed him . . . What was holiest and most powerful of all that
the world has yet owned has bled to death under our knives. Who
will wipe this blood off us? . . ." Here the madman fell silent and
looked again at his listeners; and they too were silent and stared
at him in astonishment. At last he threw his lantern on the ground,
and it broke and went out. "I come too early" he said then; "my
time has not come yet. This tremendous event is still on its way . . .
it has not yet reached the ears of man. Lightning and thunder
require time, the light of the stars requires time, deeds require
time even after they are done, before they can be seen and heard.
This deed is still more distant from them than the most distant
star—*and yet they have done it themselves.*"—It has been related
further that on that same day the madman entered divers churches
and there sang his *requiem aeternam deo.*

I went on to Hamburg for an older, younger, more childish
memory. Twenty-three years earlier, Hamburg had been my
temporary home, my roots away from the sea, when, as a Trotskyist, I was dreaming or acting out the permanent proletarian revolution. It got me a bullet wound, jail—and expulsion from Germany. What a world it was then! What dreams at twenty! What
conceits, dramas, class wars, self wars and diagrams for the
future! How long it took to grow up!

And where was Anna whom I had known here? Her street off
the Reeperbahn, Hamburg's Pigalle, was gone. A third of Ham-

burg had disappeared during the ten Royal Air Force July 1943 "Gomorrah" raids. Then a hundred thousand people had been killed by magnesium and phosphorous bombs. There was no street where Anna had lived. There was nothing. No one knew anybody of another time; 1927 was too long ago—a war ago, and a hundred thousand deaths ago. There was no Anna.

My motorbike was at the railway station. The night before I had slept in a hotel revamped from a deep bomb shelter. It was hundreds of feet below the earth, in silent, blank darkness. A humming fan drew in air from Hamburg above the shelter. But I did not sleep. I lay awake thinking of Hell—Hamburg revisited, Anna not found, Nietzsche in his madness, God alive and God dead; God supervising the bomb shelter and the darkness. It was God *uber alles* and Man *unter alles*.

Later, unable to sleep, I dressed. I went back to the railway station, to sit out the night until a morning train would take me to Copenhagen. There I hoped, from some strangely distorted Jewish humanism, to see Céline. I would reason out his petty revenges and his racist idiocies.

As I was about to put my motorbike aboard the train, a thin, badly dressed German, under thirty, shouted out to me. His voice drummed through the station like the voices of the Thirties, when the brownshirts were marching through stations, streets and towns. He yelled, "Under Hitler it was better! Now Germany is full of shit!"

In Denmark, I could not see Céline.

"No," said the Copenhagen police, "Céline does not wish to see anybody!" They had told him I was a friend of Milton Hindus'. What, another Jew come to bare his Mogen David soul?

I entrained for Paris to end my holiest year. Paris, Rome, Germany, and I was ready for New York.

A day later, I was back in Paris. Diana was ten pounds heavier, ten pounds happier. We packed our mélange of scholarly books and our bequeathed, random art collection, ready for the *Île de France*. We gave our last cat away—the mother cat—to the bistro across the street. We packed some cognac bottles and gifts for friends. We tipped the waspish concierge. At the entrance to our house were friends who were staying on in Paris forever —Zao Wou-ki and Lan-Lan, and some Americans—fortunate, we

thought. Paris, ah! Paris, oh! Paris, *merde!* Paris, high! Paris from
a train leaving Paris. The windows of slums were slums for the
icebox in your head. There was champagne for the sentimental
heart. There were visions—exteriors of still lifes. It was Paris of
Racine, Rimbaud and Baudelaire—a city of statues, heroes and
flesh made into one gamey mixture. It walked and smelled so
many miles in all directions of the twenty arrondissements. It
had 800 hotels, 22 major Catholic churches, tens of thousands of
demimondes, 174 nightclubs, 112 minor churches, and over
5,000,000 Parisians using all these human aids to remaining
Gallic. I had learned, intimately, these common statistics, as if
to compare, with despair, what we would find when the *Île de
France* arrived in New York. There we would, once again, look
for roots, to grow with the macadam roots on Sixth Avenue and
56th Street.

The ship docked at West 48th Street. The river looked worn
out—with dirt and flotsam. It was October, gray, raining, stinking and polluted. It was grimmer at the docks, mad with passengers anxious for their baggage, their taxis, their planes and
trains. We were home but we did not have a home. Mr. Bastard,
as I now called the bastard who had sublet our apartment, refused to leave. He said it was now his apartment, lease or no
lease. Now, homeless, staring out at the North River, we said to
our purser, "We want to go back to Paris. We'll keep the same
stateroom. How much will it be?"

"Three hundred and twenty dollars. Shall I have the tickets
made out now?" asked the purser, acutely sympathetic. "It is hard
to live in New York after Paris, no?"

We had, all together, a hundred dollars left. We went ashore,
suddenly in New York, suddenly in the pollution of a city. A
friend, going away, let us have her apartment. We would, we
expected, go right back to the Voice of America. We were ready
to be rooted—bedded, boarded and jobbed. It was another error.
At the Voice of America, they said: "You will have to wait until
the FBI investigates your past. It may take a week, a month or
a year, with luck."

We had no luck. Senator Joseph McCarthy was, hit and miss,
wandering throughout the alleged Leftist land, but missing
mostly. Though we were not his political targets, we got hit with
his investigatory grapeshot when my past was recalled. But I

had made peace with capitalism long ago. It was much more revolutionary than socialism and more inventive. But we were not inventive enough for the senator's stentorian wildness. When we appealed to a friend, Professor Paul Hays, now a federal judge, Paul reached out to Senator Herbert Lehman. Senator Lehman soon informed me that I "could go to work for any other department in the government but not for the Voice of America"—then under the State Department.

Senator McCarthy's methods involved some of my close friends, who thought that he was right, studious, able and dedicated in finding communists. I thought he was stupid, opportunistic—and dedicated to Senator McCarthy. His grab bag of legal aides were no better. He was a grotesque self-creation. He convinced, if briefly, some Republicans and Democrats. He was loved by some Irish for his Irish folkways in politics. He used a few Jews, who disgraced themselves soon enough. Robert Kennedy was also there. It was a hell of a way to fight communism. Overly ambitious, professionally inept, Senator McCarthy was scaring some sad liberals, some proper patriots and uncertain conservatives. I had contempt for McCarthy aloud, and I had said so regularly to my friend Max, who had come over to Paris that spring.

Now Max met us at the *Île de France*. He took us to lunch at a French restaurant. It was like sailing back to Paris—easier over steak, garlic, long bread, salad and wine. It was like Rue de la Sablière or a garden on Rue Moulin Vert or Chinese-French impressionism. It was a hundred Frenchmen, Americans and expatriates—Zao Wou-ki, Giacometti, Jean-Louis Barrault, C. F. MacIntyre, Gen-Paul, Foujita, Tristam Tzara. It was the poetry of the senses made all the more illusive. But I had no illusions. I was in New York.

Even the young in New York were old. Who had roots anywhere? The houses their fathers had been born in were being bulldozed into social statistics. The new houses were tall, institutional and anonymous. The city was beginning to die—for all of us. It would become another anonymous place, emptier as it grew tighter and taller. And the country, outside the city, had lost its natural relationship. It was an extension of the city, engulfing everything and everyone. The roads, in every direction, were going everywhere to Anonymous.

There was a war in Korea. There was General MacArthur in Korea. China was gone. President Truman was in the White House. The Russians were on their way to the Bomb, and the permanent terror and "revolution" were on. All of us, from Saigon to Moscow, from Paris to New York—were *the terrorized*.

It was 1951 in the world, in the city. New York, my city, Cherry Street—a disappearing birthplace, was becoming an alien place. There were no roots. All our faults, past and present, were still all our fancies. They came together with the remnants of an older idealism.

I wrote six months of speeches for senators, congressmen and men-of-good-will—for the United Jewish Appeal. The poet became the propagandist for Israel, for the growth of a new state. The professional spirit briefly moved in the amateur Jew. It was my first and last Jewish job as a Jew.

Let those who lived with their professional souls write the speeches for senators, congressmen, after-dinner orators—the rabbis and Sunday-supplement priests and ministers.

Christ and others had taught poverty. The Mosaic Laws, and the Ten Commandments, taught me other virtues—not always fiercely held to. I would, without doubt, remain as poor as an ex-poet. I was, too, the Jew out of the synagogue, the Jew to myself. . . .

COLLEGE OF THE SEQUOIAS
LIBRARY